THE HUMANIST IMPERATIVE IN SOUTH AFRICA

EDITOR | JOHN W DE GRUCHY

SUN PRESS

The Humanist Imperative in South Africa

Published by SUN PRESS
www.africansunmedia.co.za
www.sun-e-shop.co.za

First edition 2011

ISBN 978-1-920338-56-5

Set in Serifa BT 9.5/12.5
Cover artwork: *Hope and Optimism, 1984* by John N Muafangejo. Used with the kind permission of the Arts Association Heritage Trust (AAHT), owner of the artwork.
Cover design: SUN MeDIA
Typesetting: SUN MeDIA

SUN PRESS is an imprint of AFRICAN SUN MeDIA. Academic, professional and reference works are published under this imprint in print and electronic format. This publication may be ordered directly from www.sun-e-shop.co.za.

Printed and bound by SUN MeDIA Stellenbosch, Ryneveld Street, Stellenbosch, 7600.

The STIAS series

The Stellenbosch Institute for Advanced Study (STIAS) was born from a simple but powerful conviction: in this part of the world special initiatives are required to create and maintain an environment where we can generate and engage with conceptual frameworks and knowledge that may guide us in tracking and co-shaping global academic developments and that will allow us to address the 'big' questions and issues South Africa and the African continent face, also in a global context.

STIAS has been moulded in the tradition of Institutes for Advanced Study across the globe. It distinguished itself by encompassing all disciplines from the natural to the social sciences and humanities (with a particular emphasis on research grounded in multi-disciplinarity), by maintaining a focus on the African and South African context, and by striving towards contemporary relevance, also by actively creating avenues for communicating the results of its research projects to a wider public.

The STIAS series publications are thus aimed at a broad public which will naturally vary with specific research themes. Straddling the academic world and the forum of an engaging public is a challenge that STIAS accepts; we trust that each STIAS publication will reflect the 'creative space for the mind' in which it is rooted, stimulate public interest and debate, and contribute to informed decision making at various levels of our society.

Further information about STIAS and its research programme may be found at www.stias.ac.za.

Hendrik Geyer
STIAS Director

Stellenbosch
June 2011

stias
PUBLICATION

CONTENTS

PREFACE | *Hendrik Geyer* 9

INTRODUCTION An invitation to a conversation | *John W de Gruchy* 11

SECTION 1 On Being Human 19

Essays
- Exploring contours of being human together | *Bernard Lategan* 21
- Complexity and being human | *Paul Cilliers* 31
- Neurobiological foundations | *Mark Solms* 41
- A Christian humanist perspective | *John W de Gruchy* 57
- Becoming more fully human | *Denise Ackermann* 67

Reflections
- At this time and in this place | *Bobby Godsell* 77
- Where I become you | *Antjie Krog* 83

SECTION 2 On Humanism 97

Essays
- Reflexive humanism | *Wolfgang Huber* 99
- The spirit of Islamic humanism | *Ebrahim Moosa* 107
- The 'Dark Sides' of humanism in South Africa | *André du Toit* 117
- Science, technology and humanity | *George Ellis* 133
- Critical issues for a new humanism | *Drucilla Cornell & Kenneth Panfilio* 145
- New music for a new humanism | *Hans Huyssen* 155

Reflections
- Indigenous humanism: Manifestations of interconnectedness | *Antjie Krog* 167
- Towards a new humanism in Africa | *Njabulo Ndebele* 179
- Relational humanism | *Jan-Hendrik S Hofmeyr* 181

SECTION 3 On Human Dignity and Rights 185

Essays
- Democracy as a community of life | *Achille Mbembe* 187
- Enough is enough: Recovering humane values | *Neville Alexander* 195
- Humane justice and the challenges of locality | *William Schweiker* 203
- Constitutional law and human dignity | *Laurie Ackermann* 211
- Human complicities | *Deborah Posel* 221
- An African theory of dignity | *Thaddeus Metz* 233

Reflections
- A dignity-enriched humanism | *Russel Botman* 243
- Human rights in a more humane world | *Mary Burton* 247
- To lead for humanity | *Peter Willis* 251

THE CONVERSATION A narrative of the second symposium | *Stephen Martin* 261

PARTICIPANTS & CONTRIBUTORS 281

INDICES
- Names 285
- Subjects 289

PREFACE

Hendrik Geyer

The *New Humanism* project at the Stellenbosch Institute for Advanced Study (STIAS), culminating in this publication of *The Humanist Imperative in South Africa*, resonates with the STIAS ethos and objectives to the fullest extent.

These objectives are in essence to advance the cause of science and scholarship and invest in the intellectual future of South Africa, to focus on Africa, and to provide an independent space where innovative ideas and original thinking can thrive.

In its choice of research projects STIAS furthermore maintains a focus on real life problems and pursues sustainable solutions for the challenges facing our country and continent. A key consideration is to facilitate the dissemination of research results to policy and decision-making environments and the broader public.

Few will contest that much of the post-1994 South African optimism for a shared, brighter future, captured so eloquently in our constitution, has gradually made way for a growing disillusion and a grappling with the reasons why things "have gone wrong" in our society.

The working hypothesis of the *New Humanism* project was that understanding what it means to be human together in South Africa today, and how this can be embodied in our social life, probably cuts as close as one can get to a common understanding of the various ills that plague our society. The perspectives on this question, offered by twenty-five scholars and public leaders from various backgrounds, constitute this book. These authors formed part of a group of thirty-nine participants in two STIAS symposia in 2009 and 2010 who engaged in dialogue and debate around the humanist traditions, their local manifestations and implications for "being human together in South Africa today".

This group was acutely aware of the fact that they were neither fully representative of the South African society, nor could they expect to identify grand answers and solutions (not to mention reach consensus on them). Rather, as elaborated by John de Gruchy, what is on offer is a serious invitation to a conversation which can delve into a depth of knowledge and wide-ranging experience (and experiences).

As the first in a new series of STIAS publications I trust that *The Humanist Imperative in South Africa* will indeed contribute to the public discourse, stimulate debate and provide practical guidelines towards the more humane society we all envisage and hope will become a reality.

I would like to thank the editorial team – John de Gruchy, Bernard Lategan, Ebrahim Moosa and Lyn Holness – for their hard work in bringing this groundbreaking publication to fruition. STIAS is particularly indebted to the project leader and editor, John de Gruchy, whose inspiration and enthusiasm for the project never waivered, also during a time of personal tragedy.

Finally, a special word of thanks to all the participants in the *New Humanism* symposia for their critical reflection and for the sincerity and spirit in which they were prepared to cross disciplinary boundaries in pursuit of a common goal.

Hendrik Geyer
STIAS Director

Stellenbosch
22 June 2011

INTRODUCTION
An invitation to a conversation

John W de Gruchy

> We, the people of South Africa ... adopt this Constitution ... so as to heal the divisions of the past and establish a society based on democratic values, social justice and fundamental human rights; lay the foundations for a democratic and open society in which government is based on the will of the people and every citizen is equally protected by law; improve the quality of life of all citizens and free the potential of each person ... (Preamble to the Constitution of the Republic of South Africa)

Everyone with a finger on the pulse of contemporary South Africa is aware of the challenges facing us as a nation. The crisis in education, health, and rampant crime and corruption are daily reported in the media. But there are more fundamental issues that also concern us. Whether we are headed for increasing racial and economic polarisation, and whether our new democracy will not only survive but flourish. Much of this has to do with how we understand what it means to be human together in South Africa today and how this is to be embodied in our social life. The way in which this was perceived by those who drafted the Constitution of our Republic is captured in the Preamble, the spirit and intent of which pervades the document as a whole. Fundamental to its aim and purpose is a commitment to "improve the quality of life and free the potential of each person". Nothing could better express the humanist moral imperative that has developed over centuries across the world and which, despite it being suppressed or distorted time and again, continues to prod and push humanity today towards a better future for all with fresh urgency.

Each of the essays and reflections in this book relates to these issues and to the humanist imperative which has shaped our new democracy. More specifically they grew out of the two symposia initiated by the "New Humanism Project" at the Stellenbosch Institute for Advanced Study (STIAS) the first of which was held in June 2009 and the second in February 2010. The story behind the Project will help clarify its genesis and evolution. At a dinner to celebrate the golden wedding anniversary of friends in Cape Town early in 2009, Dr Mamphela Ramphele challenged those present to stand up and be counted in shaping the future of South Africa. She addressed her challenge specifically to "white males" whom, she said, had been engaged in the struggle against apartheid and contributed to the transition to democracy, but since then become conspicuous by their silence in responding to current debates around the future of South Africa. Whatever the reason for this reticence, the time had come, Ramphele said, to break the silence and speak to the issues, especially those that threatened the values championed by the Constitution.

I was one of those challenged by Ramphele's words and pondered on how I could respond as a "retired" academic, yet still active in research, writing and lecturing. Ramphele's words brought to mind what Njabulo Ndebele had said in his Steve Biko Memorial Lecture in September 2000: "An historic opportunity has arisen now for white South Africa to participate in a humanistic revival of our country through a readiness to participate in the process of redress and reconciliation" (Ndebele 2007:137). In reflecting on the challenge I recalled a series of symposia held in Switzerland after the Second World War when European intellectuals from a variety of ideological perspectives and academic disciplines gathered to discuss the rebuilding of Europe from a humanist perspective. Included amongst their number were existentialist and Marxist philosophers, Christian theologians, and natural scientists. This recollection, together with Ramphele's challenge, ignited the New Humanism Project. Professors Hendrik Geyer and Bernard Lategan at STIAS warmed to the idea and so the project was launched.

The purpose of the project was not to remain trapped in an intellectual discussion about humanism, but to get to the heart of the matter as it affects daily life within our present-day context. It is surely what the South African Constitution is also concerned about in talking as clearly as it does about justice, human dignity and rights, and social relationships. Before we can really address the question of national identity, what it means to be South African, we must surely give our attention to what it means to be human beings living together in this space which we call our home. If we start with difference instead of our commonality as human beings, difference will become divisive; if we start with our common humanity then difference may become mutually enriching, something that we learn to treasure and respect. Being human together precedes and should supersede all other identities. Too often this basic identity is forgotten, neglected or rejected with disastrous consequences for all of us.

Although Ramphele's challenge was to white males, it was essential that participants in the project should be more inclusive of race and gender; that it should be widely representative of scholarly disciplines; that it should include both secularists and committed members of faith communities; and that there should be some input from beyond the borders of South Africa. Not everyone invited to participate in the first symposium was able to attend, including some from faith traditions other than those represented in the book. But the overall response was remarkably positive, indicating that the project was regarded as both timely and appropriate. Its success led to the holding of the second symposium which evoked an equally enthusiastic response amongst a slightly different group of participants. Once again we did not succeed in securing greater representation and as previously we were always aware of absent voices. Perhaps they spoke more clearly than they might have done if they had been present, but we were sorry that this had to be so. Trade unionists, workers, students, the unemployed and poor, were key constituencies whose absence we continually felt. Not too far from where we gathered, people lived in squalor, trapped by poverty exacerbated by the failure of service delivery, bad housing, children unable to obtain a reasonable education, the prevalence of disease and violence. We did not bluff ourselves that we were representative of the demography of South Africa or the wider world. We were privileged, well-educated, and financially secure even in these times of economic downturn. We sometimes wondered whether we had anything to say that would make a difference to our society, let alone what we could do to embody our words in action.

The dilemma in planning the symposia was therefore simple: do we remain silent because such voices are absent? Or do we speak as clearly as possible and with as much integrity as we can muster from our own perspectives and positions in the hope that our words may make some contribution to the national debate and even to the wider global discussion of which it is a part? The dilemma was by no means new to most of us. Similar questions often arose during the apartheid years, and many a proposed gathering was cancelled or fell flat because it was difficult to get adequate representation across the racial divide. But we knew that we could not simply sit back in such a time and abnegate responsibility for future generations; that we could not allow the limitations that define us become an excuse for saying and doing nothing. We also knew that we had a wealth of collective experience, a wide range of knowledge and a fair dose of wisdom, and at least a willingness to make a contribution to the humanisation of our society.

This book, then, is an outcome of the conversation that occurred during the five days of intense discussion at the two symposia held at STIAS. But it is at the same time a reflection of the experience, knowledge and insight from a range of perspectives that the participants brought to the table. Participants were invited to submit for publication either substantial essays or shorter reflections based on papers they had presented at the symposia or drafted in response to the discussions that took place. Readers will be able to trace the way in which the discussion at the second symposia unfolded and track in broad strokes how key interventions contributed to the emerging outcome by reading the narrative account of the conversation provided at the end of the book. There is also an analysis of the discussion that refers to salient issues and themes that arose.

The conversation began around the theme of a possible and appropriate "new humanism" for today; it traversed many subjects reflecting the interests and disciplines of the participants, and eventually found focus around the question "what does it mean to be human in South Africa today?" We neither sought nor achieved consensus on all matters, though there was often agreement on what mattered most for our life together, even if expressed differently. The divisions of opinion on the questions at hand were not so much determined by culture or ethnicity but by life experience, academic background, ideological perspective, and religious commitment or absence of it. But intense debate did not undermine the discussion, for honest disagreement is of the essence of productive conversations as it is of being human, and there has been no attempt in these pages to gloss over them. The reader will soon notice where the differences lie and be able to enter the debate. Clearly neuro-pyschologists, constitutional judges, public leaders, poets and musicians, to say nothing of philosophers, scientists, theologians and social scientists, are not always on the same page; even those within the same discipline do not always manage that. But put together in the same room for a few days, sharing thoughts at meal time, and laughing together, sometimes works wonders. After all, what brought us together was a strong commitment to exploring the humanist foundations and moral character of the new South Africa for the sake of contributing to its future well-being. There was, in other words, a humanist moral imperative that we all recognised and to which we were responding in one way or another.

The nature of the essays and reflections is such that they cannot easily be separated and placed into neat categories. Although many reflect a life-time of research, the collection as a whole might be described as an impressionist mosaic derived from the intentionally interdisciplinary nature of the project and the conversational process that helped give them birth. Most of them traverse the whole gamut of our conversation around humanism, being human, and questions relating to human dignity and the building of a sustainable and just democracy. But for the sake of giving the book a structure, I have grouped together essays that focus more especially on the subject of being human in the first section, those on humanism as such in the second, and others that have to do with human dignity, rights and related issues in the third section. The reflections have likewise been spread across the sections with this in mind. Let me say something about the themes of each section.

What it means to be human, the focus of the first section, is a subject that has stirred controversy ever since human beings began to think about themselves. In fact, to speak about "being human in South Africa" must begin by acknowledging that humans have been around in this part of the world for more than three million years. The Blombos Caves, situated on the south east coast of South Africa not too far from where I live, contain the earliest evidence of human life as we now know it. In the north, about an hour's drive from Johannesburg are the more famous Sterkfontein

Caves and the Cradle of Humankind Heritage Site at Maropeng, a word that means "returning to the place of origin". In all likelihood, this is the birthplace of humanity. This gives some perspective to the conversation contained in this book, as several of the essays in the book remind us together with some selected quotations that reflect the remarkable indigenous humanism of some of the earliest peoples of the land. The humanist impulse in South Africa has a very long genealogy.

The issues in understanding what it means to be human are complex and become increasingly so as scientists explore the cosmos and research the brain; social scientists study questions of identity and sociality; lawyers clarify the articles of the Constitution; creative artists express their insights; and theologians consider the meaning of their faith traditions in terms of contemporary issues. This is universally so, especially in our increasingly multi-cultural world where issues of ethnicity and race, class, age and gender, power and poverty impinge on our lives in ways that too often threaten our sense of common humanity and the common good of our various nations and societies. For those of us who are South Africans, this is sometimes frightening, often exciting, and always challenging. Our future as human beings together is continually being negotiated as we seek ways to achieve the goals embodied in our Constitution.

Humanism, the theme of the second section, has evolved over the centuries within different historical and cultural contexts, driven by various philosophical perspectives, political agendas and religious traditions, and described in varied terms. Invariably each form of humanism, however appropriate in its context, has proved inadequate to the unfolding course of events and new knowledge, and thus has had to be critically reformulated and embodied. Humanism has certainly been a central driving force in the historical development of the post-apartheid democratic Republic of South Africa. But there have been several humanist trajectories within our earlier history, not all of them in agreement, but each claiming the title. Many have written and spoken about the humanist character of *ubuntu*, a term much romanticised but one which nonetheless expresses key elements of a genuinely African and indeed global humanist vision. There was, as anticipated, much debate about its significance as well as its appropriation by non-Africans, something that is reflected in the essays, but the term could hardly be avoided. The quotations to which I referred earlier indicate how deep the roots of this vision are in southern Africa.

The humanist spirit has also been driven by a more socialist commitment that reflects in part African tradition, but also the social democratic vision that perhaps more than others, has shaped our Constitution. A further trajectory is liberal humanism which energised European opposition to slavery and continued from then on to shape liberal opposition to the racial segregation of society and the anti-humanist apartheid ideology – an ideology which equally resisted and rejected "humanisme, liberalisme, en kommunisme". Woven through each of these humanist trajectories are religious perspectives and commitments that have often had to counter the misuse of religion in impeding the establishment of democratic values, the affirmation of human dignity and the entrenchment of human rights.

The third section, on human dignity and rights includes a range of essays on subjects related specifically to these fundamental issues, indicating that just as the struggle against apartheid was an affirmation of human dignity, so the ongoing struggle to ensure that the gains of that struggle are made secure in our new democratic society is equally so. The Truth and Reconciliation Commission and its contribution to the ongoing debate about justice and reconciliation in South Africa is part of that scenario. But so, too, is the HIV/AIDS pandemic, crime and corruption, bad housing and poor education, unemployment and land distribution, and much else that is currently on the agenda for making South Africa the country for which all of us hope.

The struggle for a more humane society is obviously not confined to South Africa. It is always both local and universal, and increasingly these are connected in our time. That is why it was so important that numbered amongst the participants were colleagues from other contexts. So while the conversation focused specifically on South Africa, our discussion was neither parochial nor insular in its scope and character. Hopefully, then, people beyond South Africa will find the contents of this book of value for them in terms of their own contexts. And while the conversation at the symposia was sometimes highly academic, the essays written for this book have had a wider readership in mind than simply fellow academics. Our hope is that the book will contribute to the current debate in South Africa on the kind of country and nation we aspire to be in living together as human beings shaped by the remarkable Constitution adopted at the birth of our new democratic republic. But our concern throughout has been how our conversation could be embodied in practice. So we invite you to enter into the conversation as you read and consider the contributions, and perhaps share with others some of the insights in your own sphere of life and work.

A Personal Note

I have hesitated to conclude this Introduction on a personal note for obvious reasons. But I have been encouraged by some involved in the New Humanism Project to do so because of the connection between what happened to our family the week of the second symposium, preventing my participation and, evidently, influencing the proceedings. I do so also because my reflections on what it means to be human together have been profoundly affected by the event, and because the editing of this book has been part of the process of coming to terms with what happened.

My eldest son, Steve, died tragically in a river accident on 21 February 2010, four days before the start of the second symposium. Instead of sharing in that event I was experiencing grief as never before. Steve was 48, a professor of theology and development at the University of Kwa-Zulu Natal, a son and colleague who celebrated life and worked for justice. I am completing this Introduction in the week of his birth on 16 November 1961, a day filled with memories of the new life I held in my arms that day. Despite all we know about the biological processes, birth remains a matter of wonder and hope just as death remains a tragic mystery. As a result of Steve's death my participation in the conversation of the symposium was reduced to reading the papers and the report some weeks after the event and more recently editing the material that is now included in this book. But I did so with different ears and eyes, seeking to understand what it means to be human when faced with the extremities of life and death and the complex mélange and interplay of tragedy and sorrow, memory and hope.

I had journeyed with others through this maze of sorrow many times; now I had to tread it myself, sometimes alone, but also and thankfully in company with my wife, family and friends. With them we shared and celebrated many memories of times past which helped us cope with the tragedy we had experienced; with them we also expressed hopes without which life would have ground to a halt. My wife, Isobel, found solace in painting and poetry, writing her own and reading that of others. Only in this way could she express her innermost thoughts, fears and hopes, and when appropriate, share them with others. She had given life and nurtured its development, now that life had suddenly ebbed away leaving memories, very special memories that continue to break upon our consciousness and dreams in unceasing waves triggered by sights and sounds, people and places.

I have learnt a great deal from the intellectual enquiry and critical reflection of the contributors and partners in this project, as I have from many other sources over many years. However, in the end, all of it has to be tested not just in the seminar room, the laboratory or the library but on the boundaries of existence, those spaces and places where human beings celebrate life and suffer death. At the end of the day, in the small hours of the night, we human beings wrestle not just with the daily problems that beset us large as they may be, or the ideas that are debated in academia stimulating as they are, but with ourselves, who we are, our relationships with each other, and what if anything is the point of the story. Does it have a satisfying outcome? Are the enigmas and ambiguities clarified and resolved? Meaninglessness and purpose mingle, fate and resistance clash, leaving us at my stage of life walking if not stumbling whether wiser or not, but certainly with a limp. The tragic sense of life increases and focuses the mind, but a hope wrestling against both depression and wishful thinking gives reason to reflect on being human afresh.

During the course of the first symposium I refrained from presenting a paper on my own approach to humanism other than by way of an introduction to the project and a brief account of what I meant by the new humanism. I have, however, written an essay for this volume on my understanding of being human as a Christian humanist. I do so in part mindful that there are people, both secularists and Christian alike, who might wonder why I as a Christian theologian initiated this project and acted as its leader. The fact of the matter is that the challenges facing us today, whether in South Africa or globally are such that we can no longer live, think and act in boxes, and hope to deal meaningfully with them. Christians, along with people of other faith traditions and those of none, should engage each other as human beings who are committed to working to make the world a place in which people are truly free, able to reach their full potential, and willing to live and act responsibly for the common good. None of us can avoid this humanist imperative, least of all, those who regard it also as a divine imperative.

As the leader of the New Humanism Project and editor of the volume I would like to express my thanks to STIAS and its director, Hendrik Geyer, for the generous support given to the project and especially for hosting the symposia and enabling this publication to come to fruition. Bernard Lategan and Ebrahim Moosa who served with me on the editorial committee have been of great support in the planning and shaping of the volume. I am also indebted to Lyn Holness for her diligence and support in helping to manage the project and compiling the names index, and who, together with Paul Schweiker prepared a detailed account of the first symposium that has been of great help as the project has developed. Lyn Holness' notes also contributed to Steve Martin's report of the second symposium which formed the basis for the account of the conversation published in the book. I would also like to thank all those who gave of their time, energy and expertise in participating in the symposia and in writing the essays and reflections that follow. I remain grateful to the National Research Foundation and the University of Cape Town for their continued research support. Finally, on behalf of all involved in the project, I thank SUN MeDIA for their professional help in publishing the book, the first in a new series on behalf of STIAS.

Reference List

Ndebele NS. 2007. *Fine Lines from the Box*. Johannesburg: Umuzi.

SECTION 1

ON BEING HUMAN

Essays

Exploring contours of being human together | *Bernard Lategan*

Complexity and being human | *Paul Cilliers*

Neurobiological foundations | *Mark Solms*

A Christian humanist perspective | *John W de Gruchy*

Becoming more fully human | *Denise Ackermann*

Reflections

At this time and in this place | *Bobby Godsell*

Where I become you | *Antjie Krog*

CONTOURS OF BEING HUMAN TOGETHER

Bernard Lategan

A dream so universal in scope, a reality so contextually defined. Burdened by the realisation that many of the high expectations we had of our young South African democracy did not materialise, we tend to forget that the quest for a more humane society has a long and multi-faceted history fed by many streams, spanning centuries, and marked by both highs and lows. Recent events in our country form but one short chapter in the history of this universal search. They provide an opportunity to re-asses what kind of society we are striving to establish and what we need to do to achieve it.

So what are some of the most prominent *contours* that should shape our living together if it is to be more humane against the backdrop of a rapidly changing local and global environment? The tension between the local and global is indicative of a deeper, more encompassing condition defining our current situation: that of increasing plurality and complexity. Things are not simple any longer (if ever they were) and things will become even more complex. Jean Comaroff speaks of a 'world of multiple abstractions and multiple mediations' while Mbembe describes it as a situation of 'multiplicity'.

The irony is that in post-1994 South Africa, plurality was embraced and celebrated. The question remains whether this plurality has ever been fully internalised and whether its implications have really contributed to the shaping of contemporary South Africa. Much of the failure of the past two decades was due to an inability to deal with plurality in an integrated way. A constructive approach to plurality requires the ability to operate in the centre of oppositional forces. A good example is how groups and individuals deal with the pervasive influence of globalisation. The usual attitude is either to embrace globalisation as the source of innovation and new development, or to resist it as the destroyer of local values and culture. But these two forces paradoxically feed on each other – the more globalisation grows, the more the need for local identities is stimulated. We have never seen the growth of local culture and identities on the scale that we are witnessing now. Moreover, we are not dealing with one set of oppositional forces, but with several simultaneously. The tension between rewarding individual excellence while retaining group solidarity, promoting global trade while trying to protect local industry, participating in the universal quest for new knowledge while insisting that this knowledge should be relevant, touting freedom of speech while preparing legislation for a media tribunal, are just a few of these opposing forces. We need to develop the ability to appreciate the synergy resulting from oppositional forces.

Multiple identities

South African society is still predominantly defined in terms of mono-identities: black or white, rich or poor, man or woman, gay or straight, privileged or underprivileged, employer or employee. Much of this is the legacy of apartheid, of patriarchialism, of exploitation. The liberation struggle sought to overcome these dichotomies – but until now with little success, due to the way in which identity is formed and how identity markers work. Identity markers establish boundaries – both inwards (who belongs) and outwards (who is excluded). In this sense, identity means how I *differ* from others. Distinctions are crucial but the problem starts when identity is tied to *one* marker or to a limited set of markers. Mono-identities do not fit well in the complex reality in which we find ourselves in South Africa. We have multiple identities – I am a husband, father, researcher, biker, etc. all at the same time. The World Cup has taught us that many of us can become football fans despite how we differ in other respects and switched our allegiances as the tournament progressed. Identity is not only about multiple allegiances, it is dynamic and changeable.

We have not developed the ability to internalise our multiple identities. A poignant example is the famous 'I am an African' speech of Thabo Mbeki. In poetic prose he identified himself with the best in each of the diverse histories and cultures of the country, but after several years of disappointment to achieve such envisaged unity, his rhetoric changed to that of 'two nations'.

A more humane society will require not only the internalisation of our multiple identities, but also the ability to utilise the overlap with our fellow citizens to build bridges and to weave a complex net of social relations that will be strong enough to function within the opposing forces of the complex world in which we find ourselves. In this regard Mbembe reminded us of that strain in African humanism which 'means negotiating people, things and knowledge in such a way that promotes future possibility and potentiality'.

Sources for being human together

Deepening our understanding of how to be human together is further hampered by another unhelpful either/or dichotomy with regard to the sources we use for this purpose. Setting up 'Western' patterns of thought versus 'non-Western' ways of thinking, or insisting on a choice between 'African' and 'non-African' traditions only serves to narrow the spectrum of sources from which we might draw inspiration. Reflecting on the essence of being human or the structuring of society is not the exclusive right of any tradition. It takes place in some form or another (as symbol, art, narrative or philosophy) wherever and whenever people live together. We are in the fortunate position to be at the interface not only between North and South, but also between East and West, and we have access to an incredible rich heritage of thought, traditions and practices.

We are heirs to the humanistic tradition of Europe and its concept of human rights – a tradition that has undergone dramatic changes over time. These changes were often triggered by a crisis that necessitated the re-thinking of current assumptions, resulting in a series of different 'humanisms' which are discussed elsewhere in this volume.

The impact of these various traditions is evident in our Constitution and especially in the Bill of Human Rights. This is not the only source that informs our ideal of a humane society. There is a rich variety of other traditions and practices that have influenced the ideal of a humane society in which every person can realise his or her full potential. Antjie Krog urges us to discover forms of humanity 'that already exist around us'. In *Begging to be Black* she describes in great detail how a leader like Moshoeshoe already in the nineteenth century personified an alternative concept of living together and of a humane society. His goal was 'to create a humane space for people to live their lives', based on three principles: 'to uplift the poor, to stabilise the area through diplomacy, and to involve everybody in decisions affecting their lives' (Krog 2009:29). This was a conscious alternative to the militaristic tradition personified by Shaka, based on violence, power and domination. Moshoeshoe bolstered this approach by numerous strategies: 'lending' cattle to the poor to empower them to become productive members of society, welcoming defeated enemies and outcasts into society, respecting cultural differences and local customs and weaving a net of social interconnectedness. Nelson Mandela thus had precursors in the history of Africa who had a deep understanding of the prerequisites of a humane society and who developed practices to implement and sustain these principles.

There are also less visible practices in the African tradition that bolster the ideal of being human together in contrast to destructive ways of behaviour: the many forms of community based co-operative support systems, the respect for the human dignity of even the most destitute, the massive and disciplined expression of human solidarity at the Easter meetings of the Zion Christian Church at Moria are just a few examples. The plurality of sources and practices supporting an inclusive and supportive environment spans continents and centuries and is a rich source to mine in our quest for a more humane society.

Looking for alternatives

The co-existence of a Constitution with one of the most expansive Bills of Human Rights and the continuing abuse of these rights on many levels of society is infuriating. The Constitution describes the Bill of Rights as 'a cornerstone of democracy' and it contains all the elements needed for a humane society. The preamble promises to 'improve the quality of life of all citizens and [to] free the potential of each person'. The 'founding provisions' stress the values of human dignity, equality, human rights and freedoms, non-racialism, non-sexism and the rule of law. The Bill of Rights concretises these principles and values in explicit detail, including living in harmony with the (natural) environment, protecting it for future generations and securing 'ecologically sustainable development'. All the building blocks (constitutionally speaking) are in place. But an exemplary legal framework and an open, democratic dispensation, that has successfully withstood the test of several elections, are not enough to bring about that elusive humane society.

A *plus* is required to energise a dispensation that on paper looks so promising. By 'plus' I refer to the idea of a surplus, of something over and above what is normally expected or required. Mbembe reminded us of another, devastating form of surplus – the production of surplus or superfluous people by the system and the need for a new humanism in terms of liberation from the production of human waste. I am exploring another form of surplus that will hopefully contribute to achieving what Mbembe has in mind.

Plus is here used in contrast to concepts like 'equilibrium', 'balance', and 'even-handedness'. The latter are basic principles of 'justice' and of the legal system underpinning our new democracy. In one important sense justice implies giving 'each his due'. In instances of injury, loss or transgression, the remedy – whether in the form of punishment meted out by the court or in the form of compensation awarded to the injured party should be comparable to and of equal worth to the loss suffered or the damage caused.

Justice as equality is a 'founding provision' in our Constitution and achieving 'social justice' is one of its explicit goals. In view of the glaring inequalities that still mar our society the principle of equality is of paramount importance. The problem starts when the principle of 'equal exchange' looses its compensatory and restorative function and begins to assume retaliatory connotations. This is not a modern problem. The *jus talionis* is already present in the *Codex Hammurabi* (96, 200) and has permeated legal systems from time immemorial (Luz 2007:275). The classical formulation 'an eye for an eye' is already a first step to restrict retaliation to a comparable response, that is, to prevent the retaliatory act from being totally out of proportion to the initial act (Luz 2007:296). But the issue is not the 'equality' or appropriateness of the response or of the legal system. The real problem is the logic of retaliation and the dynamics of the process once it is set in motion. The shift from (equal) compensation to (equal) retaliation is a subtle but devastating move in the sense that it signals the beginning of a repetitive retaliatory cycle. 'An eye for and eye and a tooth for a tooth' does indeed uphold the principle of equality, but triggers a social practice that forms the basis of all feuds, private or public, that have haunted individuals, families, groups and nations in every century of our history. It feeds a destructive cycle of repetitive retaliation from which there is apparently no escape.

The rhetorical strategy of the Sermon on the Mount is significantly different. The antitheses introducing each statement ('You have heard that it was said ... but I say to you ...') have been the subject of exhaustive analysis and debate (Ridderbos 1936; Betz 1995). Important for our purpose is the strategic intent behind the formulation of the antitheses. The intention is not to abolish or replace the Jewish Torah whose authority is assumed, but the alternative possibility ("but I say unto you ..."), or what is elsewhere described as the 'most excellent way' (1 Cor. 13:1). What is at stake here is not the rejection or replacement of the Torah, but the finding of *creative alternatives* to its current interpretation. These alternatives are demonstrated both in terms of a different understanding of the prescriptions of the Law and in an ingrained attitude of constantly looking for alternatives.

This ongoing quest for alternatives is of crucial importance for our efforts to give content to a more humane society. It provides the key to renewal in all aspects of the 'human condition' – in personal attitudes, in social relations, in interpreting the Constitution and in politics. In fact, the (relatively) peaceful transition to an inclusive democracy in 1994 remains one of the most celebrated examples of the conscious decision to opt for an alternative solution and to follow the route of negotiation and reconciliation rather than continuing with military and physical confrontation.

Alternative applications

One of the most dehumanising aspects of life in South Africa today is the endemic use of violence in both the private and the public sphere. Violence against women and children is perhaps its most visible manifestation, but there are many less visible forms of violence and the abuse of power that permeate society.

It can be argued that inter-family violence is the direct consequence of the lack (or perceived lack) of alternative options of behaviour. Male youths socialised in families and communities where violence is the default way to deal with any crisis (domestic, financial, marital, gender or sexual) have had very little chance to develop alternative ways of conduct. This violence cuts across all racial groups as can be seen from the almost daily reports of the abuse of partners, children and even the execution of whole families. If there are no role models and no concrete examples of the pursuit of alternatives readily available, we should not be surprised that the lack of respect for human dignity continues on this scale. The ability to pursue and implement alternative options of behaviour is therefore critical in the quest for a more humane society. The ethics of the alternative is as important for other spheres of life as can be illustrated from the following examples from jurisprudence, values discourse and the process of dealing with the past.

Since the implementation of the new Constitution we have witnessed some interesting examples of what can be called 'creative jurisprudence'. A famous example is the Grootboom case (Government of the Republic of South Africa and Others vs. Grootboom and Others. CCT 11/00). First the Cape High Court and then more extensively the Constitutional Court delivered a groundbreaking judgment that went beyond the normal way formal legalities regarding property rights, illegal occupation and eviction orders are treated. It was a concerted effort to forge an *alternative* way by giving effect to the housing rights provided in section 26 of the Constitution. By applying what has been described as 'the progressive realisation of the right' the Court has opened new possibilities and offered a very ingenious interpretation of the right of access to adequate housing – and at the same time brought the responsibility to give concrete effect to this right back to where it ultimately belongs, namely to the State itself. Sadly – and not without bitter irony – these laudable intentions were never implemented by the state and Mrs Grootboom died while still living in a shack.

Another area where creative jurisprudence has already made its mark, is that of property rights – a contentious field in itself. In an incisive analysis, André van der Walt discusses the underlying principles and the creative space that exists for venturing into uncharted territory and for alternative interpretations and decisions – while taking the intent of the law seriously (Van der Walt 2007:258 *ff*). This is a secular equivalent of the 'You have heard that it was said ... but I say to you' approach.

The discourse on values offers a further example of the creative pursuit of alternatives. Unfortunately it is marred at the moment by fatigue and ineffectiveness. Every time there is a new incident of dehumanising behaviour, a call for the return to 'values' is heard but this remains hollow without a clear understanding of how values function in society and without a clear strategy on how to turn laudable principles into changed behaviour on the ground.

The problem is that 'foundational' values like equality, freedom and human dignity are far too generic to be of any effective impact. They need to be made more specific. In this regard Laurie Ackermann argues that our understanding of human dignity will be extended as our knowledge of the human being increases, and as we view the human being in the context of the development of the modern natural sciences. Human dignity issues posed by the genetic, embryo, stem-cell and similar branches of the natural sciences, will challenge us continuously to reflect on our understanding and protection of the human being. This does not only apply to jurisprudence, but to every form of values discourse, as Metz illustrates in his discussion of African concepts of human dignity.

In the corporate world, the need to 'translate' generic values into more specific and contextual forms has long been recognised. Here specific processes have been developed to describe a value like 'respect' in terms of *concrete behaviour* that will be recognised as respectful. In situations of cultural and other forms of diversity, a process of dialogue and negotiation is needed in order to reach consensus on what will constitute respectful behaviour in the workplace (Lategan 2004).

A third area where the search for alternative understanding is of critical importance, is in the re-assessment of the past in order to develop an alternative understanding of the self, of our identity and of the future. Interesting work has been done on the ambiguous nature of historical memory and on ways to deal constructively with a troubled past. The TRC process is a case in point. It would seem that a 'future oriented memory' has the best chance to successfully negotiate the past – perhaps one of the most radical examples of an 'alternative understanding' (see Diawara, Lategan & Rüsen).

A fourth and most intriguing area was introduced by Solms during our discussions: the very powerful effect of our basic instincts on our behaviour, especially in situations of stress and danger. At the same time, there was general consensus that we are not merely the product of our instincts. Here another form of 'alternative' emerges – a conscious effort to reflect and to choose an alternative form of behaviour.

A necessary precondition for the successful development of alternative understandings is the effective use of imagination – not in the sense of dreaming up something illusionary, but following the trajectory or thrust of a concept or tradition as it projects itself into the future in order to find interpretations in new situations that retain the integrity of the concept or tradition (Lategan 1996:213-232). An attitude of constantly looking for alternative ways of understanding and acting, and the ability to implement these should form an important component of any New Humanism. These abilities are closely linked to some of the other salient features such as the style of dialogue and negotiation (which in themselves embody the pursuit of alternatives), as well as the embracing of plurality itself. Plurality needs to be appreciated as a way to discover new possibilities and alternative understandings (Lategan 2007).

We can only break free from the cycle of violence, of retaliation, of the 'equal' response to injustice if something more is added to the process. To disturb this equilibrium something more is needed, a plus, a surplus of humanity. The pursuit of alternatives might be one track that could lead us in this direction.

De-centering the human subject

The most fundamental change between the 'classical' and a 'new' humanism is the position of *homo sapiens* itself. In the former, (rational) man is the measure of all things and the unquestioned centre of the universe. Whether inspired by the secular ideal to free humans from all forms of subservience and external authority – be that from superstition, ignorance or religious belief – or whether bolstered by theological concepts like our God-given duty to reign over creation, the central position of the human being remained unchallenged.

This dominating role of human beings is fundamentally challenged by a growing awareness of what we are doing to our planet and to a new, all-encompassing understanding of life itself. Hofmeyr's option for the *Gaia* concept is a conscious effort to understand the planet as a living organism or system with its own physiology.

When humanity is reduced to a commodified thing, we have to move beyond this to understand ourselves as part of the web of life. Ellis shows how the developments in science (and technology in particular) are constantly changing our understanding of human beings, while Solms challenges us to face up to the fact that the search for the good life is not the exclusive possession of Europeans or the Judaic-Christian tradition, but rather rooted in biology. Our behaviour is more strongly influenced by basic instincts than we are prepared to acknowledge. Although these instincts *can* be overcome (not without difficulty) and although it does not means that humans can be *reduced* to biology, this has serious consequences for how we view ourselves and the interconnected web of life itself.

The shift from a mono- to a more complex and inclusive understanding of life is yet another facet of the plurality that characterises our present context. The implications of this shift – described by some as a move from 'anthropocentric' to 'bio-centric' thinking – are still emerging, but any new attempt to re-conceptualise our living together with other human beings and with nature will have to take these implications into account. There is a growing awareness that there is no central point from where everything can be controlled. To the contrary, human existence and survival are intricately linked to the wellbeing of nature, the physical environment and all other forms of life.

Critical awareness and humility

One consequence of the preceding is that any whiff of triumphalism or arrogance will be totally misplaced in a new version of humanism. What we need is a humble, self-critical engagement with others and with nature. Huber talks of a *reflexive* humanism that situates itself in dialogue with the multiplicity of humanisms, critically evaluating them to discover overlaps, but also unmasking the ingrained anthropocentrism in each, and questioning how each relates humans to the wider reality of creation.

At the same time, this calls for a new style of dealing with other participants in this all-encompassing network – a style of engagement, participation and dialogue. But then the enabling conditions for such dialogue must also be in place. As Neville Alexander reminds us, the process is constantly frustrated by the remaining serious inequalities (economic, social, educational) that still characterises South African society and that continue to make a dialogue among 'equals' impossible.

Inter-connectedness and solidarity

A final contour has to do with the relational aspect of human existence. This has always been very prominent concept in African thought and tradition. Ndugane emphasises that humans are always in relation – to others and to God. This interconnectedness is expressed in *ubuntu*, in the relationship with previous generations, with animals, with geographical locations and with the land. Like Cornell, he insists that this relationality goes 'all the way down' in the sense that we stand in a plurality of relations. Denise Ackermann considers relationship as the key to becoming human. This is something normative and innate in that to be human is to be created in and for mutuality. The potential for forming relationships marks humans as special and enables not only shared identity, but more importantly, solidarity with the suffering and need of others.

This very ancient African idea of interconnectedness is reinforced by recent developments that compel us to reconsider existing concepts of humanity. The rise of the network society has shifted the focus from the nodes in the sense of fixed points in the network to the *relationship* between the nodes. This is the key in dealing with complex systems. Furthermore, advances in biology and the study of the phenomenon of life itself have also highlighted the interconnectedness of all that constitutes the 'web of life'.

The ethical dimension

Community, interrelatedness and solidarity will of necessity be prominent features of any new understanding of what it means to be human in the twenty-first century. When we contemplate a new way of living together, the emphasis on communality does not diminish the importance of individual responsibility in any way. Kunneman reminds us that there is a tension between autonomy and solidarity and that humanist values can be turned to horrible use. Human agency was the main reason why previous attempts to establish a more humane society failed. Neither can we (as Du Toit reminds us) ignore the 'dark side' of humanism – the Declaration of Independence was made in a society where slavery was still practised; Smuts, so prominent in the drafting of the Preamble of the UN Charter in 1945, held racist views; the blatant lip service paid to human rights by totalitarian regimes.

Throughout the previous sections, the ethical dimension of any new imagining of society was a recurring theme. The very existence of plurality forces us to make choices and these choices are in the final analysis ethically informed. In fact, as Godsell points out, the idea of the 'common good' and the concept of 'wealth' have ethical dimensions. 'Wealth' has to do with 'wellness' and cannot be defined merely in terms material possessions. It refers in a much more profound sense to the 'healthiness' of a society or of individual relationships. 'Wealth' should therefore be understood as a normative moral concept. In the same way the quest for finding more creative and more humane ways to live together in South Africa remains in essence an ethical undertaking that challenges us all.

Reference List

Betz HD. 2002. *The Sermon on the Mount.* Minneapolis: Fortress.

Diawara M, Lategan B & Rüsen J (eds). 2010. *Historical Memory in Africa in Intercultural Context*. New York: Berghahn.

Government of the Republic of South Africa and Others vs Grootboom and Others (CCT 11/00, decided on 4 October 2000). http://www.saflii.org/za/cases/ZACC/2000/19.html

Krog A. 2009. *Begging to be Black*. Cape Town: Random House Struik.

Lategan BC. 1996. Imagination and Transformation. *Scriptura* 58:213-232.

— 2004. Threat or Asset? Dealing with Diversity and Values in the Workplace in Deeply Divided Societies. Unpublished paper.

— 2007. In Praise of Plurality. Paper read at the Wissenschaftskolleg zu Berlin.

Luz U. 2007. *Matthew 1-7. A Commentary*. Minneapolis: Augsburg Fortress.

Ridderbos HN. 1936. *De Strekking der Bergrede naar Mattheüs*. Kampen: Kok.

Van der Walt AJ. 2001. Dancing with Codes – Protecting, Developing and Deconstructing Property Rights in a Constitutional State. *SA Law Journal* 118(2):258-311.

IMAGINING BETTER FUTURES
Complexity and creativity

Paul Cilliers

If we acknowledge that we live in a complex world, this has important implications for how we understand that world and act within it. Complex systems are constituted through a vast amount of non-linear relationships. In order to comprehend such systems, we cannot take all these relationships into account, we have to simplify. This process reduces the complexity of that which we want to understand. There is no objective way of doing this since that would assume a position from where we have access to all the complexity. This has two implications. In the first place, it means that our knowledge of complex things is always limited and incomplete. Since the reduction is not objective, but based on choice, we have, in the second place, to acknowledge that normative issues are always involved when we deal with complex things. Some aspects of this can be described by what one can call an "ethics of complexity".

I will develop the idea of an ethics of complexity with reference to the question: what is it to be human? Since our engagement with complex things cannot be reduced to simple calculation, such an ethics is fundamentally provisional and emphasises the responsibility we have to assume for our decisions, despite not being able to predict their outcomes completely. Since our predictions cannot be formal extrapolations, they will contain an element of creativity (as opposed to calculation). We have to imagine aspects of the possible outcomes of our acts. The imagination thereby acquires a central position in our engagement with the world, also when we do science. We have to attempt to imagine better futures in order to create the conditions in which they may perhaps be realised. The nature of this creative act will also determine what kind of persons we are.

Living in a complex world

Human existence has always been complex, but in our time this complexity takes a unique form. The process of globalisation and the role played by an internationalised media industry has thrown us into an ocean and we have difficulty in keeping afloat. Moreover, the technological advances we have made has enabled us to do much that was impossible before, but has also provided us with the means to do harmful things on an unprecedented scale. The problem is that we do not, and perhaps cannot, understand all this complexity, and yet we act as if we are in control.

Complexity manifests itself in different aspects of our existence. Culturally and socially we have to cope with an extremely wide array of different paradigms. Different understandings of ethnicity, race, gender and religion form part of our daily interaction with others. Even such basic things as good manners, civilised behaviour and what one should and should not eat are contested notions. We do not have the luxury of simply retreating into the familiar, or rather when that happens, it is often a way of elevating our own understanding and habits to a privileged level, that of being somehow the correct way of doing things.

Economically our world has become a quagmire. The divide between the rich and poor is as stark as ever. Vast amounts of money are spent on trivial activities – luxuries for the well-heeled, symbolic acts by national states, rampant consumerism by all ages (just think of all the resources used by computer games, sporting activities, clothing, accessories and electronic gadgets) – while people die of hunger and curable diseases. Unbridled capitalism has broken the world open, creating wealth for some whilst exploiting others. If one looks at the bigger picture, it is a system out of control.

The complexity experienced on the social, technological and economic fronts has resulted in a way of life which is not sustainable in the long run. The effects that our ways of living have on the environment are becoming clear to even the most stubborn, yet we still use economic and political arguments to justify the way in which we are raping the planet. Part of the problem is that many agencies – agencies of government, of business, of other social institutions and individuals – decide and act, as if they understand the complexity of the world, as if they can predict the outcomes of their decisions.

This attitude is not only wrong, but it is dangerous. The failure to acknowledge the complexities of the world, to deal with them as if our conventional scientific models are adequate is not only destroying the world, it is destroying our humanity. As we slip more and more into a linear, instrumental kind of thinking, a kind of thinking which relies on oversimplified models of society, economics and even scientific understanding, we become more like those models: linear, one-dimensional, machine-like, self-centred, heartless. What is more, the things people do to escape our instrumental existence or our daily drudgery, things like popular consumer culture or religion, are in themselves superficial and dehumanising. How much meaningful human interaction take place in a club where you are bombarded with distorted noise? How much do we benefit from a commercialised spirituality? How many of our human relationships are not defined by a contractual framework?

These questions should be addressed on a number of levels. Nevertheless, some may argue that the pursuit of pure scientific knowledge is an activity separated from everyday human life, that in the laboratory or doing simulations on a computer, we are busy with activities which are objective and neutral. I wish to argue that this is not the case and that even our pure scientific activities need to be re-evaluated in the light of the complex things they are dealing with. This argument rests on the nature of complex systems, and the implications this complexity has for our knowledge of them. Let us examine some of these issues.

What is complexity?[1]

A "general" notion of complexity involves a host of epistemological problems. Not only is it difficult to define complexity, it is, at least philosophically, difficult to find a language to talk about it at all. This does not mean that one cannot say some substantial things about it. One can make a number of distinctions which will constrain the meaning of the notion without pinning it down in a final way. The characterisation developed in this way is thus not final – in specific contexts there may be more characteristics one could add, and some of those presented here may not always be applicable – but it helps us to make significant claims about the nature of complexity, claims that may shift our understanding in radical ways.

In the first place one should recognise that complexity is a characteristic of a system. Complex behaviour arises because of the interaction among the components of a system. One cannot, therefore, focus on individual components, but on their relationships. The properties of the system emerge as a result of these interactions; they are not contained within individual components. A second important issue is to recognise that a complex system generates new structures internally. It is not reliant on an external designer. This process is referred to, somewhat problematically, as self-organisation. In reaction to the conditions in the environment, the system has to adjust some of its internal structure. In order to survive, or even flourish, the tempo at which these changes take place is vital.[2]

1 See Cilliers 1998 for a detailed discussion of the nature of complex systems.

2 See Cilliers 2006.

An important distinction can be made between "complex" and "complicated" systems. Certain systems may be quite intricate, say something like a jumbo jet. Nevertheless, one can take it apart and put it together again. Even if such a system cannot be understood by a single person, it is understandable in principle. Complex systems, on the other hand, come to be in the interaction of the components. If one takes it apart, the emergent properties are destroyed. If one wishes to study such systems, examples of which are the brain, living systems, social systems, ecological systems and socio-ecological systems, one has to investigate the system as such. It is exactly at this point that conventional analytical and reductionist methods fail.

If we follow an open research strategy – a strategy which is open to new insights as well as to its own limitations – we cannot dismiss the argument above in any final way. Nevertheless, until such time as the emergent properties of a system are fully understood, it is foolish to treat them as if we understand them already. Given the finitude of human understanding, some aspects of a complex system may always be beyond our grasp. This is no reason to give up on our efforts to understand things clearly. It is the role of scientific enquiry to be as exact as possible. However, there are good reasons why we have to be extremely careful about the reach of the scientific claims we make. In order to examine these reasons in more detail, a more systematic discussion of the nature of complex systems is required. The following characteristics will help us to do this:[3]

1. Complex systems are open systems.
2. They operate under conditions not at equilibrium.
3. Complex systems consist of many components. The components themselves are often simple (or can be treated as such).
4. The output of components is a function of their inputs. At least some of these functions must be non-linear.
5. The state of the system is determined by the values of the inputs and outputs.
6. Interactions are defined by actual input-output relationships and these are dynamic (the strength of the interactions change over time).
7. Components, on average, interact with many others. There are often multiple routes possible between components, mediated in different ways.
8. Many sequences of interaction will provide feedback routes, whether long or short.
9. Complex systems display behaviour that results from the interaction among components and not from characteristics inherent to the components themselves. This is sometimes called emergence.

[3] The following characterisation is based on material used in Cilliers 2005. It is provided in order to substantiate the general epistemological and ethical claims made in the following section.

10. Asymmetrical structure (temporal, spatial and functional organisation) is developed, maintained and adapted in complex systems through internal dynamic processes. Structure is maintained even though the components themselves are exchanged or renewed.
11. Complex systems display behaviour over a divergent range of timescales. This is necessary in order for the system to cope with its environment. It must adapt to changes in the environment quickly, but it can only sustain itself if at least part of the system changes at a slower rate than changes in the environment. This part can be seen as the 'memory' of the system.
12. More than one legitimate description of a complex system is possible. Different descriptions will decompose the system in different ways and are not reducible to one another. Different descriptions may also have different degrees of complexity.

If one considers the implications of these characteristics carefully a number of insights and problems arise:

- The *structure* of a complex system enables it to behave in complex ways. If there is too little structure (i.e. many degrees of freedom), the system can behave more randomly, but not more functionally. The mere 'capacity' of the system (i.e. the total number of degrees of freedom available if the system was not structured in any way) does not serve as a meaningful indicator of the complexity of the system. Complex behaviour is possible when the behaviour of the system is constrained. On the other hand, a fully constrained system has no capacity for complex behaviour either. This claim is not quite the same as saying that complexity exists somewhere on the edge between order and chaos. A wide range of structured systems display complex behaviour.
- Since different descriptions of a complex system decompose the system in different ways, the knowledge gained by any description is always relative to the perspective from which the description was made. This does not imply that any description is as good as any other. It is merely the result of the fact that only a limited number of characteristics of the system can be taken into account by any specific description. Although there is no *a priori* procedure for deciding which description is correct, some descriptions will deliver more interesting results than others.
- In describing the macro-behaviour (or emergent behaviour) of the system, not all the micro-features can be taken into account. The description on the macro-level is thus a reduction of complexity, and cannot be an exact description of what the system actually does. Moreover, the emergent properties on the macro-level can influence the micro-activities, a phenomenon sometimes referred to as "top-down causation". Nevertheless, macro-behaviour is not the result of anything else but the micro-activities in the system, keeping in mind that these are not only influenced by their mutual interaction and by top-down effects, but also by the interaction of the system with its environment. When we do science,

we usually work with descriptions that operate mainly on a macro-level. These descriptions will always be approximations of some kind.

These insights have important implications for the knowledge-claims we make when dealing with complex systems. Since we do not have direct access to the complexity itself, our knowledge of such systems is in principle limited. The problematic status of our knowledge of complexity needs to be discussed in a little more detail.

Complexity, knowledge and ethics

The argument that our understanding of complex systems is problematic in principle can be made in the following way: to fully understand a complex system, we need to understand it in all its complexity. Furthermore, because complex systems are open systems, we need to understand the system's complete environment before we can understand the system, and, of course, the environment is complex in itself. There is no human way of doing this. The knowledge we have of complex systems is based on the models we make of these systems, but in order to function as models – and not merely as a repetition of the system – they have to reduce the complexity of the system. This means that some aspects of the system are always left out of consideration. The problem is compounded by the fact that that which is left out, interacts with the rest of the system in a non-linear way and we cannot, therefore, predict what the effects of our reduction of the complexity will be, especially not as the system and its environment develop and transform in time.

We cannot have complete knowledge of complex systems; we can only have knowledge in terms of a certain framework. There is no stepping outside of complexity (we are finite beings), thus there is no framework for frameworks. We choose our frameworks. This choice need not be arbitrary in any way, but it does mean that the status of the framework (and the framework itself) cannot be used as the basis for objective knowledge. The generation of knowledge of complex systems is an exploratory process. As the context in which this knowledge is to be useful changes, we will have to continually revise the framework which generates this knowledge. Our knowledge of complex systems is thus always provisional. We have to be modest about the claims we make about such knowledge.

An understanding of knowledge as constituted within a complex system of interactions would, on the one hand, deny that knowledge can be seen as atomised "facts" that have objective meaning. Knowledge comes to be in a dynamic network of interactions, a network that does not have distinctive borders. On the other hand, this perspective would also deny that knowledge is something purely subjective, mainly because one cannot conceive of the subject as something prior to the "network of knowledge", but rather as something constituted within that network. The argument from complexity thus wants to move beyond the objective/subjective dichotomy. The dialectical relationship between knowledge and the system within which it is constituted has to be acknowledged. The two do not exist independently, thus making it impossible to first sort out the system (or context), and then to identify the knowledge within the system.[4] This co-determination also means that knowledge, and the system within which it is constituted, is in constant transformation. What appears to be uncontroversial at one point may not remain so for long.

One should also be careful not to interpret this state of affairs as somehow inadequate, as something to be improved upon. There is a necessary relationship between the imposition of a limiting framework and the generation of knowledge. One cannot have knowledge without a framework. Despite the fact that our knowledge is of necessity limited, these limits are enabling, they allow us to make claims which are neither relativistic nor vague.[5] At the same time, however, such knowledge is not the result of free-floating truths; it is contextualised in time and space. Because it is not objective, and because we know that, we cannot use this knowledge as if it were objective. There is always a normative dimension to the claims we make, and we have to stand in for them. We cannot shift the responsibility for the effects of our claims onto some process we call "scientific".

The argument for the inevitability of an ethical position when dealing with complexity can be made in the following way: since we cannot have complete knowledge of complex things we cannot "calculate" their behaviour in any deterministic way. We have to interpret and evaluate. Our decisions always involve an element of choice which cannot be justified objectively. What is more, no matter how carefully our actions are considered, they may turn out to have been a mistake. Thus, acknowledging that values and choice are involved does not provide any guarantee that good will come of what we do. Complexity tells us that ethics will be involved, but does not tell us what that ethics could actually be. The ethics of complexity is thus radically or perpetually ethical. There is no *a priori* principle we can follow, nor utility we can compute. We do not escape the realm of choice.

It is clear that, beyond the realisation that we are always in trouble, this position does not generate universal or even general ethical guidelines. It constitutes a radically critical position, the main component of which is self-critique. The question is, can it be made more substantial? A first response would be that it is better to make the value judgements explicit than to claim a false objectivity. In this way the complexity of the problem can be opened up and the differences respected. But perhaps the critical position itself constitutes a kind of ethical strategy. This should still be developed in some detail, but some initial ideas can be presented here.

The critical position

A radically critical position does not entail negativity or inaction. It is not an excuse for being dismissive or lazy, nor is it anarchistic or parasitic. It contains a strategy for action and it demands taking a stance, not with arrogance or confidence, but with modesty and determination. It is not only a strategy which aims to address the unsustainable state of affairs in the world, but also one which may redefine aspects of our humanity. From the perspective which acknowledges complexity, we know

4 See also Morin 2007.

5 See Cilliers 2005.

that we cannot criticise from a position which knows in any objective sense what it is criticising, or what the alternatives would be. The critique itself is provisional and open to transformation. Despite the fact that we cannot give any *a priori* content to the critical position, we can say something about the attitude and style involved, something which may provide a kind of moveable platform from which to work. Four such aspects are worth elaborating on.

In the first place, every claim we make or position we take should be provisional. Our understanding of the world should follow from principles which are in principle revisable. This does not mean that we should take in vague, unclear or relativist positions, that is, we should not argue that any position is as good as any other. We should take in clear, understandable, defensible and falsifiable positions, but we should defend these positions with modesty. To acknowledge that we may be wrong, in part or in whole, is not weak, it is the only responsible attitude we can assume in a complex world. The moment of critique is not a humiliation, it is an opportunity to learn, to change. It opens up the possibility to leap into a different future.

A critical position informed by complexity should, in the second place, be transgressive. It has to challenge. It can never simply re-enforce that which is current. Let us be more precise. Our actions are legitimated by current structures of power. It is in the nature of these structures to maintain conditions which provide them with the platform from which they operate. It is not in their interest to question these platforms, let alone to criticise or dismiss them. There is thus a force at play whose aim is not only to maintain the status quo, but to convince us that the status quo is good for us. If we wish to change paths in a truly transformative way, we cannot allow that the conditions for this transformation be determined by those whose interests lie in resisting such transformation. We should resist the macho nature of most current political and economic cultures, irrespective of whether it is politically correct to do so or not. We should not be coerced, frightened or shamed into a state where we relinquish being transgressively critical.

Can this be done with the modesty which the complexity perspective demands? I think that it can only be done with modesty. Although the stance we take should be transgressive, it should not do so as if a new arrival is foreseen. The transgression itself should be provisional in the sense that it would have to be transgressed again. There is thus a double movement at stake here. We have to act beyond the limits determined by the status quo. This transgression has to be decisive, but should not inaugurate a new status quo. The critical position argues for a perpetual transgression.

In order to keep the double movement alive, a critical position will, in the third place, have to be ironical. Neither the current state of affairs, nor any state resulting from our attempts at transformation, can be justified objectively. We cannot take the position of others, nor our own positions, as the final measure of anything. To prevent this realisation from becoming disabling, we have to think and act with some irony. This does not mean that we should avoid judgements or actions, it just means that when we do so, we should also have our tongue in our cheeks. If we take our position too seriously, we are not far away from introducing new dogma.

Many may find this position controversial. We are faced with serious problems which need serious attention. However, the argument for irony does not mean that we thumb our noses at the horrors of the world in any way. What it does mean is that we take no position so seriously that we are not willing to criticise or transform it. If this cannot be done with an element of humour, we become revolutionary machines which trample over others on the way to our lofty goals. In order to maintain our humanity, we also have to laugh, but always at ourselves first.

In the fourth place, a central role for the imagination is indispensable when we deal with complex things. Since we cannot calculate what will or should happen, we have to make a creative leap in order to imagine what things could be like. Aesthetic and creative activities are thus not interesting diversions, they open up the possibility of imagining better, more sustainable futures.

Traditional philosophy has often argued that there are different forms of knowledge – empirical, ethical and aesthetical, for example – and that they have to be kept apart. The perspective from complexity does not want to eliminate the differences between different forms of knowledge, but it does argue that there are relationships between them which should not be trivialised. A scientific theory, especially one which makes interesting claims about the world, does not simply carry its meaning on its face. It has to be developed, investigated and interpreted. In this respect it shares certain properties with a poem, for example. As a matter of fact, if we say that in a complex world we always have partial knowledge, that there is more meaning than that which can be reduced to calculation, then the idea of the "poem" becomes generalised. The world is a poem to us, we are poems to ourselves. An acknowledgement that creative interpretation forms a fundamental part of our engagement with the world opens up the possibility to be less machinelike, to be more human in everything we do, including science.

Becoming more human

A critical stance which is provisional, transgressive, ironical and creative should be seen as challenging and liberating, as an attitude which opens up the future. It argues that we should not fall in the trap of the "present". The present is contingent, it could have been otherwise. The future can thus also be something vastly different than simply an extrapolation of the present. We should not be determined by the status quo, we should not privilege the probable over the unlikely, or the existing over the imagined.

The acknowledgement of living in a complex world and the critical stance it implies does not simply confront us with a number of practical problems; it confronts us with questions about how our humanity is constituted. We have to reflect on how we engage with the world on a very basic level: Which systems do I participate in? With whom do I associate? What do I invest my time in? What kind of a person am I? These are "first" questions, questions which precede questions such as: How much influence do I have? How do I further my cause? What do I own? How do I get better? This shift in priorities is essential. We will not first fix the world, and then become better human beings. We have to transform our understanding of what the central components of being human could be. Once we have shifted these constitutive components away from instrumental, reductive, materialistic and self-centred issues, it may just be possible for a more human and a more beautiful world to emerge.

Reference List

Cilliers P. 1998. *Complexity and Postmodernism. Understanding complex systems.* London: Routledge.

— 2005. Complexity, Deconstruction and Relativism. *Theory, Culture & Society* 22(5):255-267.

— 2006. On the importance of a certain slowness. Stability, memory and hysteresis in complex systems. *Emergence: Complexity & Organization* 8(3):106-113.

Morin E. 2007. Restricted complexity, general complexity. In: C Gershenson, D Aerts & B Edmonds (eds). *Worldviews, science and us: Philosophy and complexity*. Singapore: World Scientific. 5-29.

NEUROBIOLOGICAL FOUNDATIONS

Mark Solms

I am painfully aware that my colleagues in the Humanities become twitchy when we discuss the biological foundations of being human. It makes them worry about reductionism and other chauvinistic tendencies ... even racism. It gives me no pleasure to be suspected of such things, so I ask at the outset that you suspend judgment and give what I have to say a balanced hearing. Fundamentally, I want to ask whether our discomfort with the discussion of our biological origins might not itself reveal something important about being human.

Evolution

The evidence that we evolved – over many millions of years – from earlier, nonhuman species is so overwhelming that I will not even present it as part of my argument. I will take this to be the self-evident starting point of what I want to say. The fact that *Homo sapiens sapiens* evolved implies that, whatever else it might mean to be human, we are in the first instance a species; we are a type of animal. I know that the word 'human' is frequently used in contradistinction to 'animal', but that is precisely the point. We all too readily forget that the distinction between human and animal cannot be a radical one. In fact, looked at from an evolutionary viewpoint, it can only be described as a rather tenuous distinction – as an exaggeration, if you like.

The tendency to exaggerate the differences between ourselves and other animals is reminiscent of Freud's (1930) conception of the "narcissism of minor differences". When closely related populations compete for the same territory, they emphasise small distinguishing features between themselves and the competing group in order to obscure the more substantial commonalities. In so doing, they feel special while they derogate the others.

While there are of course a few important things that do differentiate humans from other animals, and do make them special, there are far more things that do not. Therefore, while I accept that a consideration of the biological foundations of being human must culminate in a description of the uniquely human features, these should not form the foundations of our analysis. It is better to first describe the features that we share in common with those animals that are most closely related to us. This contextualises the uniquely human features and enables us better to understand them.

Mammals

Where, then, should we start; which non-human animals are sufficiently close relatives to provide the necessary context? I suggest that we begin with the biological class to which we belong – namely that of mammals – which diverged from the other lines roughly 200 million years ago. What distinguishes mammals, perhaps above all, is the fact that they suckle their young. This is made possible by the anatomical fact that mammals possess mammary glands. Mammary glands are wonderful things, but they are not our only distinguishing anatomical feature. The features I would prefer to focus on are those that have the greatest impact on mammalian *behaviour and mental life*. I think this is the aspect of being human (or being mammalian) that concerns us most. We all know what humans and other mammals look like from the outside; this is not what concerns us here. What concerns us more is what makes us tick, from the inside; what makes us human *beings*.

The distinguishing mental and behavioural characteristics of animals are inscribed anatomically and physiologically in their brains. This is true even if the brain and nervous system are ultimately inextricable from other bodily systems. Thus, for example, although mammalian suckling evolved in tandem with changes in the mammalian endocrine and reproductive systems, suckling itself (the inclination to suckle and knowing how to suckle) is mediated by the brain. This, then, is the aspect of mammalian anatomy and physiology that we shall focus on: the brain mechanisms that mediate the being of a mammal.

Instincts

Before doing so, however, I want to set out two basic assumptions. Firstly, I am not going to revisit the tiresome debates surrounding the mind-body relation. I take it for granted that the structure and functions of the mammalian brain mediate mammalian behaviour and mental life. This assumption applies to all behaviour and mental life. But, secondly, I do not intend to describe the whole brain. I want to focus particularly on the brain structures and functions that mediate the *instinctual* tendencies of mammals. I focus on instincts because they are the aspects of mental life and behaviour that are most stereotyped. Of course mammals are shaped by other things, too – differences in the individual endowment and environment – but these differences influence a pre-existing 'default' plan. The default plan of mammalian behaviour and mental life is determined by the mere fact of being a mammal. Mammals do not learn to suckle (for example); they just do it. They are constituted that way. This instinctual part of what it is to be a particular type of animal is the common denominator that applies to the type as a whole. It is therefore the most essential part of what makes them tick – and the part that we shall take as our starting point.

What, then, are instincts and where do they come from? Instincts are inborn behavioural and mental tendencies. They are inborn for the reason that they are fundamental to the reproductive fitness of a particular type of animal. To put it differently, animals that behave in particular ways which increase their chances of surviving to reproduce (increase their reproductive fitness) will for that very reason pass on the genes that incline them to behave that way; and those that are inclined to behave differently, will not, or will be less likely to. This is called natural selection. Thus the genes that predispose animals to act in ways that enhance their reproductive fitness are passed down from generation to generation. They are evolutionarily conserved. A type of animal is thereby 'bred' to behave and feel in particular ways. These are the instincts of that type of animal.

Values

Of paramount importance in all this, in my view, is the fact that by dint of the existence of instincts, an inborn system of *values* underpins the way in which all animals behave. The most basic of these values is the very principle that it is 'good' to survive and reproduce. This principle is not preordained; it simply follows, blindly but directly, from the facts of natural selection, as just outlined. We are therefore, by default, in consequence of the fundamental biological fact of natural selection, inherently inclined to do and feel those things that enhance our reproductive fitness. This is no small matter. It implies that what 'is' and what 'ought to be' are not as radically distinct as some philosophers would have us believe (Hume 1739). It also implies that our most basic values were laid down a very, very long time before Moses descended Mount Sinai.

I am well aware that readers are at this point thinking of counter-examples from their own lives which prove that they personally do not always act in accordance with the laws I have just outlined. I therefore ask you to remember that I am starting with the broader context – not with what applies to you personally but with what applies to mammals in general. Then I will discuss the case of humans in particular, from which you may extrapolate the complexities of your own personal circumstances.

Feelings

I turn now to the manner in which the biological system of values embodied in our instincts is communicated to each individual animal. It is communicated through *feelings*. As a general rule, when an animal behaves in accordance with its instincts (i.e. when it acts in ways that enhance its chances of surviving to reproduce) it feels 'good'; when it does not it feels 'bad'. This seems to be what feelings are for. They motivate us to act in accordance with our instincts (see Freud 1911; Damasio 1999).

This, in a sense, defines the most basic instinct of all; we are compelled to act in ways that make us feel good, and to avoid things that make us feel bad. Freud called this the 'pleasure principle'.This, the most basic motivational principle, evolved long before mammals did. We know this from the fact that the brain region that mediates this basic form of hedonic consciousness – feelings of pleasure and unpleasure – namely the periaqueductal grey (PAG), evolved long before mammals differentiated from the other classes of vertebrate. In fact the PAG is conserved in all vertebrates. It is therefore at least 525 million years old. This ancient structure can still be found today, in you and me (Fig. 1), for the very reason that it is so fundamental for our survival.

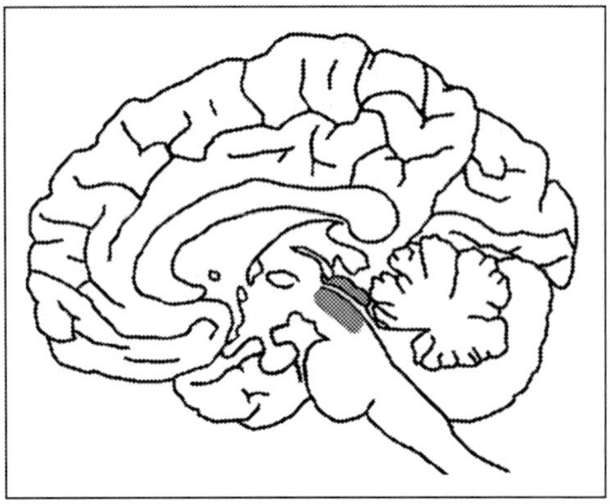

Figure 1

It has a columnar structure, with the dorsal (back) columns generating profoundly unpleasant feelings, and the ventral (front) ones generating what can only be called orgasmic delight. Important to mention, but perhaps needless to say, is the fact that the columns that generate these primitive feelings are closely connected with other cell groups that generate primitive movements. In this way pleasurable feelings are connected with compulsory 'approach' behaviours, and unpleasurable ones with compulsive 'withdrawal'. This tight connection between instincts, emotions and behaviours ensures that we act in accordance with our innate values.

But the simple dichotomy between good and bad feelings (and their associated behaviours) cannot possibly do justice to the complexity of the world. Thus, for the same reason that the pleasure principle itself evolved in the first place, more subtle and elaborated instinctual mechanisms developed subsequently. As far as mammals are concerned, seven such instincts have been identified to date. These are not exclusive to mammals (we share some of them with birds, for example) but they do apply to *all* mammals. They are our common ancestral inheritance. We should be grateful for this inheritance, because without it we would not exist at all. The phylogenetic lines that selected the genes that inclined our ancestors to behave and feel in these ways are the reason that we humans evolved. For this same reason, all seven of the basic mammalian instincts that I am about to describe are still conserved in the human brain today. Instincts, once they have evolved, are very hard to shake off; they are profoundly conservative things. These seven instincts are, as already conveyed, approximately 200 million years old. For reasons that should be self evident, they are all anatomically connected with the PAG; they are all in a sense rostral (upward) extensions and elaborations of the PAG.

1. Seeking

The first and perhaps most important of the seven mammalian instincts is given different names by different scientists. Rolls (1999) for example calls it the 'reward' system, while Panksepp (1998) calls it the SEEKING system, and Berridge (1996) calls it the 'wanting' system. Anatomically, this system overlaps strongly with the medial forebrain bundle (Fig. 2). Its origin is the ventral tegmental area (VTA) and its major terminus is the shell of the nucleus accumbens, in the ventral striatum, but it also projects to several other brain regions. Chemically, its command neurotransmitter is dopamine.

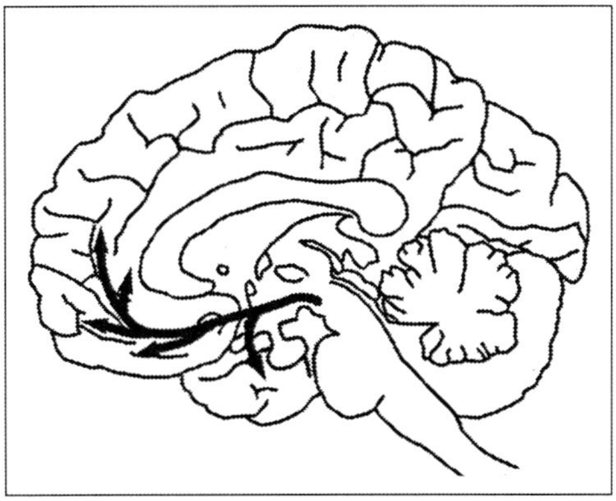

Figure 2

I will follow Panksepp's terminology here, but the common denominator underlying the range of different names for this system convey the essential quality of what it does for the animal. It compels it to engage with the environment in response to appetitive needs. It is obvious how fundamentally important this instinct is, because everything that we need – biologically speaking – is to be found in the world around us. The fact that we cannot satisfy our own needs and have to find the objects of our desire in the world outside of our selves (and consequently engage in struggle, competition, and risk, etc.) is one of the most fundamental facts of life. If it were not for the existence of the SEEKING instinct, we would never learn this basic lesson ('go forth and multiply'). We would expire in the narcissistic haze of entitlement that characterises 'his majesty the baby' during the earliest phase of pre-ambulatory dependency. (For more about the neurobiology of this dependency, see Sections 5 & 6.)

Typical mammalian SEEKING behaviours are foraging and similar generalised exploratory activities. (Imagine a dog in an open field.) An interesting and important fact about the SEEKING system is its primary 'objectless' quality. It does not drive the animal to seek specific objects in response to specific needs. No matter what the currently active needs may be (as detected by the relevant nuclei in the medial hypothalamus) the SEEKING system responds in the same way: it motivates the animal to go out and explore, to look for something – anything – interesting and nice. It propels the animal to investigate the world and engage with it, in the firm belief that whatever it needs or wants, it is 'out there'. Accordingly, the feeling tone that accompanies the exploratory and interactive behaviour triggered by SEEKING is energised, expectant optimism, or exuberant, curious interest. If and when the animal does then – accidentally, as it were – find what it needs, it *learns* that relief of a particular urge (consummation of a particular appetite) is causally linked with the particular object that it came upon. The SEEKING system (in conjunction with the system to be described next) therefore leads to the establishment of causal connections.

For this reason, the SEEKING instinct is closely tied to meaning-making; it could also be described as an epistemophilic instinct. Meaning-making and intentionality are absolutely fundamental properties of the mind. It is perhaps not surprising, therefore, to learn that over-activation of this system produces mental illness: psychotic symptoms like hallucinations and delusions (excessive meaning-making, and finding causal connections where none exist) (see Kapur 2003).

Amphetamines and cocaine stimulate the SEEKING system very directly. Anyone who is familiar with the over-energised 'cruising' behaviour of someone who has snorted cocaine at a party will know from personal experience what the SEEKING system does. It is also not surprising to learn that this system is heavily implicated in almost all forms of addiction (see Volkow *et al* 2009). This system is the fundamental vehicle of craving. (An understanding of the instinctual mechanisms of the human brain holds many important lessons for psychiatry.)

The meaning-making process just described (i.e. linking specific needs with specific objects and thereby learning how to meet one's needs in the world) is obviously pivotal to all learning. It is in fact the driving force behind learning. This demonstrates how instincts, which are stereotyped and inflexible things, nevertheless underpin open-ended, flexible cognitive processes like learning.

The primordial values that the SEEKING system generates are something like the following: it is 'good' to go forth, explore, interact, engage with the world, to investigate, to work, to find meaning in the world. It is 'bad' to be inert, lazy and apathetic.

2. Pleasure

Berridge (1996) distinguishes between the 'wanting' system just described – which is the basic mammalian *appetitive* system – and the 'liking' system – which is the basic *consummation* system. (The affective distinction between wanting and liking is fundamental; think for example of the difference between the pleasure of sexual arousal and the pleasure of orgasm.) The term 'wanting,' however, implies wanting something in particular; it is therefore perhaps not a good name for the primary, objectless SEEKING instinct. Berridge's term 'wanting' only makes sense in connection with 'liking'; wanting in this sense is a consequence of learning. Learning, as I have already said, arises from an interaction between SEEKING and PLEASURE; it is not an instinct in itself (Solms & Panksepp 2011).

Chemically, the PLEASURE ('liking') system is primarily opioid mediated. (For artificial equivalents of the feeling states it produces, try opium and heroin.) Not surprisingly, it is connected directly with and is the primary anatomical destination of the SEEKING system; and it projects back downward to the ventral PAG (Fig. 3). Also not surprising is the physiological fact that activation of the PLEASURE system leads to deactivation of the SEEKING system. They are reciprocally interactive. This is how we learn to connect the various needs with specific objects in the world – how we learn to meet our needs in the world.

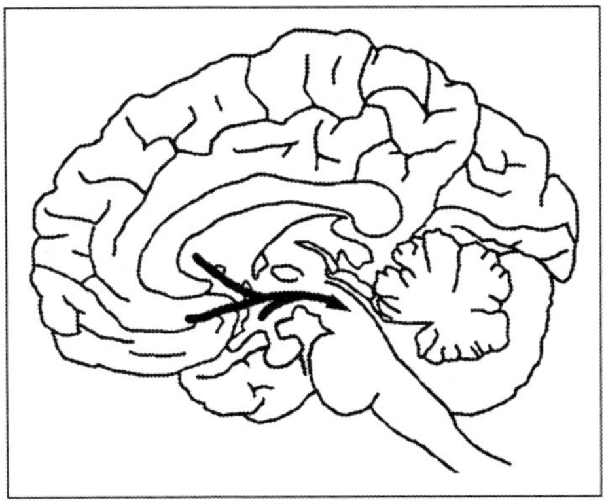

Figure 3

The primordial value system that PLEASURE encodes is that it is 'good' to meet one's needs, or conversely, that unrequited need is 'bad'. Combining the action of the SEEKING and PLEASURE systems, we learn also that pleasure for its own sake never really satisfies, that pure hedonism is less 'good' than actual satisfaction of need through appropriate action in the world. These are of course things that we all know; but that is precisely my point. The evolutionarily conserved brain mechanisms that I am describing are where such innate knowledge, such innate systems of value, come from.

3. Anger

The third of our primordial values dictates that it is 'bad' to be prevented from getting what you need or want. Irritation and anger are readily evoked in such circumstances; and these responses are directed towards the obstacle in question. The purpose of an aggressive attack is to get rid of an obstacle to satisfaction – in a word, to annihilate it.

The ANGER system in the mammalian brain has its origins in the medial (inner) parts of the amygdala, and it terminates in the dorsal PAG (Fig. 4). Like all the other instincts, activation of this system evokes a particular set of behaviours. In this case, full-blown 'affective attack' behaviours include baring the teeth, raising the forelimbs, extending the claws (if you have them), piloerection, and lunging towards the object of your wrath. More muted anger behaviours include, for instance, pacing and growling. Such behaviours are always guided and accompanied by particular feeling states – in this case, feelings of irritability, anger or rage.

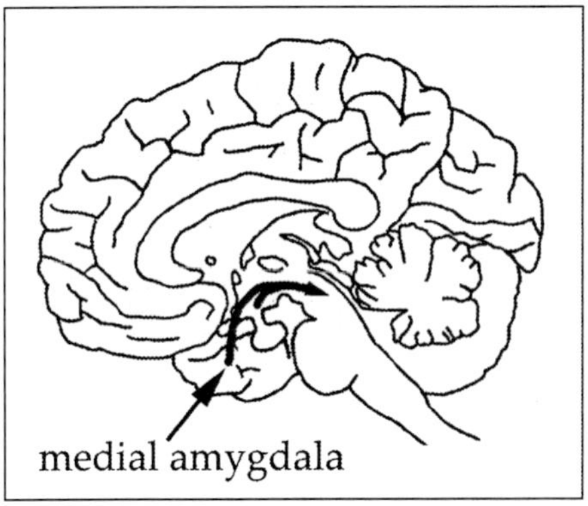

Figure 4

These feelings do not accompany all aggressive behaviours. Neurobiologists distinguish between 'hot' and 'cold' aggression. Cold aggression is also known as 'predatory' aggression. Cold aggression is associated with activation of the SEEKING system, not ANGER. A lion chasing a springbok is not angry; it is hungry. The feeling associated with predatory aggression is more likely to be invigorated anticipation than blind hatred. This distinction has forensic implications in humans.

4. Fear

The so-called 'fight or flight' response reflects the fact that attack is not always the best way to deal with an adversary. The close link between these two responses is, however, embodied in the fact that the FEAR system, like the ANGER system, has its epicentre in the amygdala, albeit in a different part of it (Fig. 5).

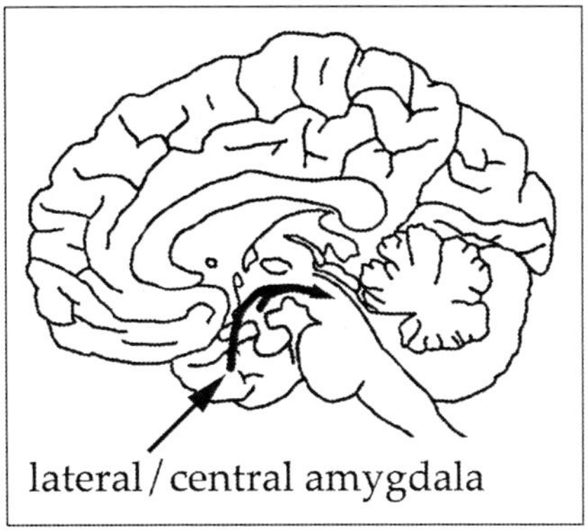

Figure 5

The most common behaviours activated by FEAR are freezing and fleeing responses. Again, the behaviours in question are accompanied and guided by characteristic feeling states – namely, in this case, trepidatious anxiety (accompanied, as are all basic emotions, by characteristic physiological changes, such as – in this case – rapid shallow breathing, increased heart rate, and redirection of blood from the gut to the skeletal musculature). Again, as with all instincts, the behavioural responses in question are not learned; they are innate. Mammals 'know' from day one that certain objects and situations are frightening. Newborn rodents, for example, freeze when exposed to just a single feline hair – even if they have never seen a cat before (let alone had the opportunity to discover their general attitude toward mice). It is easy to see why this is the case; if mice had to learn from experience how to respond to cats, that would be the only experiences mice ever had before they were killed! And that would be the end of mice. That is how evolution works.

However, again, as with all instincts, we also learn from experience to associate certain objects with FEAR; we learn to classify objects of our experience in accordance with the resemblance between their properties and those of innate instinctual FEAR stimuli. Electric sockets, for example, could not possibly have been innately encoded as objects of FEAR; they have to be associated with it on the basis of individual experience. In this way, we classify all the objects in the world in accordance with a primordial taxonomy – something akin to Kant's (1781) 'categories'. There appear to be seven such categories; seven major varieties of 'good' and 'bad'. The category of objects that we classify as deserving of FEAR are 'bad' in a particular way.

It is 'bad' to be attacked or to be otherwise treated in a manner that might cause mortal harm (that might reduce one's chances of surviving and reproducing). This, presumably, is the evolutionary origin of Freud's infamous 'castration anxiety'.

It is important to mention that once we have learnt to fear (or desire, or hate) a particular object, situation or place, the instinctual classification of that object, situation or place is irreversible. Fear conditioning is, as LeDoux (1996) memorably put it, "indelible". This fact has important implications for our understanding of human mental life and behaviour, as we shall see below.

5. Panic/grief

The fifth basic mammalian instinct is the attachment instinct. Panksepp calls it the PANIC/GRIEF instinct. This dual name reflects the fact that the experience of loss (in the context of attachment) produces a biphasic instinctual response. The initial response of a juvenile mammal to separation from its mother is one of PANIC. Panic is of course a feeling state (but please note: it is different from FEAR). Ethologists describe the associated behaviour as 'protest' behaviour. Protest behaviour is characterised above all by 'distress vocalisations' – that is, by crying. Each mammal species cries in its own way. While emitting these distress vocalisations it wanders around anxiously looking for mum. (The mum, too, emits distress calls, and looks for the missing infant.) But if this initial behaviour does not lead to rapid reunion, protest gives way to the second phase of the separation/loss response, namely 'despair'. Now the lost juvenile gives up hope. The feeling of panic is replaced by the feeling of sadness. This, we believe, is the normal prototype of depression (Solms & Panksepp 2010). Giving up hope (the transition from protest to despair) seems to have evolved in order to prevent isolated juveniles from announcing their vulnerability to predators (and perhaps also to prevent metabolic exhaustion).

Feelings of panic and sadness (the pain of social loss) appear to be the evolutionary price that we mammals pay for the biological advantages bestowed by attachment. The most basic attachment is the mother-infant bond, the evolutionary advantage of which to the infant (especially in a suckling species) is obvious. It is important to recognise that the biological advantage to the mother of this bond is the survival of her genes via her offspring; hence the specificity of the mother/infant bond, and hence also the apparent altruism of parenthood.

The PANIC/GRIEF system, like the PLEASURE system, is opioid mediated. It is interesting in this respect that it appears to have evolved out of the brain's primitive analgesic system (Fig. 6). The mental pain of social loss in mammals seems to have (quite directly) evolved from the physical pain mechanisms of lower vertebrates. The pain associated with loss of a loved one is ameliorated by reunion (indeed, the pain motivates the seeking of reunion) in the same way that physical pain is ameliorated by morphine.

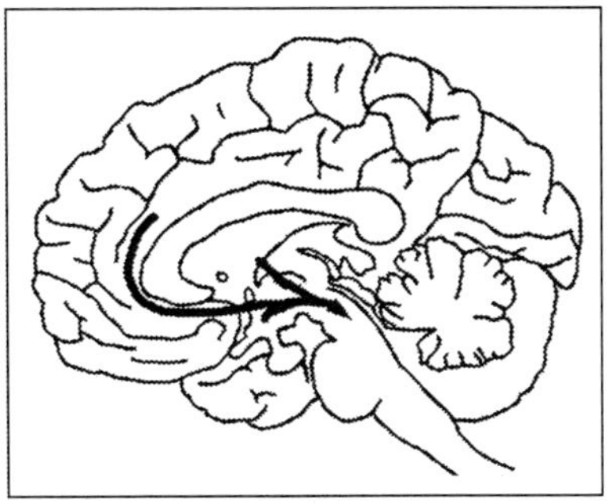

Figure 6

Although the PANIC/GRIEF system is paradigmatically activated through the formation of mother/infant bonds, it also underpins other bonds of biological significance, such as the formation of mating pairs and family groups. The primal values that arise from this system are that it is 'good' to be together with loved ones and 'bad' to be separated from them, or to lose them. Nobody has to teach a mammal that it is 'bad' to separate a pup from its mum. We acquire this knowledge with our mother's milk ... in fact before, for without this innate knowledge (this innate system of values) the milk would not have been provided in the first place. This leads to the sixth and penultimate mammalian instinct, namely maternal CARE.

6. Care

This instinct is more active in females than males. The same applies to the PANIC/GRIEF system, which the CARE system primes (via massive release of oxytocin, prolactin, progesterone and the like) during pregnancy. These sex differences are (in the average case) undeniable, as indeed they are with respect to the clinical consequences in humans. Depression, for example, is almost three times more common in females than in males; and this applies especially to females of child-bearing age. ANGER, by contrast, is more prevalent in males of all ages. Likewise whereas oxytocin (a 'female' peptide) facilitates loving trust and social bonding, vasopressin (the 'male' equivalent) mediates relentless persistence.

The values attached to the CARE instinct are that it is 'good' to care for one's offspring, to love, protect and feed them, and that it is 'bad' to neglect them. It is likewise 'good' to be cared for and to be cared about; it is 'good' to feel safe, secure and loved and to be groomed, stroked, held and carried. The addictive quality of love relationships is not as readily recognised as is the addictive character of dependence upon artificial opiates like heroin and morphine. Love is surely the primal addiction.

7. Play

The seventh and final mammalian instinct is the PLAY instinct. People are often surprised to learn that this is an instinct, but all juvenile mammals *need* to play. If they are deprived of their quota of play on any particular day, they will make it up the next day – as though by homeostatic rebound. We all know what rough and tumble play is, although it varies slightly from one type of mammal to another. The play session starts with an 'invitation' posture or gesture, then the game is on: the one animal exuberantly chases the other, then jumps on the other's back; then they roll over together and wrestle or tickle each other – always accompanied by peels of laughter (or the equivalent vocalisation) – then they are back on their feet again, and chasing each other in the reverse direction. The associated feeling state is equally universal: it feels like *fun*. Children just love to play. On the other hand, play commonly ends in tears (or in some form of negative emotion). This provides an important clue as to what PLAY is all about; it is about finding the limits of what is socially appropriate, tolerable, acceptable. When play is no longer fun for one of the participants, they don't want to play anymore. The limit has then been discovered. A very important criterion in this respect is *dominance*. In any play situation, one of the participants takes the lead role and the other the submissive role. (And yes – on average – the male becomes the dominant one.) This is fun for both participants so long as the dominant one does not insist on being 'on top' *all* of the time. The maximum acceptable ratio seems to be roughly 70:30.

This reveals a second, related function of PLAY, namely the establishment of social hierarchies – of a 'pecking order'. Accordingly, juvenile rough and tumble play increasingly gives way to *competitive* games, and also (in humans) to 'pretend' play, in which the participants 'try out' different social roles (Mum, Teacher, King of the Castle). We do not know what goes on in the imagination of other mammals when they play; but I would confidently suggest that they, too, are 'trying out' different social roles.

All of these facts reveal some of the innate values encoded in the PLAY system: it is 'good' to have fun, but 'bad' to do so selfishly; it is 'bad' to be a bully (and to be bullied); it is 'good' to compete and win; it is 'good' to be on top, but not all the time, etc.

We don't like to recognise that groups of humans, like all our closest animal relatives, naturally form complex hierarchies, with clear social rules (those governing primate behaviour are remarkably complex). The structures of families, clans, villages, even nations – almost any social group – are undeniably hierarchical, and have been so throughout history.

As with all of the instinctual tendencies I am describing here, this is not a matter of my personal preference; it is a matter of fact. If we do not face such facts we cannot begin to contend with them. The fact that instincts exist does not mean that we can do nothing about them, that we are obliged to simply indulge them. But we ignore (or deny) them at our peril. This leads me to the final section of my contribution.

Prefrontal lobes

The uniquely human aspect of our brains is not, then, a matter of its basic design. The basic design of the human brain is remarkably similar to that of all other mammals. It is more than 200 million years old. It is also not a matter of size, or ratio of cortex to subcortex (consider for example the brains of elephants, or whales). It is not even a matter of body/brain size ratio (mice beat us on that measure). It is a matter of the volume of the *prefrontal lobes* in relation to the rest of the brain. The miniscule amount of genetic difference between ourselves and chimpanzees (approximately 1%) boils down, neurobiologically speaking, to the relative size of our prefrontal lobes – the part of the brain above the eyes; the part behind the forehead (Fig. 7). This anatomical distinction – our evolutionary pride and joy – is less than one million years old.

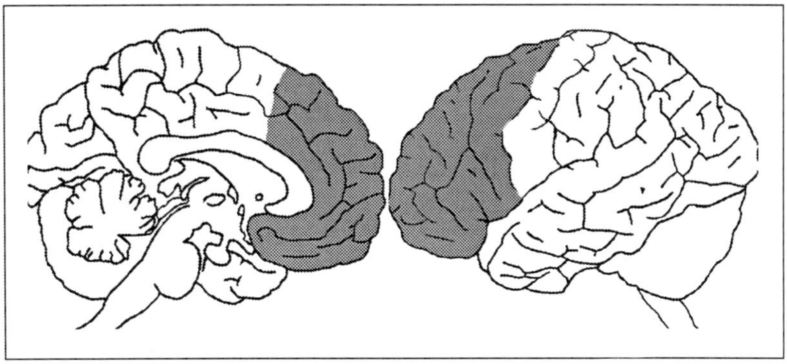

Figure 7

So what do the prefrontal lobes do? First and foremost, they *inhibit*. The ventromesial parts inhibit the outputs of the instinctual systems described above. This means that they block both the feelings and the motor actions normally associated with these instincts. Please note: they do not actually cancel them; they can only moderate their efferent expression. This means, for example, that inhibition of the 'indelible' conditioned FEAR responses mentioned earlier consists not in a failure to activate the learned association (the amygdala) but rather in a *co-activation* of structures which control the outputs of the instinct (the prefrontal cortex) which blocks the expression of fear and of the motor stereotypes of running or hiding. This is one of the reasons why some neurobiologists speak of 'free won't' rather than 'free will' (Libet 2004). Free will consists in freedom *not* to act in an automatic and preprogrammed fashion (Solms & Turnbull 2001).

Thus prefrontal inhibition permits *choice*; but it is important to recognise that choices in the real world are not totally free. They are still guided by underlying, aim-inhibited instincts, which necessarily remains active until the situation which triggered them in the first place is dealt with. Free will is in this sense a lot less free than we like to believe. One is always free to walk into a lion's den, but the degrees of freedom (the chances that you will actually do so) are greatly reduced by the FEAR activation that is associated with it.

The second major function of the prefrontal lobes, which flows directly from the first, is *thinking*. Instincts are compulsive and automatic; they are thoughtless. Thinking involves deliberation and choice. It is easy to see how choice can be achieved only if instinctual responses are inhibited – or at least delayed. Thinking intervenes between instincts and actions. This additional 'delayed response' phase in voluntary action essentially consists in *virtual* actions. In the safety of the virtual space of the mind (via what neuropsychologists call 'working memory', associated primarily with the dorsolateral parts of the prefrontal lobes) the animal can 'try out' the various options open to it, without any real consequences. Based on prevailing conditions, filtered through past experience, it can thereby *predict* the various likely outcomes, before making a considered choice as to which course of action it will follow in reality. (Thereafter it can similarly monitor progress toward the desired outcome, and flexibly alter the course of action in an ongoing fashion.)

One of the first tasks of prefrontal thinking is to synthesise conflicting instinctual responses to the same object (ambivalence). Consider for example feelings of ANGER toward a CARE object.

This is what prefrontal lobes do. It is clear what an enormous adaptive advantage is bestowed by such inhibitory and predictive capacity and the behavioural flexibility that flows from it. These are not uniquely human capacities though (other mammals have prefrontal lobes, too). But they are especially highly developed in humans. This additional (human) capacity produced the increased efficiencies of thought that are bestowed by *language*.

Language re-represents the virtual activity of thinking at even higher levels of abstraction, within a fixed system of logico-grammatical rules. These latter capacities, too, flow from our greater prefrontal volume. The dorsolateral prefrontal level of representation is, in a literal sense, the farthest removed from the concrete physicality of the autonomic core and the sensory periphery. This allows for the highest level of meta-representation. Language is a product, not a cause, of this enhanced capacity for abstraction and the higher systems of rules for thought that it inevitably generates. Language developed very, very recently in our evolutionary past (apparently between 40,000 and 80,000 years ago). It therefore must certainly have been preceded by other rule-based systems of abstraction – systems, for example, of a kind that enable us to govern the behaviour of large social groups. (Human social groups greatly increased in size following the transition from hunter-gatherer to pastoral/agricultural economies.) The formation of large social groups almost demands the creation of artificial systems of rules – civilisation – for the simple reason that our ancient instincts equip us to cope only with hunter-gatherer-sized groups. Indeed, the domestication of animals and the ability to cultivate crops must itself have resulted from our increased prefrontal capacity (from the capacity to forego short-term gratification in favour of greater – predicted – long-term rewards).

We are rightly proud of our highly developed prefrontal capacity. However, I would like to end this chapter by pointing out that increased inhibition and thinking (and all the flexible artifices and other benefits that flow from them) also come at a price. The price is this. Because the prefrontal lobes necessarily inhibit not only instinctual actions but also the affects (feelings) that accompany them, we humans are *uniquely ignorant of our own motivations*. We do not know why we do what we do. Our actions are so far removed from the instincts that motivated them (and unconsciously guide them) that we no longer know what we are trying to achieve.

If we could ask the remarkable human being who etched the first symbolic patterns into those pieces of ochre at Blombos cave, some 75,000 years ago (Henshilwood 2006), why she did so and what the patterns mean, I am confident that she would not be able to answer the question. She would have to admit, in uniquely human fashion, that she has no idea why she does such things. (The whole 'meaning of life' is a mystery to her.) Or, perhaps more likely, and again in uniquely human fashion, she would deny the mystery and make up a story about it. She would invent an explanation. She would confabulate. And no doubt she would eventually come to believe her own confabulations. The human capacity for opaque motivation, self deception and hypocrisy is *truly* unique.

Reference List

Berridge K. 1996. Food reward: brain substrates of wanting and liking. *Neurosci Biobehav Rev* 20:1-25.

Damasio A. 1999. *The Feeling of What Happens*. London: Heinemann.

Freud S. 1911. Two principles of mental functioning. *Standard Edition* 12: 218-226. London: Hogarth Press.

— 1930. Civilization and its discontents. *Standard Edition* 21:64-145. London: Hogarth Press.

Henshilwood CS. 2006. Modern humans and symbolic behaviour: Evidence from Blombos Cave, South Africa. In: G Blundell (ed). *Origins*. Cape Town: Double Storey. 78-83.

Hume D. 1739. *A Treatise of Human Nature*. Oxford: Oxford University Press.

Kant I. 1781. *Critique of Pure Reason*. London: Palgrave Macmillan.

Kapur S. 2003. Psychosis as a state of aberrant salience. *Am J Psychiatr* 160: 13-23.

LeDoux J. 1996. *The Emotional Brain*. New York: Simon & Shuster.

Libet B. 2004. *Mind Time*. Harvard University Press.

Panksepp J. 1998. *Affective Neuroscience*. Oxford University Press.

Rolls E. 1999. *The Brain and Emotion*. Oxford University Press.

Solms M & Panksepp J. 2010. Why depression feels bad. In: E Perry, D Collerton, F LeBeau & H Ashton (eds). *New Horizons in the Neuroscience of Consciousness*. New York: John Benjamins.

— 2011. Neuropsychoanalytic notes on addiction. In: G Ellis, D Stein, E Meintjies & K Thomas (eds). *Substance Use and Abuse in South Africa*. University of Cape Town Press.

Solms M & Turnbull O. 2001. *The Brain and the Inner World*. London: Karnac Books.

Volkow N, Fowler J, Wang G, Baler R & Telang F. 2009. Imaging dopamine's role in drug abuse and addiction. *Neuropharmacology* 56 Suppl 1:3-8.

A CHRISTIAN HUMANIST PERSPECTIVE

John W de Gruchy

Our lives are a minute yet significant part of a cosmic story and the evolutionary processes that are central to it. These could, as Martin Rees eloquently surmises, "spread (life) through the entire Galaxy, evolving into a teeming complexity beyond what we can conceive" (Rees 2010:484). While located in this story at a particular time and place, as humans we are bound together by birth and death irrespective of time and place. Whatever else we may have in common with each other and the natural world, whatever the particularities of our own historical context or place on the evolutionary chain that precedes us and will continue after us, we share this origin and fate. But the hopes and potential of a new life that stretches into a future as yet unknown, and the reality of suffering and the inevitability of death that brings separation and closure to a personal story, raise serious queries about the meaning of life and the significance of being human.

Religious traditions and science share a common interest in these questions, but approach and answer them differently, though often in complementary ways. In this essay I will briefly offer a Christian humanist perspective. Underlying my approach is the conviction that this is not primarily about origins or where we come from however important that is, but more about how we should live today as we journey together into the future. How we do this shapes who we are and how we perceive reality and relate to others and the world. This, in turn, is informed by an ongoing conversation with others past and present whereby we find the ideas, words, images and narratives that give structure and meaning to our lives. In so far as we ask questions of meaning and significance, we seek answers from different perspectives shaped by culture, experience and education within a given historical context, and try to achieve some coherence in doing so even if this ultimately eludes us.

Most of us engaged in the New Humanism Project (NHP) share a common South African identity shaped by having lived through apartheid and having experienced the birth of our new democracy. Yet, we are South Africans differently. Ethnicity, gender, class, upbringing, education and, not least, age, are all variables that influence the way we perceive and relate to reality. Another important variable is religion or its absence. The different religious traditions and the variety within them demonstrates that this variable is itself complex, but for some it often appears the most significant of all in defining what it means to be human.

The Christian variable

Christianity, diverse as it is, is the religious tradition to which the majority (some 70%) of South Africans adhere, some with passionate conviction, others more nominally. We cannot ignore this when considering what it means to be human together in South Africa today anymore than we can ignore the other faith traditions that shape values and determine the way in which people relate to each other and to society. Apart from anything else, this is acknowledged and upheld by the Constitution.

Within the nexus of religious traditions in general and the Abrahamic faiths (Judaism, Christianity, Islam) in particular, the core narrative of suffering and redemptive love in Jesus Christ, witnessed to in the New Testament, gives Christianity its distinct character. It is undoubtedly a "grand" narrative; if it were not so nobody would meaningfully choose to embrace it, and I would not understand and tell my own story in relation to it. But I do not regard it as an exclusive narrative as though all truth is confined within its boundaries or communicated through its symbols. In this respect my understanding of Christianity is at variance with fundamentalism. For me, Christianity is inclusive and orientated to the future in dialogue with the past and with other voices in the present. But it only remains explicitly Christian in so far as it embodies and witnesses to its core narrative.

In recent years I have described myself as a Christian humanist, a description with a long pedigree and contemporary significance (De Gruchy 2006). Secularists might consider "Christian humanism" an oxymoron, and fundamentalists would undoubtedly regard it is as sell-out. But I believe that Christianity is properly understood as humanist at its core, albeit humanist in a particular sense. What could be more humanist than the audacious *faith* claim that God in Christ became fully human or that human beings are made "in the image of God"? Moreover I would argue that the purpose of Christian faith is not to make us more religious, but to help us to become more truly human.

My reasons for naming myself a Christian humanist are more than theological; they are also strategic and polemical. They are strategic because I believe that all people, whether committed to a religious faith tradition or not, who work for the welfare of the planet and the common good of humanity should engage with each other in this critical task. The reasons are polemical because I cannot accept the absolutist and exclusive assertions of fundamentalist or triumphalist religion any more than I can the equally strident and dogmatic claims of secularism and scientism. Religion, not least Christianity, has a sad and deplorable dehumanising record, but so, too, have these other -isms. Irrespective of their historical record, they are now part of the broader crisis of modernity, emptying life of responsibility and meaning, and sometimes plunging us into violence.

Theology amongst the sciences

Scientific investigation and rational enquiry are essential tools in understanding reality, including the reality of being human together. The amazing advances in cosmology, biochemistry and technology are fundamental to the conversation. But the social sciences and law equally ground our reflections in reality, and the humanities help us to understand our past, communicate with each other, and engage with social and political reality. The fine and performing arts are likewise essential in expressing what it means to be human, providing the modes of what we traditionally call the aesthetic. Collectively all these disciplines inform our perception of reality and our conversation about being human. The reality is the same for all, but the perceptions, paradigms and discourse are different. Theology functions best at the interface of rational enquiry, social reality, aesthetic creativity and religious tradition embodied in a particular historical narrative, faith experience and communal life (Holness & Wüstenberg 2002). The flourishing of dialogue between scientists and theologians over the past decades is evidence of a shared concern for human well-being and the future of our planet. The same is true of the dialogue between theologians and lawyers, social scientists, literary critics and artists.

The "God-debate" that has in recent times become such a media event and popular pastime has freshly challenged the validity and credentials of theology especially for people unaware of the constructive dialogue between science and theology. But in any case, the statement that human beings need to be understood in relation to God is problematic if not nonsensical for many people. The problem is compounded by the fact that the word "God" has its own complex history and is used in so many varied and even contradictory ways that it no longer conveys the cosmic mystery beyond human grasp which is perhaps best expressed through negation. Yet, the word is given content in religious traditions embodied in narratives that enable us to understand the world and who we are in terms of that which transcends us and "the other" who encounters us amidst daily reality.

While the reasons for the conflict between science and theology have often been foolish and misinformed, there is sometimes good reason for the tension between them when it concerns the welfare of human beings and the planet. The simplistic and foolish polarisation that has occurred around "creationism" and evolution has led the popular debate between science and religion into a cul-de-sac where many, who rightly accept the latter as fundamental to science, fail to recognise the philosophical and ideological inadequacies of Darwinism as a creed that explains everything. There is often blindness to its destructive social consequences, something reflected in the original subtitle to Darwin's *Origin of Species* namely "the preservation of favoured races in the struggle for life". This worldview informed the most destructive forms of social engineering of the twentieth century, Nazism and Soviet Communism, as it also influenced the architects of apartheid. Capitalism in its own way and often misusing Jesus' words that the "poor are always with us" as its legitimation, has its own dehumanising consequences: the rich grow wealthier because they deserve it at the expense of the poor and vulnerable.

It is these consequences that bother me and other Christian theologians, along with religious and secular humanists and scientists who reflect on the issues and seek alternative ways of understanding the human project. So when that concern is shared, and when there is mutual respect and honesty amidst critical debate, the engagement is mutually instructive and helpful not simply for the sake of religion or science, but for the common good. This does not dissolve the tensions between the disciplines, nor should it, but it can make them creative in serving a larger purpose.

Sociality and the new humanity

Much is said in this book about human relationality, for without being-in-relation we are not truly human. I do not wish to repeat what is said elsewhere, but as human sociality is fundamental to a Christian understanding of being human I must briefly say something else the rest of what follows will be subject to distortion. Likewise something must be said at the outset about the Christian vision of a "new humanity", for it is this vision of sociality that informs and drives Christian social engagement.

The Christian understanding of the sociality of humanity stands in contrast to two alternative views: the primacy of the individual as in liberal humanism and democracy, and the primacy of the collective, as in Communism. Christianity as I understand it is about building community, insisting that human beings always exist in relationship to and for others, but equally insisting that no one should be absorbed into a collective, denying personal rights and freedoms. It is for this reason that, despite its undoubted faults and failures, there is a strong affinity between social democracy and Christianity even though Christianity cannot be equated with any political order (De Gruchy 1995).

The ongoing struggle to establish communities in which the common good and the good of each is achieved, lies at the heart of what is meant by the church as an agent of a new humanity. Understood in this way (though much in Christian practice contradicts it), the church is not a closed conglomerate of like-minded individuals or an institution in which individuals forfeit their personal being. Rather it is meant to be a community always in the process of formation in which human beings relate to each other beyond the divisions of race, class, culture or gender, yet in ways that respect difference. As such the church should provide a model of reconciliation for the broader human community as well as a basis for solidarity in the struggle for a more just world. For the Christian humanist such a community is not closed or exclusive in character, but exists for and in solidarity with others. This understanding of human sociality is fundamental to all that now follows.

Body and soul

Without bodily existence we would not be human. But religious traditions also speak of "spirit" and "soul" as that which makes us distinctly human. These are slippery and contested terms, the meaning of which is not universally accepted. The debate has gone back and forth from earliest times when humans first thought about their being human and celebrated their humanity in dance and image, to our day as we explore the brain, debate the mind and engage in cloning experiments.

"Soul" suggests a dualistic understanding of our humanity in which body and soul are discrete entities. Coupled with this is the idea of the "immortality of the soul" by which is meant that there is an entity that survives death. This is a popular notion in Christianity but it is not as central to the biblical record as usually assumed. The Bible conceives of the human being in a more holistic way, emphasising the interconnectedness of all dimensions of existence rather than any clear-cut separation between them. Rather than the body being denigrated it is affirmed as good, as therefore is sexuality and materiality. There cannot be life without procreation or food and drink. Further, "soul" is not understood as an entity or substance, but as being-in-relation and in the process of becoming, being as a life-long project beset by ambiguity, perplexed by suffering, and ending in the dust of death even for those who live in hope of the "resurrection of the *body*", a phrase that emphasises the persistence of identity.

Though the word "soul" is contentious it remains useful in expressing the various dimensions of human subjectivity and inter-subjectivity, whether these are rational, affective or creative. It has to do with "who we are" in ourselves and in relationship. To reduce our understanding of being human in a way that excludes such subjectivity and the spirituality associated with it by subsuming it within a solely materialistic paradigm is, from a Christian point of view, highly problematic. In her essays on modern thought entitled *The Death of Adam*, Marilynne Robinson, the Pulitzer Prize-winning novelist, provides a trenchant critique of such dangers, linking it to the loss of "soul", or the "human spirit" which, as she says, was of the essence of Renaissance humanism and as such "once an object of unquestionable veneration". This loss is the death of Adam, the demise of being human. Robinson acknowledges that much past veneration of the "soul" was romantic, yet it connected religion and humanism in a remarkable enterprise at once aesthetic and scientific which demonstrated "the heights which human beings can attain" (Robinson 1998:8).

The recovery of the humanist vision today is not unrelated to the recovery and embodiment of "soul" in a way that draws on a range of knowledge and experience appropriate to the complexity of the subject. Without the language of "soul" it is difficult to speak of love and hope, let alone express it in music and art. It is also difficult to respond to the reality of death in a life-affirming hopeful way without denying its awfulness. A Marxist by conviction, Terry Eagleton speaks to this in his phrase "tragic humanism" which is able to express love, beauty and hope even in the face of human frailty, mortality and wretchedness (Eagleton 2009:163). But how are we to understand this "wretchedness" which is often the result of destructive human choices, and the attendant suffering which calls "God" into question and challenges any optimistic account of being human or vision of a new humanity? What about "sin", that bogey of liberal humanism and yet the most empirically verifiable of all Christian doctrines, the theological equivalent of the "selfish gene"?

The myth of Adam

One formative narrative in shaping self-understanding in Christian tradition is the myth of Adam. Simplistically reduced by most to a story of origins, it is much more a complex analysis of being human in relationship. As such it is a tragic story which describes not just the loss of innocence in human development, but also the human inability to achieve utopia and live in paradise without engaging in self-destructive behaviour. Compromised relationships marked by hubris and greed lead to the destruction of nature and inevitably destroy global civilisation (Babel).

The myth is not dogmatic but evocative, enabling us to see ourselves, and not just some primordial predecessor, as if in a mirror. Reflecting on what it means to be human in front of it, it is difficult to disentangle the bondage of the will, which seems to freeze responsible action from the freedom to choose and act responsibly.[1] But it is clear that being human is characterised by both – by irresponsible and destructive choices and the will-to-power, and by freedom to love, to create beauty, and discover truth. Through our own choices we are too often unable to choose and act rightly even if we know what is good for us and the world we inhabit. This leads to compromise if not self destruction in our actions. Living with the unresolved tension between our finitude and our desire for control, between the use and abuse of power, between meaning and incoherence, freedom and bondage, hope and anxiety, we either resign ourselves to the way things are, or seek ways to overcome and transform them that are too often motivated by self interest. In all this we remain the problem.

Despite its bad press and misleading interpretations, the doctrine of sin is a bold attempt to unpack these ambiguities, to understand the ongoing struggle between the will and desire to live and act in ways that are true, good and creative, or false, evil and destructive; ways that enable us to become more truly human, and ways that make us less so. We should not think more highly of ourselves than we ought, claiming the right to dominate in ways that destroy the environment and engender spurious aspirations of becoming superhuman, instead of becoming

1 The best account of the human predicament or "fallenness", to my mind, remains that of Reinhold Niebuhr's *Nature and Destiny of Man*. For a contemporary statement of Niebuhr's "Christian realism" in relation to the "new realities" of our own time, see Lovin (2008).

more truly human. Such will-to-power is nihilistic, cynical, senseless, the curtailing of possibilities of fulfilment for future generations and the future of the planet. It threatens every attempt to build community in a sustainable and just way.

If there is this constant danger of "over-humanization" (Schweiker 2010:8) there is also a danger of an "under-humanization" which denigrates human being. We should not think less of ourselves than we ought to think. The fact that 94% of our DNA is shared with animals or that all life is interconnected and evolving, does not mean that humans do not have a distinct role to fulfil as human beings in the unfolding cosmic story. To insist that this is so is not the same as claiming a status that gives humans the right to dominate other forms of life or destroy the planet, nor to deny our place on the evolutionary spectrum, but simply the recognition that humans are responsible for being human-in-relation to the "other", and becoming more truly so. As such they are accountable to something that transcends self or group interest whether described as moral law, transcendent claims, or God. Fallen we may be, but we remain responsible and have the potential to make a difference to the world even if our solutions are penultimate, and the societies we construct are fragile and impermanent.

The biblical insistence that humans are "in the image of God" is not a description of substance but of relation, responsibility, freedom and significance. Despite our "fallenness" this conviction adds infinite value to being human without which there would be far less reason to protect the weak and vulnerable, or equally to oppose unjust and oppressive power, sometimes at great cost to the self or the group. Human beings have significance; that is why we can speak of human worth and dignity, and of the rights that flow from that. It has taken centuries to recognise these rights and the freedoms associated with them, and it is always a struggle to uphold and entrench them. In fact, religion is often their worst enemy, and the appeal to God in support of injustice, violence and greed the ultimate idolatry. Human rights are not just the product of history; they have to do with what it means to be human and build community. To achieve certain goals in the struggle for such rights and freedoms may be salutary, but the struggle continues to maintain them and take them further for the common good. But this assumes that there is good reason to do so, that there are values worth defending which give meaning to life beyond the motivations of group and self-interest.

Nihilism is the rejection of any meaning to life and therefore any ultimate values that define being human and challenge our will-to-power. The ruthlessly honest nihilist commits suicide, choosing death rather than meaningless life. Nihilism also expresses itself in greed, the exaltation of the weapons of war, the torture of the prison cell, in other words, the death of "the other". But nihilism is more than a *philosophy* of negation; it is reality as many people experience it, not only through choice and addiction, but more often through circumstances beyond their control. It is being without hope, living with dreams shattered and aspirations denied. We see it in the eyes of the millions of victims in our world whose families have been washed away by flood or destroyed by earthquake; refugees fleeing rape, genocide and war; AIDS orphans and the homeless. That is why the suffering of the innocent challenges any facile understanding of faith or God, any naïve reading of the texts of tradition, any humanism that is not tragic in character even in espousing hope and expressing love. Faced with such reality, the temptation for all of us to become nihilists is great. We counter it by seeking meaning both within and beyond ourselves as we live between memory and hope.

Memory, hope & transformation

Memory binds us together as human beings; even very personal memories are invariably linked to others and keep us in relationship with them. The loss of memory does not make someone less human, but it does make relationships and togetherness problematic and painful. That is one reason why we in South Africa have to learn together about how to deal with our past, how to remember slavery, colonialism and apartheid, but also the achievements of democratic transition and the tentative but real steps towards transformation. Not to do so prevents us from becoming truly human together as a nation. There is no way forward toward justice and reconciliation without a journey backward, no hope without memory. Memories are seeds of hope marking our being human and giving rise to both reflection and transformative action.

Memory in Christian as well as in other traditions or literary discourse is not something that refers to the past in such a way that it is always receding into the background until it loses all reference to the present. Memory is that which informs the present; it is the past always re-inventing itself in ways that relate to present experience. That is why a living tradition is a dynamic process that is always being transformed even as it transforms us. When a tradition ceases to do this it becomes a relic. That is why Christianity or "the democratic tradition" or "humanism" ceases to have meaning and transformative significance when bound to the past.

The struggle against apartheid in South Africa was motivated by "a humanist vision" (Ndebele 2007:58) nurtured by memory and hope. So, too, is the present struggle to ensure a more just and democratic society in which all those who live in South Africa are enabled to live meaningful lives and develop their potential in ways that are personally fulfilling and contribute to the common good. This democratic and personal transformation and all that contributes to it in terms of land, economic justice, gender equality and the rest, is critical for becoming more fully human together in South Africa. And it is central to the Christian humanist perspective and agenda which is political at its core, but political in a distinct sense.

The memory at the heart of the Christian narrative keeps hope alive of a more just world in which oppression is overcome and peace becomes a reality. In this regard, some theologians refer to the "dangerous memory" (Metz 1980:88) of Jesus whose life and ministry threatened established religious and political order to the extent that it led to his death, as also happens to many prophets and advocates of justice not least in our own country. It is true that the utopian vision of a new humanity embodied in this "dangerous memory" sometimes leads to misguided action, unrealistic expectations and totalitarian experiments. Yet, without such vision and the drive that it inspires, the longing for and realisation of human and social transformation, however limited, is stymied. How to avoid the former without losing the latter is one of the challenges facing Christians (and not only them) in their engagement with social and public life. The loss of hope for a better life for all undermines attempts to live meaningfully and creatively into the future. This is as true of us as individuals as it is of us as citizens of South Africa and the global community. Those of our compatriots who have lost hope of a better future find it difficult to be human together with those of us who have not lost hope.

Spirituality and human fulfilment

Being human is a complex evolutionary process of becoming in which we continually change physically, mentally and spiritually. Human beings do not all change in exactly the same way or at the same pace, but there are discernible stages of physical growth from childhood to old age through which all who live that length of time pass. Mental and spiritual growth is related to these stages, but there is variation and not everyone develops to his or her full potential. Even so, as the Preamble to our Constitution declares, we are committed as South Africans to "improve the quality of life of all citizens and free the potential of each person". This is one of the building blocks of a united and democratic South Africa. But how is this to be understood and achieved?

Human fulfilment can be understood as reaching personal goals that are self-centred and achieved at the expense of others. But we can also understand it as growth towards embracing the other, deepening relationships, developing potentials, enhancing gifts for the common good, exercising responsible freedom, expressing gratitude, becoming compassionate, offering forgiveness, creating beauty, standing for truth and justice, and respecting the needs and rights of future generations and their inheritance – in short, anticipating the birth of a new humanity. All of which is, from a Christian perspective, necessary in becoming more truly human together.

The development of integrated and mature people of such character depends to a large degree on nurture. There may well be innate predispositions and contextual circumstances that help, but human fulfilment in this holistic way cannot be programmed. From a humanist perspective, education has always been fundamental to the nurturing process, but education understood as formation of character rather than simply the accumulation of knowledge. Knowledge without the wisdom to use it well can be dangerous. Being truly human together in a way that contributes to human and social well-being and builds community requires more from our educational system than it presently offers or can possibly offer. In this regard the role of home and parenting, of faith communities and other institutions that seek the welfare of society is critical.

Christian humanism speaks of the need for a spiritual formation that engenders practical wisdom and enables love and compassion to flourish. The process is not about becoming more pious and religious, but becoming more truly human and therefore more responsible in relation to the world, to others and to the transcendent. Of critical but of forgotten importance in this process is the recovery of what Dietrich Bonhoeffer called "aesthetic existence" under whose rubric he included art, friendship and play (Bonhoeffer 2010:268; De Gruchy 2001:136-168). All of these are indicative of the spirituality that fosters human fulfilment in community. They feed the "soul" and enable us to live in ways that are truly free and responsible, meaningful and fulfilled as human beings. From this perspective, the human project becomes a work of art, a creation within the evolutionary process that expresses itself in creativity as well as in compassion and justice. Children at play are truly human; adults making war, despite the heroism that we may celebrate, are being dehumanised even as they dehumanise others. That is why becoming childlike, not in naïve innocence but in wisdom and creativity, is central to the Christian humanist understanding of the human project and its future.

Reference List

Bonhoeffer D. 2010. Letters and Papers from Prison. In: *Dietrich Bonhoeffer Works in English*, vol. 8. Minneapolis: Fortress.

De Gruchy JW. 1995. *Christianity and Democracy*. Cambridge: Cambridge University Press.

— 2001. *Christianity, Art and Transformation: Theological Aesthetics in the Struggle for Justice*. Cambridge: Cambridge University Press.

— 2006. *Being Human: Confessions of a Christian Humanist*. London: SCM; Minneapolis: Fortress.

Eagleton T. 2009. *Reason, Faith, and Revolution: Reflections on the God Debate*. New Haven: Yale University Press.

Holness L & Wüstenberg RK (eds). 2002. *Theology in Dialogue: The Impact of the Arts, Humanities & Science on Contemporary Religious Thought*. Grand Rapids: Eerdmans.

Lovin RW. 2008. *Christian Realism and the New Realities*. Cambridge: Cambridge University Press.

Metz JB. 1980. *Faith, History and Society: Toward a Practical Fundamental Theology*. New York: Seabury.

Ndebele NS. 2007. *Fine Lines from the Box*. Johannesburg: Umuzi.

Niebuhr R. 1949. *The Nature and Destiny of Man: A Christian Interpretation*. New York: Charles Scribner's Sons.

Rees M. 2010. Conclusion: Looking Fifty Years Ahead. In: B Bryson (ed). *Seeing Further: The Story of Science and the Royal Society*. London: Harper.

Robinson M. 1998. *Death of Adam: Essays on Modern Thought*. New York: Picador.

Schweiker W. 2010. *Dust that Breathes: Christian faith and the New Humanisms*. Oxford: John Wiley & Sons.

BECOMING MORE FULLY HUMAN
Aspects of the relational

Denise Ackermann

A sentence in a paper presented by John de Gruchy at a Conference on the Reformer and humanist John Calvin held at Stellenbosch University in September 2009, has stayed with me and will be the focus of this contribution. It reads: "In the end, the project towards a new humanism is all about recovering the human soul in an age that would reduce us all to machines, that is, about *becoming more fully human in relation to others and the world as a whole* [my italics]" (De Gruchy 2010:378). Why the need to "recover the human soul [by] becoming more fully human?" The answer is self-evident. The world we live in struggles to find its soul and hence its humanity – value systems are inverted, poverty, need, suffering, wars, violence and the abuse of power, abound. Nuclear disarmament is still a far-off dream, the earth is groaning, and uncomfortable questions raised by bio-ethics confront us. To become more fully human and to live in mutual relationship with others and our world in these circumstances is more than a challenge. It is an imperative if we are to survive present crises; hence the call for a revived humanist spirit that enables living in mutually enhancing relationships with one another and with our environment.

Humanism and relationship

I would like to explore the idea of relationship as essential to becoming more fully human with specific emphasis on communities that adhere to the Christian faith. This focus comes from a profound concern that religious institutions[1] are riddled with fault lines: the separation of people that still echoes our geographically separated past, hierarchical structures that separate clergy from laity, sexism in church structures that exclude women from practising their calling to ministry at all levels, homophobia that deprives gay people of their dignity and rightful place in their faith communities, the rising number of fundamentalist and right wing churches some of whom are unashamedly proclaiming economic prosperity as a goal, and a profound lassitude, if not ignorance, in taking up the vital issue of climate change and the future of our planet. Ecumenism is at an all-time low, and inter-faith dialogue limps along bravely carried by a few open-minded spirits. John de Gruchy's conviction – that when the Reformed tradition loses "touch with its humanist origins and fails to maintain the creative tension between them, it becomes trapped in a dogmatic fundamentalism and moralism – to the detriment of the Church, humanity and society" (De Gruchy 2009:40) – is sadly true for most religious communities today.

Yet, relationship is central to the Christian faith. Christians are taught to love God and to love their neighbour (across all boundaries) as themselves. In practice this means sustained caring and just actions on the part of faith communities for the common good of all.[2] Actions – whether intellectual, moral or acts of friendship – are to be in accordance with that which makes us more fully human, that is being in mutual relationship with one another. Relationality, I argue, lies at the heart of things. The active making of just and caring relationships in order to make a better world, is where the encounter between Christian and humanist concerns can take place.

The terms 'humanism', 'relationship' and 'becoming more fully human' are undoubtedly contested, tentative ideas that can appear indeterminate, if not shadowy. 'Relationship' in particular needs rescuing from romantic obtuseness.

I understand *humanism* as a movement originating in the 5th century BCE when the Sophists and Socrates, in the words of Cicero "called philosophy down from heaven to earth" (Honderich 1995:375). Social, political and moral questions should

---

1 'Religious institutions' is a deliberately vague term as such communities are hugely diverse in South Africa. Those with whom I am best acquainted are what are traditionally called the 'mainline churches' though that term is increasingly contested.

2 According to Aristotle, "... the good has rightly been declared to be that at which all things aim" (see *Nichomachean Ethics*, Book 1, Chapter 1). Anthony Kenny comments: "Aristotle, like all moral philosophers, is of course interested in the question 'What shall I *do*' [my italics]." Philosopher Martha Nussbaum ("Aristotle" in T. J. Luce (ed), *Ancient Writers*, New York, 1982, p. 403) explains what Aristotle means as follows: "Throughout books 1-10 [of the *Nicomachean Ethics*] Aristotle has indicated that the human good is an inclusive plurality of actions according to excellence, in which intellectual activity will be one component, side by side with other constituents of intrinsic worth, such as activity according to excellence of character and activity benefiting friends."

be introduced into common discourse. During the Renaissance, humanism aimed to direct attention away from theoretical speculation to the study of the works of man [precisely] found in literature, history and art. This was a movement away from God as the centre of interest. The Renaissance humanists saw God's activity as a general controlling influence of the universe. Scientists were freed to explore the universe and its laws. Principally, humanism encouraged the ability of human beings to explore the universe by their own efforts, and to draw on ancient philosophy and other more recent sources in their reflections.

At that time, humanism emphasised studying the works of the classical era. Particular attention was paid to the nature of rhetorical language, the role of social context, the love of classical literature and philosophy. Despite presenting the church with challenges, Renaissance humanism failed to reform the church or society (De Gruchy 2009:38). It was only in the late nineteenth century, largely because of conflicts between Darwinism and a fundamentalist reading of the bible, that the term 'humanism' became associated with atheism or agnosticism (Honderich 1995:376). The search for a contemporary humanist spirit will, in my view, require a broader, more inclusive, critical and self-reflective understanding of the nature of humanism that is open to the role that faith perspectives can play in its recovery.

The word '*relationship*' needs qualifying – relationships can be domineering, exploitative and abusive, or they can be mutually satisfying and freeing. Relationship that is life enhancing is characterised by an innate mutuality – by a 'do unto others as you would have done unto yourself' – one that emphasises equality of being. In his Gifford lectures, John Macmurray deals extensively with the ethical consequences of being in relationship (Macmurray 1961). Human beings, he argues, are relational beings who have agency and thus have the ability to act. Our actions are defined by our intentions and our motivations. Since we are agents our relations are realised in our actions. We cannot duck the responsibility of making choices – choices that lead to life-affirming actions, or choices that do not. We can choose to be moral agents that promote relationships that are characterised by mutuality and freedom and that emphasise the unity of the common life, or not. Our relationships thus have the potential to be life enhancing or life denying, depending on how we live them. However we act, we cannot live wholly outside relationship, as relationship is profoundly constituent of being human.

"Becoming more fully human" is shorthand for human striving to choose goodness, wholeness and what affirms life, rather than to submit to what is destructive, injurious and even lethal to human existence. "Becoming fully human" is an aim tempered by the reality that we can only aim at being "*more* human". According to Christian understanding only Jesus Christ was truly and fully human.

Toward a theology of relation

The idea of relationship can, in present times, seem faddish and trendy with interminable workshops run at considerable cost on 'building relationships' for the benefit of greater economic production – transforming relationship into a packaged commodity. For women theologians, however, relationship is a key concept and considerable effort has been devoted to developing a *theology of relation.* This is understandable given the history of sexist hierarchical relations that have dominated traditions and practices in the Christian faith. Such a theology posits the interrelatedness of all life. Nothing is self-contained. All life is part of a cosmic web and no theology (or philosophy) that fails to envisage reality in this way will be able to understand the implications of living, acting and making decisions in the diverse and complex realities in which we live. A theology of relation is about becoming more fully human by enhancing life-affirming relationships.

This is not new to the Christian tradition. Living in relationship characterised the faith of the Israelite communities, centred on the covenant. God speaks, the people respond; God acts and the people then act with God – for righteousness and justice. Justice is understood as right relationship between Creator and creature and is reflected in relationships between human beings. Our relation to God makes us responsible for creating a just world. Despite the negative aspects of a covenantal understanding of relationship such as the notion of exclusivity, what was remarkable about the covenant was its voluntary character. Human acts for justice and righteousness are formed around the covenant, and are voluntary and agreed to by both parties, in the interest of justice. Thus ancient Israel understood the meaning of the law of love and all God's commandments.

In the life and ministry of Jesus Christ, justice as right relationship, is also a requirement for the fulfilment of the law of love. He often reminded his followers that he came not to abolish but to fulfil the law (Matt. 5:17; 7:12). But pursuing righteousness would not be easy. In the Sermon on the Mount he advocates a radical reversal of accepted values and warns his followers: "Blessed are those who are persecuted for righteousness sake, for theirs is the kingdom of heaven" (Matt. 5:10). Christianity lost the intimacy, immediacy and the voluntary nature of the covenant. Classical theism "... there is God (contrary to atheism) ... God is one (contrary to polytheism), and ... the one God is not to be identified with the world (contrary to pantheism)", (Johnson 1992:19) deeply affected the way in which relationship with God was understood. God became "wholly other", a God who was "being in itself", and who in a certain sense no longer needed relationship with human beings. The recovery of the Christian notion of the Trinity as a relational concept – a relationship of persons-in-relation with one another open to the joy and pain of the world – overcomes the theistic focus on the transcendence of God to the exclusion of relationship (Moltmann 1982). The symbol of the triune God is a relational concept. Each trinitarian person is unique, but it "is only by their reciprocal and mutually exclusive relationships" that they are really distinct from each other (Johnson 1992:216).

Reclaiming the relational in theology calls for a more specific understanding of what is meant by relationship. As already noted, relationship can be appropriate or inappropriate, distorted, abusive and dominating, or mutual, liberating and life-giving. Thus a theology of relation begins with a critique of the historical forms in which relationships have been constructed. Clearly, women's interest in the relational is based on millennia of women's domination by men, and our desire for change. The same need for change applies, however, to relationships between different races, cultures, and classes of people. Thus, understanding the nature of relationship will begin with an analysis of what constitutes 'otherness' – in this sense a coded expression for the treatment of those who are different and thus less worthy of respect. This is only the beginning. Thereafter, a theology of relation takes up a positive stance to understanding relationships among people and the criteria by which they can be evaluated. A theology of relation explores a paradigm for human relationships that is characterised by "equality of power, mutuality of freedom and responsibility, love that is other-centred and yet neither neglectful nor destructive of the self, and fidelity", writes Margaret Farley (Farley 1996:239). What is at stake here is mutually enhancing relation in an equivalence of persons that entails a valuing of one another, and a common regard of affection, respect and trust, in contrast to any assertions of dominance or superiority. The ultimate aim of a theology of relation is the flourishing of all people as well as the environment in which we live and that nurtures us.

Can this vision of 'being in relation', often accused of simply being utopian, become rooted in our faith communities, as an ethical call for a better future? Can it contribute to the renewal of spirit of a contemporary humanist spirit?

Relational praxis

Contributing to the spirit of a 'new' humanism depends quite simply on what we *do* about 'being in relation'. All theoretical or doctrinal musings on the origins and nature of 'being in relation' must be rooted in relational praxis that is mutual, just and liberating in the interest of the common good of all. How can this come about?

First, 'being in relation' starts with understanding that no human being, no community, no society exists in some independent sphere. We are all *interrelated and interdependent*. The realisation of this rather self-evident truth is foundational for actions that are just and liberating. Moreover, anthropocentrism is the death knell of 'being in relation'. We are made of stardust; we survive only by being sustained by the environment. Absolute interdependence is our reality. Creation is about the making and maintaining of a web of interdependent relations. It is also a mistake to think that relationship is only possible between persons who know one another. For example, I am dependent on a host of people I have never met, nor am likely to meet, for food – those who produce, transport and deliver food to the local supermarket. When I pay for food I contribute, in some measure, to the personal lives of these people. Thus our interrelatedness exists on both a personal and an impersonal level. Such is our reality.

Second, being-in-relationship is an *embodied* concept. We live embodied lives and our relationships are embodied. Our senses are the source of what we know. All knowledge is mediated through our bodies. We learn in the body because our experiences are embodied. The body is synonymous with the self. Women know this: we do not *have* bodies, we *are* our bodies. I have written elsewhere on a cautionary note: "Body talk as I understand it, is not primarily concerned with what bodies look like. Bodies are who we are, the most powerfully tangible aspect of our shared humanity" (Ackermann 2003:66). Thus our relational praxis is embodied praxis, subject to both the limitations and possibilities of being embodied beings.

My bodily dependence has to be assessed in terms of what is just and good for all, and what is not. Again the economic argument illustrates this fact. If my appetite craves strawberries out of season, it can be assuaged by eating imported strawberries. These strawberries may come from arable land where beans and maize were previously grown, land that is now owned by foreign companies who plant strawberries for export, while the local populace now has to buy maize and beans at inflated prices in order to survive. I do not know these peasant farmers but I cannot take refuge in the impersonal nature of my relationship with them. Their needs are as embodied and dependent as mine, and raise the question: What will make for just relationships between us?

The very idea of an embodied divinity permeates the Christian faith. Denigrating the body or the idea of a disembodied existence is foreign to the Christian faith. "The Word became flesh and lived among us, and we have seen his glory, the glory as of a Father's only Son, full of grace and truth", writes the Evangelist John (1:14). Sallie McFague points out that "The body matters, says the common creation story; in fact, it is the main attraction. Likewise, from the point of view of the common creation story, right action or praxis begins from embodiment as well" (McFague 1993:48). According to McFague, the needs of bodies provide the primary context for obligation. An embodied perspective is simply a reflection of our common, shared, embodied humanity – we and all life-forms are radically embodied – and this moves us towards an inclusive sense of justice for the needs of all (embodied) human beings. "In an embodiment ethic, hungry, homeless, or naked human beings have priority over the spiritual needs of the well-fed, well-housed, well-clothed sisters and brothers" (McFague 1993:48). And an environment that is depleted and over-exploited cannot feed the hungry.

Third, our bodily interdependence raises the issue of the praxis of *justice*. Justice here is understood as right relationship with self, with God, with others, and with creation. The scope of justice as right relationship is broader than simply giving to each what is due. It calls for attention to and an option for groups of people who experience oppression and poverty. It requires solidarity with those who suffer and struggle for liberation from social and economic structures that are oppressive and designed to keep people powerless. This may sound like old-fashioned liberation theological talk, but it is as poignantly valid today as it was fifty years ago –a pressing need in a society such as ours in which the difference between those who 'have' and those who do not, grows daily.[3]

Christianity itself has a long and painful history of injustices. It has contributed too often to the rupture of justice, instead of being the author of peace, love and freedom; it has authored discrimination against 'the other' such as Jews, women,

3 There are multiple areas of human life that are unjust: racism that is ethnic injustice, rape that is sexual injustice, repression that is political injustice, robbery that is economic injustice, removal that is cultural injustice, and so on (see Lebacqz 1987).

and gay people and perpetrated repression, even terror such as the crusades and the mediaeval witch-hunts. Christian views on poverty have been ambivalent, and too often the poor have been blamed for their poverty using biblical texts[4] to justify keeping the poor in 'their place'.

These examples show a lamentable lack of historical consciousness and biblical remembrance in dealing with the idea of justice in Christian communities (Schüssler 1984:114). The Christian story that emerges from the biblical texts shows that the experiences of the poor and the oppressed are the point of departure for the praxis of justice. The struggle, then and now, is for a just and equitable society in which people can live with dignity and be agents of their own destiny. The teaching, the life and the ministry of Jesus Christ, reveals the need for liberating and just Christian praxis that is true to his story – one that speaks from the underside of history. Thus the praxis of justice is grounded in remembrance of the contexts of those early stories and how Jesus sought to side with those who suffered injustice. Humanising praxis is deeply a justice issue in which relationships will be judged according to the degree to which they contribute to right relationships.

Fourth, respect for rights is a hallmark of justice. However, because the praxis of justice involves intention, it entails *responsibility*. We are responsible for both our actions and our intentions. Being responsible for our intentions means accepting moral culpability for what we intend even if we do not carry out our intentions. Although a person who forms the intent to murder, but goes no further, is not guilty of the crime of murder or attempted murder, such a person is morally responsible for his or her intention to commit murder. The good will, Kant insisted, wills what is good, and *vice versa* (Kant 1996:49). Because doing justice is a continuous process of correction, accepting the responsibility for the constant restoring of justice rests on the human community.

Fifth, problems arise in relational praxis when we are confronted with persons who are radically *different*. Humanity has a sad history of viewing different people as a problem. Those who are different from us in terms of religious affiliation, race, gender, sexual preferences, class or nature, are all too frequently met with attitudes of indifference, suspicion or fear. Instead of emphasising the positive values of diversity and otherness, difference is seen as threatening, even alienating. Dealing well with difference is a serious challenge for a new spirit of humanism. Can we really relate to those who are very different from ourselves in ways that are at all meaningful? (Ackermann 2003:14-15).

Our interrelatedness across our differences arises from our shared humanity. Creation is shot through with diversity. The very creation story itself is one of difference and similarity in an intricate pattern of being separate but nonetheless utterly interdependent. Michael Welker speaks of the "pluralism of the Spirit". He argues that the outpouring of the Spirit on the early communities in Acts was a specific witness to difference. He writes: "The unity of the Spirit becomes a reality not by imposing an illusory homogeneity, but by cultivating creaturely differences and by

---

[4] Such as, for example, Mark 14:7 – "For you always have the poor with you ..."

removing unrighteous differences". This requires an awareness of difference and a sensitivity to difference (Welcker 1994:25).

As our societies become less homogenous by the day, living with difference is inescapable. How we relate across difference is a matter of intention. "To look at something [or some one] is to see it with the intention of knowing it [or her], and this transforms the seeing from matter of fact to matter of intention," writes Macmurray (Macmurray 1961:128). Intentional knowledge of the 'other' deepens knowledge of the 'other'. If we do not try to understand or have knowledge of what constitutes our differences, our efforts at relationship will flounder. Living well with difference is accepting the moral responsibility that comes from knowing that human beings are interdependent and that in order for humanity to live in peace and harmony, our relationships must be characterised by justice and by caring.

In sum, a contemporary humanism calls for a fresh look at what it means to be a vulnerable human being attempting to live more fully in a complex reality of conflicting interests. People who attempt to live according to the precepts of their different faiths are an integral part of this complex reality. There are distinct commonalities between humanist values and the basic tenets, traditions and practices of the Christian faith. If Christian communities can embrace a theology of relation that translates into relational praxis, there will be no room for an 'us and they' mentality, for exclusivist or triumphalistic views on the 'rightness' of a particular faith perspective, or for bizarre views on rationality and scientific thought.

In a well-known statement, the World Council of Churches summarised the truth of our interdependence in the phrase "the integrity of creation". This phrase means "The value of all creatures in and of themselves, for one another, and for God, and their interconnectedness in a diverse whole that has unique value for God" (McFague 1993:165). A contemporary humanism that encourages us to become more fully human underscores the intrinsic value of each living being as a creature created and loved by God, living in a web of life-enhancing relationships that includes the environment. Then we may hope to be more fully and truly human.

Reference List

Ackermann DM. 2003. *After the Locusts; Letters from a Landscape of Faith*. Grand Rapids: Eerdmans.

De Gruchy JW. 2001. John Calvin, Karl Barth and Christian Humanism. *Nederduitse Gereformeerde Teologiese Tydskrif* 51 (Supplementum).

— 2009. *John Calvin: Christian Humanist and Evangelical Reformer*. Wellington (RSA): Lux Verbi.

Farley M. 1996. In: LM Russell & JS Clarkson (eds). *Dictionary of Feminist Theologies*. Louisville Westminster: John Knox Press.

Honderich T (ed). 1995. *The Oxford Companion to Philosophy*. Oxford: Oxford University Press.

Johnson EA. 1992. *She Who Is: The Mystery of God in Feminist Theological Discourse*. New York: Crossroad.

Kant I. 1996. *Practical Philosophy*. MJ Gregor (transl & ed). Cambridge: Cambridge University Press.

Lebacqz K. 1987. *Justice in an Unjust World: Foundations for a Christian Approach to Justice*. Minneapolis: Augsburg Press.

Macmurray J. 1961. *Persons in Relation*. Atlantic Highlands, New Jersey: Humanities Press.

McFague S. 1993. *The Body of God: An Ecological Theology*. Minneapolis: Augsburg Press.

Moltmann J. 1982. *The Trinity and the Kingdom: The Doctrine of God*. New York: Harper and Row.

Schüssler FE. 1984. *Bread not Stone: The Challenge of Feminist Biblical Interpretation*. Boston: Beacon Press.

Welker M. 1994. *God the Spirit*. JF Hoffmeyer (transl). Minneapolis: Fortress Press.

AT THIS TIME AND IN THIS PLACE

Bobby Godsell

One of the defining characteristics of *homo sapiens* is the interest she has in reflecting on who she is. That these reflections change over time and are intimately connected with place is clear. What then can be said about the nature of *being human* in this time and in this place?

The twenty-first century is producing evidence aplenty of a move beyond the *industrial age*. This *age* was remarkable for much more than its revolution of the patterns of economic activity, at first in Western Europe and then around the world. This *age* saw new forms of knowledge and, in particular, the rise of the natural sciences, new concepts of political order in the form of the *nation state* and *democracy,* and a new battle between science and religion.

Perhaps the apogee of this age occurred in the late 19th and early 20th century: in the expansion of railways; the triumph of the republican nation state; the conquest of empire outside of Europe and North America; the rise of the United States of America, and the promise that the natural sciences would succeed in unravelling even the last questions about existence in this age of Darwin and Einstein. Two world wars, the atom bomb, the failure not only of colonialism, but also of decolonisation, and the rise and subsequent failure of consumer economies and societies have forced us to enter the new millennium with a high measure of anxiety and humility.

What then of place? What does it mean to be human in South Africa? This place has a confused if not schizophrenic geographic DNA. For Jan Smuts this "dark far corner" of the world held the hope of creating a "good society" on the tip of the African continent. Clearly, for as long as the country remained a race-based aristocracy, his aspiration was hubristic. Thabo Mbeki's African Renaissance envisaged a distinctly African concept of humanity, progress and civilisation that would restore Africa to a central seat at the table of global history.

Globally, we watch the leading "Western" societies grapple with an economic instability that sometimes verges on the edge of collapse; with social decay and political stalemate. The command communist societies that provided an alternative view of being human in the industrial age now offer no alternative vision, but seem intent on catching up with their Western competitors. Now more than ever, a new view of being human, here and elsewhere, is needed. Could this new view come from the intellectual, genetic, ethnic and cultural meeting point that is South Africa?

If the values of a country are most evidently displayed by the lifestyles of their elites, then the humanism of the new South Africa seems deeply unattractive. Our political and economic elites look more and more like their Russian equivalents: wanting wealth in excess; ready to act without any reference to values or ethics in order to get wealth; and, once wealth is acquired, determined to live a lifestyle of ostentatious consumption, essentially placing themselves "outside" the rest of society. Yet, if this is the media-captured surface of our new society, there is more and better at work beneath this surface. Three fragile new conceptions of what it means to be human in this 21st century give hope.

The prospect of hyphenated identities

The age of Napoleon, and its despatch of Europe's *Ancien Regime*, created a new kind of personal identity. Europeans had seen themselves as defined by occupations, class or place (as in village or valley). This is evident in the names they gave themselves, such as Smith, Van der Merwe, and Godsell, derived we think from God's Hill in Hampshire, England. Now, through the deeds and words of the Napoleons, the Garibaldis, the Metternichs and Bismarcks of this world, people became French, Italian, Austrian and German.

In the colonies, colonists clung to the national identity of their homelands, though they occasionally adopted another "name" as in the *pieds noirs* of the French settlers in Algeria. The more indigenous populations quickly embraced a colonial nationalism, in the sense of national identities defined by the boundaries and borders of colonial conquest. The speed and depth of this embrace is evident in the failed attempts of Kwame Nkurmah to create even the smallest part of his vision of a United States of Africa.

In the context of this new world of national identities, South Africa is a case apart. In the context of what was indeed a colonialism of a special type, white settlers developed an identity separate from their country of origin, whether this was Lithuania, Holland, France, Germany or Britain. I suspect that the development of a new African language (Afrikaans) was of critical importance in this regard. This Dutch-derived but now fully-developed language remains the sole linguistic footprint of a Dutch colonial empire that straddled three continents. Of course, this new identity, arising boldly out of the ashes of a bitter war, excluded then three quarters of the people living in the new country that emerged in 1910. This act of racial exclusion, in turn, defined and forged an inclusive South Africanism amongst black, Indian and coloured South Africans which found voice at the Congress of the People in 1955 and remains framed in the words of the Freedom Charter adopted at the Congress *"South Africa belongs to all who live in it Black and White"*.

Clearly, the old exclusive identity is buried (at least formally) in the ashes of the Apartheid project. The new inclusive and non-racial national identity is clearly entrenched (again formally) in our new Constitution. Yet, an identity lives first and foremost in the minds and hearts of a population. Here the evidence is much more ambiguous.

Many (most?) white South Africans are at ease with the label *South African*. They have long seen themselves as such. The inclusion (formally) of black South Africans has done little to change or dilute this identity. Many (most?) black South Africans appear more comfortable with the description *African*. Perhaps South Africanism is just still too new and alien. Many (most?) white South Africans could not easily describe themselves as *African*. And yet, if this does not fit, on which continent are they living? The *continental exceptionalism* is deep-seated, and is not entirely limited to whites. So South Africans who travel often speak of *"going into Africa"* as if their starting point was somewhere outside Africa.

The *green shoots* of a new and existentially-grounded inclusive identity are apparent. This was evident during the Football World Cup: first in the Friday soccer jerseys, then in the car-bedecked flags and finally in a stadium containing at least 50,000 South Africans (at least half of whom were white) who from first to last whistle gave their hearts and souls to black African Ghana, against (white-looking) Uruguay. These shoots are evident in workplaces, schools and universities, and of entertainment where friendship groups across race lines have begun to emerge. They are (just) evident in sporting teams where quotas are beginning to be applied to minority groups, as well as majority groups.

Will this new inclusive South Africanism obliterate the lines of cleavage produced in the past by race, ethnicity, language, class and religion? This seems very unlikely. The best we can hope for is a hyphenated or complex identity that embraces a signifier of both clan (race, ethnicity, language) and nation (South Africa). This dual identity is clearly what our nation needs, both to cohere as a national identity, but also to provide the cultural, linguistic and indeed ethnic resources needed to make this *place* or *nation* the place it both is and can be. Such an identity will grow organically from the "bottom" of our society, as both black and white discover what unites them with their fellow South Africans, and also what separates them. It will grow as they embrace the commonalities and respect these differences. Such a dual identity can also be promoted or undermined by the way the institutions and elites of our society manage the symbols of national identity: flags, anthems, place names, national events and holidays.

A new meaning to the term "wealth"

Between September 2008 and March 2009 a very strange thing happened to the world's wealth. A very large part of it (some would argue as much as half) disappeared. Where did it go? Was it there in the first place? Perhaps we experienced during this turbulent six months an economic equivalent of Einsteinian physics: that is the complex relationship of time and money. How do you value a 30-year contract to supply gas (as investors in Enron discovered both to their own and everyone else's cost)? And if you dice and splice 10,000 sub prime house mortgages, what is the effect of this aggregation on the real value of these mortgages. These epistemological (and accounting!) uncertainties reveal a much more important problem with the twentieth century concept of wealth. This word has its old English roots in a stem that is also captured in the concept *weal* and *well-being.*

Incipient debates about the purpose of business (as evident in many of the values embraced by the King III code of corporate governance) and the levels of wealth accumulation and wealth expenditure that are acceptable are evidence of an attempt to create what the American sociologist, Talcott Parsons, once described as a shared normative consensus. Societies are struggling with concepts of stakeholder capitalism and sustainable development. In South Africa, a concept of wealth that is also well-being not just for individuals but also for society as a whole, is of immediate and clearly national importance. It is central to government efforts to define a New Growth Path, as well as the creation of a National Planning Commission whose task it is to define a national vision. This new concept of wealth/well-being will need to express itself in the life experiences of 50 million South Africans if it is to accommodate the shared endeavour, which makes a society possible.

Embracing the "I" and also the "we"

To an extent, the late 20th Century may be described as the conquest of the "we" society, as embraced most dramatically by communist style organic states, by the "I" of individualist capitalism propagated by Margaret Thatcher and Ronald Reagan. This tidal wave of hyper-individualism dissolved the ties of working class societies. It destroyed collective economic institutions, such as the defined benefit pension fund with its generational risk-pooling character. Increasingly, interests were defined and pursued in individual terms. It is still too early to say what China's 1979 embrace of market economics will do to social cohesion, while Russia's post-communist experience also does not provide a clear alternative to the self-centered individualism of "advanced" Western societies.

This contrast between "I" and "we" societies is not trivial. The emergence of an "I"-centred consciousness in Western European societies made possible social orders where individual accountability was both possible and required. "I"-centred economic systems gave space to both entrepreneurs and crooks in the market place, along with freedom of expression. It is also at the heart of the concept of the Rule of Law. However, when the "we" is banished to the periphery, social cohesion dissolves and collective action, except in the frenzy of greed or fear, becomes impossible.

What then of South Africa? Will black *Captains of Industry* run their companies with the same social values as their white compatriots? Will programmes of broad-based economic empowerment produce owners with different concepts of profit and wealth to those of "Wall Street"? Can social welfare programmes be designed that balance individual and collective interests and contributions? Can employment and honest economic activity become central to our society's concept of economic progress?

These three challenges: national identity; an appropriate concept or value of wealth and well-being, and a societal balance between individual responsibility and collective solidarity are South African challenges with global relevance. To the extent that we answer these effectively, we will be playing our role in creating a way of being human in this new century and on this great continent that works.

WHERE I BECOME YOU
"WAAR EK JY WORD"

Antjie Krog

"WAAR EK JY WORD"

1.

jy kom my omhaal
aan die anderkant van die wêreld
jou roep hoor ek
bibbernagblou en ge-
blind aan stralende gebeentes

by jou my snerpende kop

onwillig behaar
geuromgord
begin jy die ek uit die self knoop
die onskendbare eens
laat jy los in vele

uit-mekaar-uit-neer-sit
losmakend die een stuk uit die ander
sodat die verbintenisse voortvouend
blyk in die ondraaglik meeskrywende a-
sem ongekloofde rose

om uit-
mekaar-te-haal
die ek
van die ook-ek
die jy
van die byna-
jou-in-my

hoor, sê jy, hoe on-
naspeurbaar treur
die dieptesig van liefde

WHERE I BECOME YOU

1.

you come to win me over
at the other end of the world
I hear your call
shivering night blue and blindly
bound by radiant bones

with you my head bitingly cold

unwillingly hairgrown
scentgirded
you begin to unfasten the I from the self
the inviolable once
you let loose in many

separating-laying-side-by-side
loosening one piece from another
so that the bonds seem incessantly to unfold
in the unbearably co-writing
breath of unsundered roses

to dis-
mantle
the I
from the also-I
the you
from the almost-
you-in-me

listen, you say, how un-
fathomably it grieves,
the profoundness of love

2.

jou vokale sterf by my verby
so naby dat dit ek
kon gewees het

oneindig die statiese lading van sterre
wat spetterend snags boeie aan ons slaan

maar jy wat ek kon gewees het
maar nog nie was nie, jy skuifel
hardnekkig skif jy tot toebedeelde veelsaamheid

elke blaar wat val
val alleen, weerlê ek

jou gesig knars tot stilstand

ek wil
die ek wat ek is
bly

maar waar
begín
die issende-ek?

op die plek
waar die ek soos jy is
of daar waar die ek anders as jy is?

my tong word doof
jou oë kirr uit die oogholtes van die verlorenes
net 'n asemlek blink
granaatpitblink
tussen waar ek-is is
en jy-nie is

ek vergaan – grint in die keel
jou vokale sterf hier verby
so naby
dat my ooglid aan jou liefde smee

2.

your vowels die passing me
so close that I
could have been the one

endless the static cargo of stars
that sputtering in the night shackles us

but you that I could have been
but was not yet, you shuffle
stubbornly you sift to bestowed profusion

each leaf that falls
falls alone, I counter

your face grinds to a halt

I want
the I that is I
to stay

but where
does it begin,
this being-I?

at the place
where the I is like you
or there where the I is other than you?

my tongue goes deaf
your eyes coo from the sockets of the lost ones
just a breathlick of light
pomegranate pip light
between where I-am is
and not-you is

I decay – grit in the throat
your vowels die passing
so close
that my eyelid welds itself to your love

3.

sterre tongblind en sterwend in gravitasie
jy kom
hartbevlek en opwaarts
kom jy
jou asem van kristal
en die mondnabye geluid van voëls

sterre tongblind
sterre sterwend
sterre asembenemend as digsbysyndste galaktiese sig

onverworwe moet ek word
losgeknip
en sterstapelend van gewrig

4.

oor-ruisend deur ons
houvassende kapasiteit
op hierdie kniebare aardmantel

kan ek nie nie-jy wees nie
jy nie niemand wees nie
ons nie nêrens wees nie
die ongehoorde behorende woord
nie nie-gesê word deur ons nie

my hart haper – gewigloser as tevore
dog brugbaar

daar waar ek anders as jy is
begin ek
dis waar

maar daar waar ek jy is
jy geword het
sing ek buite myself
ligte polsslae kwiksilwersingend
iets anderkant alle mensheid gekaats

3.

stars tongueblind and dying in gravitation
you come
heartstained and upwards
you come
your crystal breath
and the mouthclose sound of birds

stars tongueblind
stars dying
stars breathtakingly closest galactic sight

unwon I must become
unfastened
with wrists that can pile up stars

4.

overwhelmed by the whisper of our
capacity to grip
this kneadable earth's mantle

can I not be not-you
you not be no-one
we not be nowhere
the unheard-of befitting word
not be unsaid by us

my heart falters – more weightless than before
yet bridgeable

there where I am other than you
I begin
it's true

but there where I am you
have become you
I sing beyond myself
light pulses of quicksilversong
a thing cast beyond all humankind

5.

ontmantelende sterreskuim
onttakeld
swierende sterrehope puin-
stof wat vormloos en maakbaar verdig

swaartekrag lê haar wil op
en weg meteens
alle geborge-wees

kwesbaar-tollend vorm die klodders hulle lemmende lig
sterre kwesbaar
sterre pokdalig

hoe draal die spiraalarms
om die pas statig-getilte teerheid
hoe chaoties die wirwar

sterre-speeksel
sterreskuimnewel
ons sou die saamwesendes kon gewees het
as ons bloeiender mekaar in die greep kon werf

maar nou kom jy my verhaal
aan die anderkant van hierdie skonkige wêreld
om uit-mekaar-uit-neer-gesit te word
die spykers in bloed
die melk in bene
die fosfor in die harsingkors
ons, ja ons bestáán uit sterrestof

sterre tongblind
sterre sterwend
so onvoorstelbaar dreun ons
so gigant dra ons ons ewewig
dat, as ons koud is
gloei ons soos ons brand

5.

dismantled starfoam
stripped
swaggering starheaps of ruin
dust that thickens latent and formless

gravity's force imposes her will
and gone at once
all sheltering

vulnerably reeling clots form their blades of light
stars vulnerable
stars pockmarked

how the spiral arms linger
around the new stately tilting tenderness
how chaotic the swirling

starspittle
starfoamfog
we could have been the ones together
if we could have recruited each other less bloodily

but now you come to recover me
at the other end of this giddy world
to be taken-apart-set-down
the nails in blood
the milk in bones
the phosphorus in the cortex
we, yes we consist of stardust

stars tongueblind
stars dying
so unimaginably we roar
so gigantically we carry our equilibrium
that, when we are cold
we glow as we burn

6.

om die punt te bereik
anderkant die sê van die ek
die punt
wat die ek so veeltallig is
dat dit nie meer saakmaak
om ek te sê nie
dat die ek nie meer sigself is nie
maar herkenbare
veelvoude

van die hopeloos beminbare skadu's
van jou sleutelbeen

7.

die winterwind
my kleine
my agtergeblewene
jasmynbedruipte skedel

beskryf ons skaduwee teen die klip
teen die wand is ons
een
maar jou wond
bly spieëlend as ek
apart
na jou kyk
vanuit die geur van jou diepste arm

6.

to reach the point
beyond the uttering of the I
the point
of the I so multitudinous
that it no longer matters
to say I
that the I is no longer itself
but discernible
multiples

of the hopelessly lovable shadows
of your collarbone

7.

the winter wind
my littlest
my leftbehind
jasmine-draped skull

describes our shadow against the stone
against the wall we are
one
but your wound
keeps reflecting if I
look at you
separately
from inside the scent of your deepest arm

8.

jy
die juiste jy
die ja-jy
die gras ruis nog van jou enkels nou net
elke keer as ek opkyk
pasrugkerende
wegstappende
geliefde
astraal gefluit   nagtelik geskort
kom!
laat 'n woord dwarsdeur jou kom
laat meer as ek kom
meer as die ondermynende myne
die meinedige myne
die eindeloos ekkerende myne
laat ons
onvergloei naak
onberoerd
wat ons nooit
alleen kon wees nie word

9.

herfs die enkelheid uit jou slaap voor dagbreek
alle sinjale swerf deur jou tong
en ons hou mekaars bloed in bewaring
my geleefde
my geloofsang verrukte

jou onbedingbare asem
maak van ons apartes
mettertyd
o my gelyfde lief
swaartekrag-talmend, almalmagtig: ons

8.

you
the true you
the yes-you
the grass still rustles from your ankles just
now each time I look up
turning away
departing
beloved
astral birdsong   wrapped in night
come!
let a word come right through you
let more come than I
more than the undermining mine
the perjuring mine
the endlessly I-ing mine
let us become
unglowing nakedly
unmoved
that which we never
could have become alone

9.

autumn the singularity from your sleep before dawn
all signals roam through your tongue
and we hold each other's blood in trust
my lived one
my faithsong enraptured

your non-negotiable breath
makes of us separate ones
in the course of time
o my embodied love
lingering in gravity, all-powerful: us

Bronnelys

Celan P. 2001. *Selected Poems and Prose of Paul Celan.* J Felstiner (vert). New York & London: W.W. Norton.

Schilling G. 2003. *Evoluerend Heelal – de biografie van de kosmos.* Leuven: Fontaine Uitgewers Davidsfonds.

Reference List

Celan P. 2001. *Selected Poems and Prose of Paul Celan.* J Felstiner (transl). New York & London: W.W. Norton.

Schilling G. 2003. *Evoluerend Heelal – de biografie van de kosmos.* Leuven: Fontaine Uitgewers Davidsfonds.

SECTION 2

ON HUMANISM

Essays

Reflexive humanism | *Wolfgang Huber*

The spirit of Islamic humanism | *Ebrahim Moosa*

The 'Dark Sides' of humanism in South Africa | *André du Toit*

Science, technology and humanity | *George Ellis*

Critical issues for a new humanism | *Drucilla Cornell & Kenneth Panfilio*

New music for a new humanism | *Hans Huyssen*

Reflections

Indigenous humanism: Manifestations of interconnectedness | *Antjie Krog*

Towards a new humanism in Africa | *Njabulo Ndebele*

Relational humanism | *Jan-Hendrik S Hofmeyr*

REFLEXIVE HUMANISM

Wolfgang Huber

The ambiguity of humanism

I will examine five examples of humanism to illustrate its ambiguity: Renaissance humanism, Enlightenment humanism, Human Rights humanism, the New Humanism, Third Culture humanism, and Cosmopolitan humanism.

Sixteenth century *Renaissance Humanism* was essentially a literary, intellectual humanism. Its conviction was that literacy and literary education are of crucial importance for the formation of the individual person. It had a special meaning for the conceptualisation of the European "occident" with its threefold cultural basis for which the names of Athens, Rome and Jerusalem stand. Therefore humanism for a long time was related to the interaction between classical antiquity and Christian tradition. The fostering of this cultural heritage was regarded as the central element of "Humanism" and the cultural superiority of "Humanists" was often assumed.[1]

1 Graduates of a "Humanistisches Gymnasium" in Germany were half a century ago convinced of their cultural superiority over the graduates of a "Realgymnasium". That false assumption was not due to the Humanists of the 16th but rather to the Neohumanists of the 19th century.

Humanism through literary learning continues to be an important concept.[2] Its scope was remarkably broadened in our times to a concept of a self-conscious and self-critical understanding of one self in the encounter with the other. Such a reflexive understanding, as Edward Said says, creates a sense of community with other interpreters and other societies (Said 2004). However, as open as this concept is, it was at its beginnings clearly Eurocentric. It gave birth to the concept of the "occident" (a term of the 16th century). Even in its contemporary transformations it has a strong emphasis on the intellectual character of humanism. It became a concept of learning, of education, of research in the "humanities".

Eighteenth century *Enlightenment Humanism* was essentially an individualistic humanism. It revolved around the autonomy of the subject. Enlightenment was understood as the self-liberation of the subject from dependence on the views of others. The human person was conceived as a rational being. Its rationality made it certain that its subjective, autonomous decisions would, taken rationally, coincide with the universal principles, which everyone has to follow. Individualism and universalism converged.

But the mono-logical concept of rationality does not take into account the historical formation and therefore cultural plurality of human rationalities. The programme of universal rationality was and still is not aware of the different, culturally embedded normative orientations of our seemingly autonomous, rational decisions. In addition, this concept did not take into account the social, relational nature of the individual human person. It underestimated the communicative character of its existence. It gave room to the development of a narrow individualistic understanding of the human being. Founded on the concept of the human person as animal, it tended to exclude the self-transcendent character of human beings.

Charles Taylor therefore calls Enlightenment Humanism and even more its later successors an exclusive humanism (Taylor 2007). This tendency has become particularly evident in modern forms of humanism which, under the name of "New Humanism", are aggressively antireligious and atheistic.[3] Critical observers therefore express their longing for the "Old Humanism" compared with this self-declared "New Humanism" (Scruton 2009). Parts of this movement are organised in an "International Humanist and Ethical Union". Of course this antireligious fundamentalism in the name of "New Humanism" finds its religious or pseudo-religious counterparts in a new "Humanistic International" with branches in Latin America, Africa,[4] Europe

---

2 "New Humanism" was the name for a school of literary criticism in the USA between 1910 and 1930.

3 *Cf* the magazine "New Humanist", edited by the "Rationalist Association" and advertising "Godlessness for free" or the activities of the "British Humanist Association" whose vice-president is Richard Dawkins. His "God Delusion" is perhaps the most outspoken expression of this kind of "New Humanism". At Harvard University you find a Humanist Chaplaincy, which mediates a "New Humanism", for which "Good, without God" is the governing formula.

4 A first Humanist African Forum took place 2006 in Dakar, followed by a next one 2008 in Nairobi. In Dakar a "New Africa" was proclaimed in the name of the "New Humanism".

and elsewhere.[5] The name "New Humanism" can obviously be used ideologically in different directions.

After World War II a new kind of humanism emerged, which I call *Human Rights Humanism*. Its interest was directed towards the development of institutions that are destined and suitable for the protection of human dignity and the fostering of human rights. There are direct links between the dialogues on "New Humanism" after the end of World War II and the United Nations "Universal Declaration on Human Rights" of 10 December 1948. Its inaugurators followed the deep conviction that after the manifold cruelties of the German Nazi-Regime, the genocide committed on European Jewry, and the suffering of so many people under the Stalinist terror in the Soviet Union, the respect for the dignity and the rights of every human person had to be firmly established.

With the Universal Declaration of Human rights a clear egalitarian universalism was established on the global level. But unfortunately this consensus was soon drawn into the global dispute between East and West and was subjugated under the ideological battle between an individualistic and a collectivistic understanding of human rights to which some time later the concept of a third generation of human rights was added, including the right to development.

This Human Rights humanism lost much of its reputation because of the cynical use of human rights in the service of power politics by the USA and others. In our days it is quite unclear whether the concept of human dignity and human rights, as evident as it is, can help to tame the wild global capitalism of our days, diminish the enormous gap between rich and poor that exists globally as well as regionally – with South Africa as a specific and even dramatic example – or foster a sustainable kind of politics and economy which takes the rights of future generations into account as well as the dignity of nature in all its dimensions.

The term "New Humanism" took on an additional meaning in the debate about the split between science and humanities. After CP Snow formulated the state of the debate as a division of "two cultures" (Snow 1959), again and again efforts were undertaken to overcome this separation and to find a "third culture" which forms a new synthesis between the two. For this new synthesis John Brockman used the

5 This movement originated in Argentina and is founded on ideas of Mario Rodriguez Cobos, known also under his artist's name Silo. Therefore the members of this movement call themselves also "Siloists". Their "New Humanism" is understood as a "Universalistic Humanism". It focuses on the overcoming of pain and suffering at a personal, interpersonal and social level. It includes sexual liberation as well as nonviolent conflict resolution. They organised a World March for Peace and Nonviolence, which started 2 October 2009 in Wellington/New Zealand and ended on 2 January 2010 in Vacas/Argentina. In France this "New Humanism" is counted under the sectarian movements. It got applause from Michail Gorbachev, the former president of the Soviet Union, and from Evo Morales, the present president of Bolivia.

term "New Humanism" (Brockman 1995:2003,2008).[6] I will call this type of humanism a *Third Culture Humanism*. It is closely bound to the academy and therefore can be characterised as an academic humanism. His impulse was taken up in different places and directions. Often the integration of science and humanities is found in a way in which the assumed insights of science show the direction. Evolution theory for instance is often used as a general key to the understanding also of society and the human person. The difference between explanation and understanding that made the differentiation between science and the humanities necessary is regularly underestimated when it comes to such a concept of a "third culture" – and it may be so under the title of a "New Humanism".

Let me finally mention efforts to formulate a new cosmopolitan ethics that broadens the perspective over the horizons mentioned so far. I take as example the philosophical proposals of Kwame Appiah, who was raised in Ghana, educated at Cambridge and teaches philosophy at Princeton (Appiah 2006). Although Appiah does not use the term "humanism", we could call this emerging concept a *Cosmopolitan humanism*. It tries to take egalitarian universalism seriously, but it combines universalism with the respect for differences.

Not all share such a connection between universalism and diversity. It is opposed by a counter-cosmopolitism, as Appiah calls it, that insists on universality without tolerance, such as occurs especially in religious forms. It is a universalism that in fact excludes all those who do not accept the truths its own claim as obligatory for all. Another counter to Cosmopolitan humanism is the way in which today's economic globalisation deepens the gap between rich and poor in the one world. Global injustice is irreconcilable with Cosmopolitan humanism because it violates the equal dignity of every human person.

Every use of the terms "Humanism" or "New Humanism" thus needs a self-critical evaluation. For this reason I speak about *Reflexive humanism*. The contextual limitations of the term *humanism*, its cultural presuppositions, its use as a means of justification, the interests it serves, and its inevitable shortcomings, have to be evaluated carefully in order to develop the normative plausibility of a concept of humanism as clearly as possible. For this purpose we must compare and critically evaluate the different approaches, and be attentive to the overlaps between them and the meaning of humanism. Reflexive humanism is characterised by the attempt to find in different cultural and religious traditions as well in other streams of knowledge enriching perspectives for enlarging the different understandings of humanism.[7] Reflexive humanism at the same time evaluates critically the traditional anthropocentrism of different humanisms in order to locate the place of human beings in the natural world. This is an ongoing process and requires continuous effort.

---

6 The term "New Humanism" is also used by *Daisaku Ikeda*, the President of Soka Gakkai, who published his University addresses under the title of "New Humanism" (new edition announced for 2010).

7 As an example for such an approach see John de Gruchy (2006), *Being Human: Confessions of a Christian Humanist.*

Motivation, pluralism, relationality

I now wish to stress my enthusiasm for a new discourse on humanism and in doing so I will discuss three points of specific personal interest.

First of all, I have no doubt that the quest for the *humane quality of human togetherness* takes on a new character in our time. That is the case because of the following:

- today's generations more than any previous ones exist in one world which means that insight into the equality of all human persons presents itself in new dimensions, and
- they experience in the one global reality the plurality not only of cultures, but of human individuals as a comparably radical plurality and therefore
- they have to address the diversity of human beings and of their life conditions more intensively than any generations before.

Humanism has to acknowledge the equality of difference. Such a statement does not seem to be controversial. That could already indicate that the problem of today is not so much a new definition of humanism, but more the practical respect for it. Simon Critchley speaks of the "motivational deficit" as a crucial ethical problem of our time (Critchley 2008:6). The ethical task is fulfilled not when you define the good but only when people are motivated to practice what is good. When this is applied to humanism the questions have to be asked: What makes it so difficult for human persons to behave towards others consistent with their conviction that all persons are equal? Why do ethical motives seem much weaker than economic incentives? The world economy produces not only goods but at the same time a growing inequality. Obviously this has not only to be attributed to systemic imperatives or to an "empire", but it is at the same time bound to the actions of many individual actors who at least should be aware of the inconsistency of their deeds and convictions or at least their obligations in the light of human dignity and human rights.

That leads to the core of a religious approach to the problem of humanism. For a religious approach has to do with the inconsistency and brokenness of human existence and the hope for liberation from this inconsistency and brokenness for the sake of the renewal of the wholeness of life. In this connection Jürgen Habermas hints at the deeper sources of solidarity in religions for which the enlightened morality of equal respect for all in forms of secular ethics seemingly do not present a motivational equivalent (Mendieta 2010).

Secondly, do we really know what constitutes the "essence" of the human being? The Renaissance humanists spoke of the "dignity of the human person".[8] They took up the classical distinction between the honour that humans deserve in different degrees, and the dignity in regard to which they do not differ.[9] But how should we define this dignity? Is there any definition in the proper sense of the word? Definitions in this case grow more problematic as they become more substantial, and only as they stay

8 Giovanni Pico della Mirandola (1463-1494), *De dignitate hominis*, Lat.-Dt. Hamburg 1990.

9 For more detail see Huber (2010).

formal are they seemingly more accepted. An exemplary formal definition was given by Immanuel Kant who understood human dignity under the perspective that the human person is not purely seen as a means to an end but as an end in itself (Kant 1956:68). The anthropocentric shortcomings of that definition are obvious. Today we are convinced that such a definition has to be comparably applied to all parts of nature and also to pieces of art. So we understand that human dignity as well as other kinds transcend the borders of its definition. And that is not a coincidence. Any closed or closing definition of human dignity would be an intervention into human dignity itself. In addition it would be a denial of the contemporary pluralistic situation to make absolute a definition that stems from a certain cultural tradition as if it could be a general definition of the term. Every definition represents only a perspective on the universal character of human dignity as such; we will never reach more than a relative universalism which is bound to a specific language, cultural code, etc. Therefore every definition has to take into account the necessary openness for different understandings and differing reasons for human dignity. Only in such a way can the complexity of the human being be acknowledged.

Thirdly, Christian theology does not ground human dignity in one or the other aspect of the "essence" of the human being, for instance rationality. Rather it understands the dignity of a human person as a relationship of recognition in a radically eccentric way. It is not that which the human person makes of herself that results in and determines her dignity, but how she is seen from the perspective of the completely other and the divine. This dignity, conceived as relational, can be understood as radically equal because it does not depend on the different qualities, qualifications or performances of the individual but is grounded in a radical differentiation between the person and her deeds. Human dignity is not justified from the "substance" of the human person, but from a relation that constitutes herself. This divine relatedness is constitutive for the inalienable and inviolable character of human dignity and opens the perspective on other relational dimensions of human existence: relations to the world, to the others, to oneself. Relatedness therefore is not a counterweight to the individuality of the human person but inherent in it because individuality itself is relational. Individuality means the relation of the person to herself; it is therefore one dimension of the multidimensional relatedness of the self.

Of course the relatedness of the self is explained and understood not only in terms of religion, but also in secular terms. But I continue to be fascinated by the radical form in which Christian religion takes the described eccentricity of the human existence as a starting point and unfolds it in the fourfold relationship of the person to God, to the world, to the others and to herself. As far as my first question – relating to the motivational deficit of our time – is concerned, I therefore argue that we should not neglect the possible motivational force of religious traditions, rituals and convictions. In this respect religious and secular consciousness do not compete with each other. Religion offers answers to questions which secular consciousness does not pose.

Reference List

Appiah KA. 2006. *Cosmopolitanism: Ethics in a World of Strangers*. New York & London: Norton.

Brockman J. 1995. *The Third Culture: Beyond the Scientific Revolution.* New York: Simon & Schuster.

— 2003. *The New Humanists: Science at the Edge*. New York: Barnes & Noble.

— (ed). 2008. *Science at the Edge: Conversations with the Leading Scientific Thinkers of Today.* New York: Union Square Press.

Critchley S. 2007. *Infinitely Demanding: Ethics of Commitment, Politics of Resistance.* London & New York: Verso.

De Gruchy JW. 2006. *Being Human: Confessions of a Christian Humanist.* London: SCM.

Huber W. 2006. *Gerechtigkeit und Recht: Grundlinien christlicher Rechtsethik.* 3rd Ed. Gütersloh: Chr. Kaiser.

Kant I. 1785. Weischedel WA (ed). 1956. *Grundlegung zur Metaphysik der Sitten vol IV*. Wiesbaden: Insel.

Mendieta E. Interview with Jürgen Habermas. 3 February 2010. Posted on *The Immanent Frame: Secularism, Religion and the Public Sphere*. www.ssrc.org.

Said EW. 2004. *Humanism and Democratic Criticism*. New York: Columbia University Press.

Scruton R. 2009. The New Humanism. *The American Spectator*. March 2009, 42(2):42-44.

Snow CP. 1959. *Two Cultures* (reprint). Cambridge: Cambridge University Press.

Taylor C. 2007. *A Secular Age*. Cambridge MA: Harvard University Press.

THE SPIRIT OF ISLAMIC HUMANISM

Ebrahim Moosa

Whether an image is a reflection of reality or the fabrication of a hostile media, there is widespread agreement that worldwide the image of Islam and Muslims is taking a horrific beating. It is, of course, risky to speak glibly and anecdotally about complex empirical realities in Muslim societies that are not easily decipherable. Whatever the causes of the anger unleashed by people who identify with Islam individually or collectively, it is true that most right-thinking people in the Muslim world and beyond are alarmed at the dehumanisation of Muslims. Even though a very small minority of Muslims perpetrates violence, yet a community exceeding 1.2 billion people is implicated by the blowback of Muslim terrorist activities.

If Muslims are so concerned about their image, sceptics and outsiders will immediately ask, what are they doing about it? There lies the rub. Suicide bombings occur not only in New York, Washington, London and Madrid, but also target the business districts of Istanbul, Karachi, and Kabul, all Muslim majority cities. The American military invasions of Iraq, Afghanistan and intense US military strikes in regions of Pakistan and Yemen all inflame Muslim sentiment. But these descriptions not only speak of a stand-off between foreign governments and groups of people; they also signify that something deeply troubling is fermenting within Muslim societies. Solutions to these intractable problems are in short supply since the diagnoses are often hastily made and are flawed.

One flawed diagnosis was made by al-Qaida and Osama bin Laden who thought they could undermine American security by attacking the US homeland. Equally flawed was the decision after 11 September 2001 by President George W. Bush to invade Afghanistan in a fit of imperial hubris in order to apprehend the criminals responsible for 9/11. That invasion soon morphed into a civilising mission via nation-building in Afghanistan of saving Afghan women from the Taliban. And once the filament of logic used to justify the invasion of Iraq withered that exercise in imperial hubris also turned into a civilising mission. For those of us who still remember colonial times the Euro-American military adventures in the Middle East and South Asia sounded all too familiar. Not only are these costly imperial adventures being paid in blood, treasure, opportunities and catastrophe for everyone concerned especially for the Afghans and Iraqis, but it also stirs anger and resentment throughout the Muslim world and perpetuates the cycle of hatred and mistrust.

South Africa, too, has had its fair share of horrific religiously-inspired violence perpetrated by people identified as Muslims who were linked to the vigilante group People Against Gangsterism and Drugs (PAGAD) that sowed mayhem and destruction in the city of Cape Town in the late 1990s. Thankfully deliberate prosecutions and sensible leadership managed to break the back of these criminal networks that masqueraded in the colours of religion. Yet, these few bad apples also managed to undermine the positive image of South African Muslims who rendered extraordinary public service and leadership in all walks of life. From leadership in government, the judiciary and business, to the arenas of healthcare and sports, South Africans of Muslim heritage have demonstrated their contribution as citizens and a people of faith in a complex and diverse country.

In many ways South Africa is both an exception and a role model. Muslim minorities in Europe, North America and elsewhere are envious of the extent to which Muslims in South Africa have integrated into national life. These overseas groups might want to study the experiences of South African Islam where efforts in faith, citizenship and service to humanity are orchestrated effortlessly and seamlessly. In part, this shining legacy of Islam is owed to the struggle of Muslim South Africans alongside people of different faiths and other convictions during the dark days of apartheid. Those struggles taught everyone the crucial lesson that we share a common humanity that transcends race, religion and ethnicity. In that struggle triumphalist and exclusivist theologies of Islam were abandoned in favour of more egalitarian and inclusivist Muslim theologies. If the South African story of Islam was shared on a larger global forum there could be something edificatory for all who are interested.

The global scene

On a global scale Muslim communities were caught in a bind of bad choices. Some Muslims resorted to violence and militancy directed at Western governments who aid a wide range of Muslim political leaders and elites, many of whom are kleptocracies, dictatorships and authoritarian rulers. The best interests of their societies and people are often furthest from their minds. The many militant and terrorist adversaries of these foreign-backed Muslim elites are determined to harm the interests of the 'far enemy', namely the Western powers, in a nihilistic fashion irrespective of the human cost of their destructive actions. In a bizarre and craven manner Muslim terrorists who attack both the 'near enemy,' namely the bad rulers, and the 'far enemy', enjoy some credibility in the 'Muslim street' so to speak. Wanton violence is far from being a solution and only perpetuates the nihilistic syndrome. When violence becomes an end in itself then we are already well past nihilism. In many places where entire communities are caught up in this violent syndrome I also question whether faith has not already been replaced by its opposite and something more sinister.

At the other end of the spectrum are the romantic peaceniks. Somewhat benign and perhaps equally misguided they imagine that by merely talking peace, without taking decisive action, the world and its genuine trouble spots will be magically transformed into some idyllic havens. Clearly this option ought to be more attractive than violence. But if peace talks, interfaith dialogues and non-violent campaigns become ends in themselves without a deliberate agenda for transformation they also become dangerous pathways. How? When dialogue becomes a commodity for consumption with no higher ends at stake, then a good thing, too, can become harmful. Often such superfluous acts breed scepticism about dialogue and undermine opportunities when conversation and exchange might genuinely be available. Well-intentioned thoughts in themselves enjoy no immunity from being delusional. Such intentions must be accompanied by a genuine will to change and make the world a better place in order to be meaningful. In the absence of a genuine will to change, peaceful processes can make us stare down the same nihilistic abyss as the perpetrators of violence do to their adversaries. That will to change via peaceful protest was demonstrated in the uprisings of the Spring of 2011 beginning in Tunisia, followed by developments in Egypt, Bahrain and Libya. These are promising beginnings that should be encouraged to flower into self-sustaining democracies.

Meaningful analyses proposing humane solutions and action to our existential dilemmas are the best guarantors of meaningful change. One crucial aspect of change requires that we ensure that governance at a global level delivers optimal justice to all societies. An international order bereft of justice is nothing short of a jungle where strong predatory states prey on weaker ones. In the international order too much emphasis is placed on the threat of force in the service of narrowly defined interests while very little energy is invested in persuasion. In the post cold-war global order, and especially after the end of the bipolar world with the collapse of the Soviet Union, liberal-capitalism has gone on a rampage. This state of affairs has inaugurated an enormous imbalance in power and has caused serious distortions to our global political, economic and cultural orders. If left unchecked, we can be sure that the resultant anger will afflict more than just the powerful; it will also overwhelm the weak and the poor. A Qur'anic passage warns of such possibilities: "Beware of an affliction that will not be restricted to the evil-mongers among you alone" (Qur'an 8:25). Neo-liberal globalisation might have its attractions but it has also bequeathed some alarming catastrophes and ticking bombs: from impending environmental degradation, the run-away gap between the 'haves' and the 'have-nots' within and between nations, and the skewed consumption of global resources for the benefit of the powerful to a lack of care for fellow humans in foreign and alien places.

Islamic humanism

What kind of resources does Islam as a tradition offer in order to heal the human spirit? Islam once played a major role in the intellectual tradition known as humanism. Muslim thinkers shared knowledge traditions with their Jewish and Christian counterparts in the Middle Ages. Muslim scholars acted as curators of the rational traditions of the Greeks in the form of philosophy and logic for a considerable time. Islam at its best also ushered in a cosmopolitan order where Muslim Arabs and non-Arabs, Jews, Christians and a host of other religious groups flourished. Muslim humanism energised Islamdom's philosophical and theological traditions for the better. Yet, more exclusivist and triumphalist theologies also reduced the capaciousness of Islam's humanistic tradition. This narrowing of the intake of the humanistic spirit also undermined the theological possibilities of creating a world shared with 'others' so that sectarian and group interests displaced the caring for humans qua humans. Furthermore, the Islamic humanistic tradition was also unable to reign in the imperial reflex of Muslim politics and ethics.

In the face of a hegemonic Muslim theology the humanistic tradition of Muslim theology provides an opportunity to critique the former. To foster critique in such a narrowing world is critical. The lack of self-critique among the mainstream of Muslim religious thinkers today and Muslim intelligentsia generally is deeply troubling. How alien would such a passive stance have sounded to the ears of humanist Muslim thinkers of the past who did posses a critical voice and directed it freely at insiders and outsiders alike? It is with breathtaking force that the humanist poet Abu al-Ala al-Ma`arri (d. 1057) could parody the self-righteous religious scholars of his day for their double standards.

> They recite their sacred books, although [the fact informs me]
> That these are fiction from first to last
> O Reason, thou [alone] speakest the truth. Then perish the fools
> Who forged the [religious] traditions or interpreted them!
> A rabbi is no heretic among his disciples,
> If he sets a high price on stories which he invented
> He only desired to marry women
> And amass riches by his lies.
> Softly! Thou has been deceived, honest man as thou art,
> By a cunning knave who preaches to the women.
> Amongst you in the morning he says that wine is forbidden, but
> He makes a point of drinking it himself in the evening.

Ma`arri and many other Muslim humanist thinkers and philosophers kept alive the flame of critique and introspection. They left a legacy that others could follow and occasionally drawing on their ideas help to shift the mainstream Muslim theological paradigm in the right direction but often not far enough.

A modern exemplar

A modern exemplar of such refreshing Muslim humanism is Abul Kalam Azad (1888-1958), a leading religious scholar and statesman of modern India (Henderson *et al* 1988). Born in Mecca to a father of Indian heritage, Azad was a child prodigy and an erudite man of letters who was trained as a traditional Muslim theologian. A master stylist in Urdu, Azad spent his early years as a journalist and as an editor of widely read learned magazines. He joined the nationalist movement for liberation from colonialism and spent a good part of his life in British India's jails alongside figures like Mahatma Gandhi and India's first prime minister, Jawaharlal Nehru. At independence Azad became India's first minister of education and the foremost exemplar of humanistic Islamic values in a culturally and religiously diverse India. Azad derived his humanistic inspiration both from the Qur'an, on which he wrote a commentary and from the oral tradition going back to the Prophet Muhammad.

It was Azad who made Indian Muslim audiences in the early part of the twentieth century aware of the humanism at the heart of the teachings of the Prophet Muhammad. Steeped in the oldest of Islamdom's humanistic tradition, namely literature, since he had an unusual mastery of three languages Persian, Arabic and Urdu, Azad grasped the essential spirit underlying our humanity. Through literature, especially his love for poetry Azad explored the manifold vistas that beckon our common humanity (Azad 1983). This talent he put to great use in order to leaven his theology for application in a culturally pluralistic India. With an intellectual apparatus honed by literature, Azad could appreciate both the particulars of Islamic theology and its universalism. Therefore, he firmly believed that Islam's teachings could not differentiate between human beings purely on the grounds of religion. In a united India, Azad believed, Hindus, Muslims, Sikhs, Jains, Parsis and Christians could all live amicably with each other. Given this humanistic vision, he was also an implacable foe of the division of the subcontinent into two religious homelands: a Muslim homeland called Pakistan and a Hindu homeland called India. While Azad was aware of the darkness of the human soul as it spilled out in religiously inspired violence on the subcontinent before the partition of his homeland, he was optimistic in his faith in human beings and human nature. He never gave up on humanity's ability to transcend limitations.

I stumbled upon Azad's particular reading of an inclusive theology while reading an essay on Azad in a collection called *Aging Lantern (Purane Chiragh)* written by Azad's much younger contemporary Abul Hasan Ali Nadvi (d. 1999). Nadvi was an influential scholar of a traditional stripe who headed a society called *Message to Humanity* attached to his influential seminary in the Indian city of Lucknow called the Nadwatul Ulama. In his essay Nadvi reminisced on a speech delivered by Azad that he had attended in which India's leading Muslim statesman talked about human equality. To demonstrate that Islam's highest authority and teachings supported human equality and friendship among all of humanity, Azad cited a benediction that the Prophet Muhammad made during his nightly vigils and after his daily prayers.

Nadvi himself seemed surprised by the proof-text Azad uncovered, just as I, too, was pleasantly surprised by my discovery. The proof-text was a tradition found in the canonical collection of the ninth century compiler of prophetic sayings, Abu Dawud al-Sijistani. For most Sunni Muslims this book is an authentic representation of the body of knowledge of Islam's Prophet. I was also reminded of how often communities read their treasured collections in ways that obscure material offering liberating insights. But it took someone with Azad's acumen and insight to retrieve from the Muslim archive a liberating insight that impressed Nadvi and continues to delight Azad's readers today.

The report Azad recovered was a benediction the Prophet Muhammad repeatedly made at the end of his formal worship five times a day: "... Oh God, our Lord and the Lord of all things, I testify that you exclusively are the Lord," he said. This was later followed by: "... Our Lord and the Lord of all things, I testify that all of humanity are brethren [family] ..." For Azad this benediction captured the spirit of an Islamic humanism. All of humanity is a single family, a fact to which the Prophet of Islam testified repeatedly, is a beacon to those followers of Islam who are committed to Muhammad's teachings with integrity. Armed with such teachings, Azad never wavered in his commitment to Islam, or in his service to all of humanity. But it is surprising how this benediction has fallen out of the benediction practices of contemporary Muslims especially at a time when such an inclusivism was needed for Muslim societies. Even within progressive Muslim circles in South Africa and beyond, this benediction is absent from the regular liturgy.

But there are other benedictions of the Prophet Muhammad that circulate within Muslim communities that speak to the human spirit across time and place and require greater attention to their meaning and implications. In a humanity broken as ours, where the emphasis is purely on the external we often neglect the darkness that overcomes the conscience and the soul. The Prophet Muhammad taught humanity to be aware of such darkening possibilities and therefore urged us frequently to reflect on the state of the soul and human conscience. Among my favourite benedictions are the following:

> O God, grant my soul piety
> And my conscience purity
> No one can rival You in purifying it
> You are the Guardian of my soul
> And the Master of my conscience
>
> Oh God, I seek refuge in You and ask you to guard me:
> From knowledge that does not profit
> From a heart that does not tremble
> From an ego that is never sated, and
> From a supplication that is never granted. (al-Nisaburi *et al* 1995)

A medieval exemplar

The exemplar par excellence who persistently excavated the ethical dimensions of Islam's teachings was Abu Hamid al-Ghazali (d. 1111), a towering figure in the Muslim tradition (Moosa 2005). Clearly Ghazali saw the value of the humanistic tradition and subtly incorporated it in his writings. There are some parallels between our condition and that of Ghazali's while there is a great deal that separates us. Like him we are better at knowing what we do not want, than fully knowing what we do want. What we do know is that we desire and seek a paradigmatic shift and that we search after emergent knowledge, both of which will facilitate transitions to alternative futures. While the awaited paradigmatic transition in its messianic calling is as yet barely discernable, we have a hunch in which direction we wish to go. What we do know is that dominant paradigms within the world system that continue to reproduce themselves have to be contested and countered with alternative ways of knowledge and knowing, as well as models of society-building and models of living.

During his time Ghazali asked what kind of subjectivity was required and capable of creating new knowledge for the myriads of challenges in his society. That subjectivity could potentially have several possibilities and iterations. Ghazali cultivated a subjectivity of a self in a unique relationship with the divine, nature and society. To cultivate the self was the goal of the paradigmatic transitions and emergent knowledge that he sought. Happily the notion of the self he aspired to could not be construed as an egotistical one, but one that was related to tradition, revelation, knowledge and society.

As Muslims explore ways to energise their knowledge traditions, in addition to being critical, robust and cutting-edge, they will have to take into account the kind of subjectivity that a shifting paradigmatic tradition aspires to produce. Prudence requires that Muslims look at their own past while concurrently exploring experiences and resources of knowledge in other cultures and traditions. It requires forging partnerships in order to form alternative societies. As De Sousa Santos so poignantly reminds us, the future has dramatically become a personal question for us, one of life and death (De Sousa Santos 1995:345). "The past is a metonymy of all that we were and were not," he says. "And the past that never was demands a special reflection on the conditions that prevented it from ever being. The more suppressed, the more present. The emergent subjectivity is so radically contemporary with itself that, by dealing with the past as if it were present, it even gains an anachronistic dimension" (De Sousa Santos 1995:345). In a most astute observation he adds: "The past is, however, made present, not as a ready-made solution, as in reactionary subjectivity, but rather as a creative problem susceptible of opening up new possibilities" (De Sousa Santos 1995:345).

The critical work that any theological project seeking a paradigmatic change has to undertake is to de-familiarise, interrogate and question the canonical tradition, and literally de-construct it. But it will have to be different from certain strands of postmodernism that only deconstruct, as if deconstruction were an end in itself. Together with De Sousa Santos, we must insist that it is only in an archaeology where the past becomes present; in other words, it is only in an encounter with the historical that a paradigmatic transition can engage in a radical critique of the politics of the possible, without yielding to an impossible politics (De Sousa Santos 1995:491).

Ghazali found inspiration in poiesis and ethos and the creativity of being in the threshold position or the border areas. In one of his important writings he spoke of the advantage of being in the threshold position, the in-between space called a *dihliz* in Arabic. As a theologian Ghazali could care less for the finery of philosophy but valued its insights. Despite his interest in philosophy he also realised a certain debt to poetry. What he found refreshing in poetry was its ability to disclose impossibilities or apparent impossibilities. Poetry held together heterogeneous knowledge: knowledge of the ends of human life, knowledge of the soul. While philosophers were disdainful of the occasional vulgarity of poetics – the ability to be creative and form something new out of the old – Ghazali understood better than some of his contemporaries, the value of this mode of discourse. And, he put it to effective use in order to mediate complex notions of truth located in the essential diversity (heterogeneity) of knowledge. For this reason he had little hesitation in mixing different grammars of thought in order to persuade and cajole his audiences. Therefore, his narrative could simultaneously sustain divine interventions in nature through miracles and also admit to the role of reason and a radical conception of order in nature – one that was primarily based on empirical observation but not on necessary causation. Thus, different kinds of discourses could co-exist within a paradigm without contradiction and paradox but one that was sufficiently capacious to accommodate different knowledge systems.

Ghazali also understood that knowledge must be emancipatory. True knowledge paved the way to the ethical in Ghazali's view. Knowledge paved the way to salvation in the afterlife and offered the fulcrum of earthly emancipation. The emancipated subject was one who was truly liberated from all material dependencies. However, an emancipated subject did not behave like a pseudo-divinity on earth who perpetrates genocide and the destruction of knowledge, two notorious crimes often perpetrated by humans in spiritual and mental bondage.

Ghazali was also an adventurer and an explorer in his thinking. He realised that all the answers to life's complex realities did not reside in a single culture, intellectual tradition or historical epoch. For that reason, he ventured outside the mainline currents, raiding archives of knowledge in order to see how he could reinforce the positive aspects of the traditions that he had inherited and invent other interpretations. Not only did he de-familiarise the canonical tradition, but he also supplemented it and re-familiarised it, adding a new gloss, in order to make the lustre and vibrancy of tradition more pronounced. This reconstructionist approach to tradition resonates well with those whose intellectual temper is predisposed to critical thinking and the intellectual renewal of tradition, just as many formalists would be offended as too presumptuous a claim to make.

Ghazali, in my view, tried to configure why so many Muslim thinkers like him in the past effortlessly engaged with an assortment of knowledge and ideas stemming from different origins without their labour and personas being rejected by tradition. He successfully adapted knowledge according to the needs of his own subjectivity. In other words, knowledge to him was intimately related to the needs of the self and his subjectivity and therefore he did not allow any verdict of authority to veto his quest.

The contemporary relevance of Ghazali to Muslim thought lies precisely in his critical engagement with tradition, but more specifically, the way in which he modified, adjusted, re-calibrated, amended and supplemented the intellectual tradition. Unlike many contemporaries who either uncritically romanticise tradition or in an apocalyptic spasm take refuge in it, he took critical thought seriously. It was important for him, just as it is for us, to critically engage with the canonical tradition, a process that culminated in radical questioning of the canonical tradition.

The Muslim intellectual tradition is not static, nor is it inert. It has its own rhythms of continuity and discontinuity by always re-calibrating itself to the imperatives of ethical, moral and spiritual integrity. For if we do not wish to see the ethical imagination lapse into a censorious puritanism that hurtles toward self-destruction, nor degenerate into nostalgic lamentation, then the ethical must be taken seriously not only in its discursive guise, but also in its poetic manifestation. What impresses and captivates any reader of the Muslim efforts in the South African liberation struggle, or of Azad's labours in British and post-independence India and Ghazali's work in the eleventh century, is how impressively each recovered poiesis – inventive making and creating – by disseminating into the reading and interpretation of texts broadly conceived, the extravagant heterogeneity of knowledge.

Where others hesitated to bring art and aesthetics to the study of ethics, Azad and Ghazali unapologetically brought the power of literature and poetry to the study of the ethical. The purest of art resides in the heart – the receptacle of subjectivity. Subjectivity here means the capacity of the soul or self to submit to all ethical possibilities, with the aid of a variety of disciplines and practices that empowered it.

If Islamdom has any hope of renewing its tradition in its manifold manifestations today then it is crucial to re-read the classical figures like Ghazali. It will be equally important to examine the way Muslim communities around the world, South Africa being only one example, deal with challenges with a modicum of success. In colonial and post-colonial India, we do well to recall, Abul Kalam Azad constructed a Muslim political theology that made diversity and the integrity of all human beings the foundation of his faith and his faith in humanity.

Reference List

al-Nisaburi, Abu al-Husayn Muslim bin al-Hajjaj. 1995. *Sahih Muslim Bi Sharh Al-Nawawi.* Isam al-Sababiti, Hazim Muhammad & Imad Amir (eds). 9 vols. Cairo: Dar Abi Hayyan, 1415/1995.

Azad, Abul Kalam. *Ghubar-i Khatir.* 2nd Ed. M Ram (ed). 1983. New Delhi: Sahitya Academy.

De Sousa Santos B. 1995. *Toward a New Common Sense: Law, Science and Politics in the Paradigmatic Transition.* New York & London: Routledge.

Henderson I, Minault G & Troll CW (eds). 1988. *Abu Kalam Azad: An Intellectual and Religious Biography.* Delhi: Oxford University Press.

Jameson F. 2002. *A Singular Modernity: Essay on the Ontology of the Present.* London & New York: Verso.

Moosa E. 2005. *Ghazali and the Poetics of Imagination.* Chapel Hill, NC: The University of North Carolina Press.

THE 'DARK SIDES' OF HUMANISM IN SOUTH AFRICA

André du Toit

At different times, being a 'humanist' has meant different things to South Africans but these have not been consolidated in a sustained 'humanist tradition'. Earlier 'humanist' initiatives and tendencies do not appear to be in conspicuous and robust health: some have entirely disappeared from the scene; others are dissipated or survive only in minimal and attenuated forms. On reflection it must even be deemed something of a paradox that the new South African Constitution has been taken to embody a distinctly 'humanist' vision and commitment. What then was the relevance and significance of earlier humanist tendencies, how should their apparent decline and even demise in post-apartheid South Africa be understood, and what are the consequences and implications for a possible 'new humanism'?

Humanism in South Africa has been notably lacking in historical self-awareness. A contemporary reflexive humanism will need to evaluate the historical multiplicity of humanisms including their cultural assumptions, ideological functions and unintended consequences. This will require not just taking credos at face value but also interrogating the 'dark sides' of actual historical humanisms. Before setting out ambitious agendas and commitments for a 'new humanism' we may do well to take critical stock of just what has happened to previous humanist initiatives and discourses in our own local context. This may best be explored concretely with particular historical references rather than in abstract and globalising terms.

For our purposes the following criteria are proposed for those who may non-arbitrarily and credibly be regarded as 'humanists':

'Humanists' are individuals, groups or movements who:

- have conceived of themselves as 'humanists' (or some closely related and/or equivalent term in the context of their own time);
- were closely associated with other 'humanists' or with 'humanist' traditions/ movements (or their equivalents) at the time, and were so regarded by others;
- are described in the literature as 'humanist' (or some closely related and/or equivalent term in the context of their own time).

These criteria need to be applied with some flexibility, especially with regard to historical changes in terminology, but taken together they may provide useful guidance on who were and are 'humanists' in the South African context.

In terms of these criteria significant 'humanists' in South African history will have to include Dr John Philip in the imperial and colonial context of the 19th century and General Jan Smuts in the early 20th century context of South African politics and international relations. There are a number of other likely candidates, from Olive Schreiner and Gandhi to Archbishop Tutu, but Philip and Smuts can definitely not be passed over in any serious investigation of who the 'humanists' were, and what 'humanism' in the South African context meant. It does not follow that in either case their 'humanism' was straightforward or uncontroversial. It is precisely these challenges that may be relevant to a critical understanding of the historical significance of 'humanism' as well as its 'dark sides'.

Dr John Philip: Evangelical humanitarian

Philip is firmly established as a controversial founding figure of the (Cape) liberal tradition. This is a retrospective misnomer since 'liberal' had not yet acquired our current usage in the early decades of the 19th century. Philip and his contemporaries saw him in relation to the evangelical lobbies which had issued in Wilberforce's Anti-Slavery Society and later in Buxton's Aborigines Protection Society with their joint headquarters in London at Exeter Hall. Under the banners of "Christianity and Civilisation" the abolitionist campaigns of the late 18th century had by the 1820s extended to encompass other issues of social reform (such as education, judicial and penal reform, treatment of the insane and poor relief) while also taking a special interest in colonial policy. This approach can more accurately be termed as that of 'evangelical humanitarianism' (Keegan 1996:75). But there is no problem in recognising this as a contemporary version of humanism: "The missionary", wrote

Philip, "sees in every man a partaker of his own nature, and a brother of his own species" (Philip 1828:I,xxxiii).

Philip's own commitments and convictions were deeply and specifically rooted in the late 18th century Evangelical Revival. At the same time Philip's thought was profoundly informed by the Scottish Enlightenment not only with regard to the primacy of free trade and markets but also in terms of the four-stage schema of progressive development from subsistent and nomadic societies towards the common goal represented by European agricultural and industrial civilisation. This intellectual scheme fitted Philip's own experience and circumstances in two major respects. On the one hand it precisely reflected the perspective of his own upwardly mobile generation on the dynamic changes of Scottish society in its 'Golden Age'. On the other hand, it also provided a ready-made framework for understanding colonial society at the Cape where the ongoing encounters of nomadic San hunter-gatherers and Khoi and Xhosa pastoralists with colonial agricultural settlers could be viewed in a longer term historical perspective as stages in the development of a common human civilisation.

Philip's humanism related in equal parts to the mutually reinforcing evangelical and utilitarian components of his outlook. Thus a key aspect of the four-stage scheme of the philosophic historians was that it applied to the evolution of civilisation conceived as a singular whole. This meant that the Enlightenment discourse of civilisation significantly lacked any pluralist conception of different culture(s) (Stocking 1987:40). Philip did not conceive the nomadic Khoisan and pastoral Xhosa as culturally different from colonial settlers but rather as still at different stages of the common evolution of human civilisation. Philip saw Christianity and civilisation as "inextricably bound together. People who truly became Christian were inevitably civilised in the process" (Ross 1986:79-80). The assumption that all people belonged to the same order of humanity as God's creatures implied that they also "shared a natural propensity to embrace civilisation" (Keegan 1996:91). It followed that the objective of mission could not be confined to spiritual salvation but inevitably contributed to the civilising process more generally. This inextricable fusion of Christianity and civilisation remained the centerpiece of Philip's evangelical humanitarianism.

Human rights as civil rights

In the colonial context Philip, as a principled evangelical humanitarian, was exceptional – indeed notorious – for his pronounced beliefs in the fundamental equality of all human beings regardless of race, colour or ethnicity. Significantly, though, he did *not* articulate this primarily at the level of equal human or natural rights but rather through a determined quest for equal civil rights.

Along with other evangelical humanitarians Philip believed that racial differences and social inequalities derived from environmental differences in circumstances and were of secondary significance compared to our shared humanity (Philip 1828:II,316). In the colonial context this had radical implications. Contrary to the assumptions of local colonists and of many officials and even some missionaries Philip insisted that, in principle and in practice, the indigenous peoples of Africa had equal natural capacities compared to Europeans. In Philip's view the primary source of oppression, social conflict, inequality and "every species of crimes and calamities" was the "barbarising effects" of the exercise of uncontrolled authority and power; the remedy for this lay in a just administration guaranteeing equal civil rights to all (Philip 1828:I,383,402). However, this did not involve the invocation of underlying natural or human rights; rather it required the imposition of a new civil order.

Philip was well aware of the universalist notion of human rights as distinct from legal rights in positive law (Philip 1828:I,xxvi). We might well expect that the colonial conquest and dispossession of indigenous societies would be prime instances of the violation of just such human rights. However, on closer analysis it appears that any such supposed human right against conquest was by no means what Philip had in mind. Philip was concerned with the prospect of equal *civil* rights for the indigenous peoples once they were incorporated into the colonial order; indeed, the very notion of equal civil rights for them presupposed their colonial incorporation. Philip's great campaign to secure equal civil rights for the Khoi was thus at one and the same time a plea for their full incorporation into colonial society. This was also the thrust and function of Ordinance 50, the major measure of colonial reform which Philip together with his allies at the Cape and in London secured in 1828. This charter of civil rights guaranteed equality in law and security of property to all free inhabitants of the Cape irrespective of colour. However, it did not bring about their social and political equality within the Colony, but "removed disabilities in order to make persons of colour legally living in the Cape equal *subjects* of the Crown" (Dubow 2010:5).

Evangelical humanitarianism and the ambiguities of empire

Much vilified in Cape circles as the foremost 'friend of the natives' and critic of all things colonial, Philip's relation to imperialism was in fact profoundly ambivalent. The first volume of his *Researches in South Africa* (1828) provided a sustained and relentless narrative of colonisation as a succession of "violent dispossession", "hopeless bondage", "wrongs and outrages inflicted on the innocent and the defenseless". At one and the same time, however, Philip also acknowledged that the missionary project itself shared the basic objectives of British imperialism. No doubt, Philip's formulations were couched with a shrewd rhetorical eye to his British metropolitan audience and should not be taken at face value (Bank 1995:118). And Philip did go on to differentiate the peaceful methods of evangelical conversion from the violence of military conquests (Philip 1828:I,x). But he also recognised that mission was intimately bound up with the spread of imperial rule. More concretely, Philip consistently supported actual extensions of empire. The crucial difference with the territorial ambitions of local colonists was that for Philip such extensions of imperial authority would not involve dispossession of indigenous land: the Xhosa, Griqua and Sotho would keep their land and colonists would not be allowed to exercise property claims in these territories. Philip's ideal was that of Classical Rome which he took as model for the British empire in her even-handed justice, equal civil rights and spread of civilisation (Ross 1986:72-73).

Evangelical humanitarianism as cultural imperialism

The core humanitarian assumption of a single and common human nature, conjoined with the evangelical belief that all people had souls in need of salvation, required and also legitimated a missionary project with global aspirations. In practice this resulted in an unreflective quest for assimilating a diverse range of peoples to (English) 'civilisation'. The starting point was provided by the 'humanist' assumption of a common and malleable human nature always amenable to 'improvement' (Stokes 1959:38). The *terminus ad quem* was provided by the similarly 'humanist' assumption that the highest levels of progress and achievement, represented by contemporary (English) culture, should in principle be accessible to all. Given the transparent beneficence of their intentions there was no need for any missionary self-criticism or doubts. Mission stations in the colonies thus functioned to transform indigenous cultures; they were "intended to become the seedbed of a new society, designed to replicate the metropolitan social order which the missionaries themselves represented" (Keegan 1996:90-91).

From the outset Philip set out to transform the Khoi people at LMS mission stations like Bethelsdorp and Theopolis into respectable and productive communities on the English model. He recognised that the habitat typical of indigenous African culture, such as the reed-and-daub huts in clusters of extended homesteads, required spatial re-organisation in order to induce wholesale cultural transformation (Philip 1828:I,209-211). Accordingly he embarked on an improvement plan for the mission stations involving the replacement of traditional reed huts by stone houses with proper windows "built in rectangular pattern along straight streets surrounding a village square. As part of the plan, trading stores were to be established and 'artificial wants' inculcated" (Keegan 1996:92). For Philip the visible signs of social and economic progress, including European modes of dress as much as literacy and education, was needed to demonstrate that they merited equal civil rights (Philip 1828:I,213). The Kat River settlement acquired special significance as a model community demonstrating the results of extending education and equal civil rights and encouraging productive enterprise under missionary tutelage. More generally the missionaries "encouraged their converts to drop their 'uncivilised' ways of life – a nomadic hunter-gatherer economy of communal forms of property – and move to the 'higher' and more 'civilised' economic and social norms of individual property, English property laws and a settled form of agriculture within European-style villages" (Evans *et al* 2003:29-30). If this clearly amounted to a sustained exercise in cultural imperialism in the name of a common humanity and of "Civilisation" it also was a (relatively benign) case of paternalism. As Ross pointed out, Philip may not have recognised the intrinsic value of African traditional belief and practices, and badly underestimated their validity and liveliness, but 'he never fell into the trap of seeing them as social evils to be removed by the force of European authority and law' (Ross 1986:225). Moreover, he vigorously represented the cause and championed the interests of the Khoi and other indigenous peoples, both at home and abroad. Still, like the humanitarianism of the Aborigines Committee, this was an essentially paternalist intervention on behalf of the victims of imperialism unable to speak for themselves.

Humanitarianism as utopian imperialism?

It might seem paradoxical to consider a humanitarian like Dr Philip, the renowned "friend of the natives", to have been an imperialist. Yet, there can be no doubt that he considered colonisation desirable (Lester 2001:44). Like other humanitarians, he was firmly convinced that the main threats to indigenous peoples were not posed by the extension of the British empire, but by anarchic, settler-led colonisation allied to unreconstructed colonial government. He had a peculiarly utopian notion of the extension of empire as nothing more than the creation of an orderly framework for facilitating the process of civilising. This assumed that such a process of civilising was endemic to indigenous African societies. That could, of course, also provide an argument *against* extension of the empire. But if the autonomy of African communities beyond the frontier was being threatened by the territorial ambitions of colonial settlers and authorities, Philip believed that the remedy lay in imperial intervention. The ideal situation was one in which, under imperial protection, otherwise untouched African societies would be transformed by 'Christianity and commerce'. All this assumed that the British imperial authorities would maintain an even-handed 'Roman' approach to the administration of its extended colonial territories, undeterred by resource constraints and not influenced by sectional interests, in order to weld many races and peoples together in one civilised culture (Ross 1986:221). This was about as far removed as possible from the realities of actual imperialism.

In hindsight it is evident that Philip never understood the full extent to which the evangelical humanitarian project depended on a particular and transient configuration of imperial power at home and abroad. At a strategic level Philip was a past master in utilising his powerful connections in London to bypass reactionary colonial forces at the Cape. In effect, though, the great humanitarian victories of Ordinance 50 and the extension of equal civil rights to the Khoi people were only made possible by the authoritarian top-down structure of imperial rule at that time. When colonial subjects increasingly began to participate in their own local governance, and even more when representative and responsible government was granted to the Cape Colony, the once potent evangelical humanitarian lobby was effectively marginalised. With the extension of democracy the paternalist assumptions of the evangelical humanitarian project were increasingly exposed. This must raise the question under what conditions a bottom-up 'humanism' compatible with the extension of democracy might be possible. It does not seem that Philip's utopian imperialism could provide a relevant answer to this.

Also in hindsight, there is the awkward question of the ideological functions and consequences of Philip's cultural and utopian imperialism. While recognising the undoubted historic achievements of Philip's critical exposure of the evils of colonial oppression, the fact remains that he, like other evangelical humanitarians, continued to support imperialism as such, both at the level of moral principle and in particular local circumstances. Even if this should not simply be equated with imperial conquest or the territorial ambitions of some colonists, it could not but provide a generalised ideological justification for these as well. If Philip was a 'humanist' then in the colonial context of his time this meant that he was also an imperialist and paternalist authoritarian.

Smuts: classical humanist

By common account Smuts was the dominant figure in South African politics for most of the first half of the 20th century and the only South African to achieve an established reputation as international statesman. A shrewd, sometimes ruthless, politician he may be regarded as the intellectual father of 'segregation' during the era of 'white supremacy'. On the face of it, he must be an unlikely candidate to be considered a 'humanist'. Surprising as this may seem, though, Smuts meets our criteria for having been a 'humanist'. He characterised himself as a 'humanist'. He closely associated with other humanists and he found his spiritual home among a remarkable group of enlightened, pacifist and humanitarian women in Oxford. A key member of their circle was Gilbert Murray, Oxford Professor of Classics, and at the time the leading exponent of 'classical humanism'. Smuts systematically articulated and developed his own philosophy of life and metaphysical views as 'holism', a variant of humanism. He played a key role in basing the Preamble to the United Nations Charter on a notion of 'human rights' in 1945 in San Francisco. Indeed, a leading study of his life and thought was published with the title *Smuts: the Humanist* (Haarhoff 1970).

Evidently, though, the notion of Smuts as a 'humanist' must pose a number of serious problems.

- Historically: how could Smuts possibly have become a 'humanist' in a context of colonial white supremacy, and what might that 'humanism' have meant?
- Morally and politically: how could Smuts have been a 'humanist' if in personal terms he was a racist with a horror of the 'intermixture of blood' and in political terms he was a leading exponent of segregation?
- Intellectually and globally: what was the significance at the time of basing the Preamble to the UN Charter on 'human rights'?

These problems can be explored in two different contexts: the relevance of classical education to South African intellectual and social life, and the historical significance of 'classical humanism' in the early 20th century.

Smuts's classical colonial education and the meaning of 'classical humanism'

As in Victorian England (and 19th century America) the model of the 'Latin School', and the ideals of *Paideia* these embodied, was a core institution of the colonial education system at the Cape. The study of Latin and Greek were not incidental aspects of this model of education but among the most powerful and consistent means of conveying notions of human formation and 'civilisation' (Jenkyns 1980; Turner 1981). This had special significance in the imperial context: a study of the classics became a requirement for senior appointments in the Indian Civil Service (Allen 2010:5-6). In 19th century South Africa the study of classical language and literature also played a formative part in colonial culture with classical ideas of moral character, moral community and rational debate informing notions of 'civilised' life (Nash 1995).

Intellectually and morally Smuts was a paradigmatic product of this 'classical' tradition of colonial education. This is the central theme of his biography by T.J. Haarhoff, long a close associate of Smuts and himself a prominent classical scholar. Haarhoff argued that Smuts's classical education provided the key to much of his personality and lifestyle, and furnished the basic categories of his moral and political thought. Smuts not only retained the Greek and Latin he studied at school and university, still re-reading the New Testament in Greek in his seventies, but modeled himself on the ancient Greek and Roman notions of simplicity and nearness to nature while aspiring to fulfil the Greek ideal of the educated man and citizen. In all sorts of ways he remained deeply committed to the classical ideal of *humanitas,* the art of civilised life. He worked closely with Gilbert Murray, a leading classical scholar of the time, to apply the principle of *humanitas* to world politics and a new international order (Haarhoff 1970:6-10), and his quasi-metaphysical philosophy of Holism can best be understood as a contemporary elaboration of Humanism constructing the evolution of humanity as a Whole to transcend all sectional and nationalist particularities (Haarhoff 1970:19-20). Politically Smuts was committed to overcoming the historical conflicts that had so bitterly divided the Afrikaans and English communities, "forming a Whole in South Africa, supplementing each other" (Haarhoff 1970:30).

Smuts's 'classical humanism' might seem a historical anomaly. Modern accounts of Renaissance humanism had, of course, stressed its orientation to the models of Classical Antiquity, but subsequent varieties of modern humanism were increasingly less concerned with classical studies as the foundation of humanist education. Still, in the decades before the Second World War there was a revival of 'Classical Humanism' with just this orientation. A leading exponent of this contemporary 'humanism' was Gilbert Murray, who was also closely associated with Smuts's group of friends (Parker 2010:10-11). Significantly, the key concept in Murray's notion of 'humanism' was that of 'Civilisation', understood in opposition to a mere struggle for survival, with the ancient Greek *polis* serving as the paradigm. Murray related contemporary society in two main ways to this Classical model: on the one hand, modern (European) culture derived from this ancient civilisation as its historical source while, on the other hand, the historic challenge was to preserve and reproduce this civilised heritage in the face of pervasive threats of extinction and/or renewed barbarism (Murray 1946:216,230-231). For Murray himself, during the period of Europe's two great wars, it was no doubt the emergent forces of Fascism and Nazi-Germany which posed the imminent threats to European 'civilisation'. But from a South African perspective and in an African context this notion of 'classical humanism', and especially its core assertion of 'civilisation' against threats of extinction and/or renewed barbarism, all too readily acquired racial connotations. This proved only too true of Smuts's own version of 'classical humanism'.

The humanist as racist?

For present purposes the key question must be whether, and if so, in what sense a 'humanist' can also be a 'racist'. Smuts's notion of 'race' has been the object of several recent historical and critical studies. These have cautioned that at the time the term 'race' was often used loosely and in different senses from what has become standard usage, so that 'the race question' could typically refer to the differentiation between the Afrikaans and English sections of the white population. Even so, it can hardly be disputed that at some level there was what Shula Marks has described as a "visceral racism" at work in Smuts's thought (Marks 2001:206). This was most blatantly expressed in his categorical rejection of the prospect of racial miscegenation. The young Smuts in 1895 looked "upon the intermixture of black and white in South Africa as in every way the darkest spot on our civilisation, the cancer which, unless arrested and kept within the narrowest limits, will ultimately corrode and corrupt the very life-centres of our society" (Hancock & Van der Poel 1966:I doc. 28,121). Notoriously, in his 1917 London address on *The White Man's Task* Smuts, as international statesman on a world stage, propounded as the principal 'axiom' of South African policy that there should be "no inter-mixture of blood between the two colours ... It is dishonourable to mix white and black blood" (Smuts 1940:13). This conception was part and parcel of Smuts's sustained double equation of whites with 'civilisation' and Africans with 'barbarism'. Already in his student writings in the 1890s "he conceived the white presence in southern Africa as a struggle to maintain 'European civilisation' against the 'barbarism' that would prevail unless the whites united" (Garson 2007:176). In 1947 he still described "South Africa [as] a little epic of European civilisation on a dark continent" (Dubow 2008:71).

While the conceptual contours framing Smuts's thought on 'race' thus remained stable throughout his long public career, key aspects relevant to both his 'humanism' and 'racism' were elaborated and developed over the decades in more sophisticated terms. Of particular note are the ways in which he (re-)configured the polarity of 'civilisation' and 'barbarism' in relation to a paternalist notion of *trusteeship*. In his political debut defending Rhodes at Kimberley in October 1895 he stressed the precarious position of barely half a million whites at the southern corner of a vast continent populated by over 100 million 'barbarians'. Even so, he posed it as the responsibility of the civilised (white) minority "to 'lift up' that vast dead-weight of immemorial barbarism and animal savagery to the light and blessing of ordered civilisation" (Hancock & Van der Poel 1966:I doc. 23,82-83,95). In his letter on the 'Native Question' to the Cape liberal statesman Merriman in 1906 he could affirm that "I sympathise profoundly with the Native races of South Africa whose land it was long before we came here to force a policy of dispossession on them. And it ought to be the policy of all parties to do justice for the Natives and to take all wise and prudent measures for their civilisation and improvement". However, he immediately went on to assert that this sympathy could not have concrete political consequences and posed an insuperable responsibility and intolerable burden. "When I consider the political future of the Natives in South Africa I must say that I look into shadows and darkness, and then I feel inclined to shift the intolerable burden of solving that sphinx problem to the ampler shoulders and stronger brains of the future" (cited in Marks 2001:210-211). In his 1917 London address *The White Man's Task* Smuts articulated the need for white supremacy in securing the values of western Christian civilisation while invoking a paternalist "moral axiom" that white rule be based on "honour, fair-play, justice, and the ordinary Christian virtues" anticipating his later concept of trusteeship (Smuts 1940).

Smuts's idea of trusteeship was more explicitly articulated in his 1929 Rhodes lectures at Oxford. Significantly, his notion of 'civilising' Africans, unlike that of evangelical humanitarians like Dr Philip, attributed some intrinsic value to specifically African customs and practices thus ostensibly avoiding overt cultural imperialism. But his notion of 'trusteeship' was equally paternalist – Smuts literally considered Africans "a child type, with a child psychology and outlook" (Garson 2007:167). In his 1929 Rhodes lectures Smuts argued that the "parallel institutions" of segregation, as a form of indirect rule, would no longer seek to scrap 'native institutions' as 'barbarous' or to 'civilise' Africans as rapidly as possible through direct rule. However, instead of following through on the pluralist implications of segregation as such an alternative system of "parallel institutions" Smuts appeared to backtrack and in his final years increasingly began to accept the capacity of at least some Africans to qualify for 'civilised' status in terms of certain educational and economic criteria (Garson 2007:173). In his 1942 Presidential address to the South African Institute of Race Relations Smuts famously declared that "segregation had fallen on evil days" and sought to enlarge on the moral obligation owed by the trustee to the ward.

We may thus conclude that it was the discourse of 'civilisation' and the paternalist notion of trusteeship which allowed Smuts to be both a 'humanist' and a racist. Significantly these same notions of 'civilisation' and paternalism also figured centrally in our account of Dr Philip as evangelical humanitarian – but in that case they contributed to his non-racialist humanist perspective. For the evangelical humanitarians and Dr Philip the notion of 'civilisation', informed by the conceptual framework of the Scottish Enlightenment, served to motivate and justify non-racial inclusion. In the case of Smuts, though, a 'classical humanism' premised on the polarity of 'civilisation' and (renewed) barbarism, served to justify racial inequality and exclusion. In the African context the 'humanism' of both Philip and Smuts was equally paternalist, if with opposite consequences. In the case of Philip the paternalist assumptions at work in bringing humanitarian reform along with the Christian Gospel to Africa amounted to a comprehensive project of cultural imperialism, even if this relied on conversion and persuasion rather than coercive imposition. For his part, Smuts's paternalist notion of 'trusteeship' served to temper outright white supremacy by implying certain moral and political obligations towards African subjects as wards. At times Smuts's notion of trusteeship also suggested that segregation, unlike non-racial assimilation, need not amount to full-blown cultural imperialism – but in the absence of clear alternatives this proved little more than an ideological mystification of white supremacist rule.

Smuts and the incorporation of 'human rights' in the UN Charter Preamble

Recent studies of Smuts's role confirm that he did play a significant part in the origins of the notably human rights-focused Preamble to the new United Nations Charter in 1945. However, if so, then that raises a number of problems. One set of problems has to do with understanding Smuts as a champion of human rights: 'classical humanism' was quite distinct, in its main concerns as well as its underlying assumptions, from the new post-Second World War discourse of human rights associated with the 1948 Universal Declaration of Human Rights. How could Smuts reconcile his 'classical humanism' with 'human rights', or did he somehow misunderstand what this new discourse of universal 'human rights' entailed? A second set of problems has to do with the glaring contrast between Smuts's role as putative champion of human rights on the international stage and his totally opposite response to the same issues in the domestic South African political arena at that time. Hypocrisy alone can hardly be the full explanation: could it be that his 'humanism' allowed an understanding of 'human rights' that might reconcile his UN stand and his South African position? A third set of problems relate more generally to the historical function and significance of the incorporation of the notion of 'human rights' in the UN Charter at the time. Retrospectively this has come to be understood in terms of the emergent hegemony of contemporary human rights discourse. However, in more recent research this interpretation has been challenged as anachronistic. In relation to Smuts this raises important questions as to the more general significance of Smuts's intervention at the founding of the United Nations.

How did it come about, in the first place, that Smuts of all people played such a prominent role in the incorporation of 'human rights' in the Preamble of the UN Charter at San Francisco in 1945? Proposals for the founding of a postwar organisation like the United Nations and deliberations on its mandate had a complicated history going back at least to the Atlantic Charter in August 1941. Significantly, though, neither Smuts nor the notion of human rights figured at all prominently in that history until a very late stage. Instead, along with the main strategic, security and economic concerns, latter-day versions of the discourse of protecting 'civilisation' still tended to prevail. Neither the Moscow Declaration of April 1943 nor the US draft Four Power plan at the Quebec Conference in August 1943 contained any particular references to human rights. These plans and proposals were given firmer shape at the Dumbarton Oaks Conference in October 1944. Significantly, the Dumbarton Oaks Proposals contained no equivalent to the Preamble and only one reference to human rights (Heyns 1995:333).

Meanwhile Smuts, in contrast to his central role in 1918 in the founding of the League of Nations (whose Covenant did not include any mention of human rights), had taken no active part in these international discussions and planning for the UN, but was merely a distant spectator (Hancock 1968:429). It was only at the meeting of Commonwealth Statesmen in April 1945 that Smuts became involved in the process by suggesting the need for a Preamble to the proposed Charter. Smuts was concerned with the overly legalistic tone of the Dumbarton Oaks charter proposals and argued that a more uplifting wording should be found that would touch the heart of the common man (Hancock 1968:431-432). Smuts then developed a formal draft which was subsequently revised into the eventual Preamble adopted at San Francisco in June 1945. His approach was that the UN Charter, unlike the Covenant of the League of Nations, must be based explicitly on respect for human rights, providing "a spiritual element ... a true confession of faith" (Heyns 1995:336-337). Accordingly the draft presented by Smuts for consideration at San Francisco pledged "to re-establish faith in fundamental human rights, in the sanctity and ultimate value of human personality, in the equal rights of men and women and of nations large and small ..." (cited in Dubow 2008:56). However, both the specific wording and the ready success of Smuts's draft proposal raise various questions. On the one hand, why was this novel proposal by someone who had not been a key player in the protracted deliberations on the UN and its Charter so readily accepted at this late stage? And, on the other hand, why did Smuts couch his proposal in terms of the new discourse of 'human rights' which had previously not been part of his own conceptual vocabulary? For the answers to both these questions we may best look to some of the contextual developments during the final years of the Second World War.

Though human rights considerations did not yet play any conspicuous part in the formal deliberations of the Allied Powers on the UN and its proposed Charter, civil society response was a different matter. As the gravity and extent of the mass atrocities by the Nazis became public knowledge, the need for special protection of human rights was increasingly acknowledged. In the US private organisations and public figures, from Eleanore Roosevelt to church leaders, were advocating the international protection of human rights in any post-war settlement well before Dumbarton Oaks. In this context the failure to include strong provisions on human rights became a focus in criticisms of the Dumbarton Oaks proposals. This surge of interest in human rights had not been widely anticipated by the major powers and, indeed, "its universalistic implications were actively resisted by countries like Britain" (Dubow 2008:73). But by the spring of 1945 it had become clear that the new Charter of the United Nations *would* have to make some reference to human rights (Mazower 2004:392).

From the perspective of the great power representatives and diplomats involved in the political deliberations and formal negotiations on the UN and its proposed Charter the public mobilisation of an effective international human rights movement of this kind appeared as a somewhat unwelcome but not altogether insuperable complication. Their particular concern was to combine the design of an effective international peace-keeping organisation while protecting the traditional domain of domestic jurisdiction and without imposing unacceptable limitations on state sovereignty in the name of human rights (Simpson 2001:255,258). Evidently Smuts's proposal was taken to be sufficiently responsive to the public demands for recognising human rights as an international objective while also being compatible with the realist interests of international relations. (We may also speculate that this had something to do with the fact that it came from an experienced and respected international statesman rather than from the advocates of some human rights lobby.) More cynically Hans

Kelsen, the foremost legal theorist of the time, observed that the much-vaunted Preamble amounted to empty phrases which made no difference in international law (Kelsen 1946:148). What transpired in the event was that the UN Charter which emerged from the San Francisco conference did include unprecedented references to human rights both in the Preamble and in the main body of the Charter itself beginning with Article 1. But this was immediately followed by Article 2 which re-affirmed the principle of national sovereignty with a stringent domestic jurisdiction clause (Mazower 2004:393). This allowed Smuts in 1946 to claim the protection of the domestic jurisdiction clause to defend his country from India's charge of human rights violations.

Still, the question remains why Smuts couched his proposal for the Preamble in terms of what was for him not only an unfamiliar but also a problematic new discourse of 'human rights'. We may speculate that, as a self-conscious 'humanist' of sorts, Smuts assumed that he could accommodate the general objective of 'human rights' within his own understanding of the core values of (European) 'civilisation'. What he definitely did not do was to connect the incorporation of 'human rights' into the Preamble of the UN Charter with the political quest for equal rights in his own South African context. That was by no means a theoretical issue only. In response to the 1941 Atlantic Charter the ANC had in 1943 issued its major rights-based declaration *Africans' Claims*, including a Bill of Rights, and with a demand for 'full citizenship rights'. The ANC President, Dr Alfred Bitini Xuma, sent Smuts a copy of *Africans' Claims*, commending him for his international stand in support of the objectives of the Atlantic Charter, and requesting an interview. However, Smuts summarily dismissed the ANC Declaration as 'propagandist', could not agree that the Atlantic Charter might be applied to African problems and conditions, and responded that no useful purpose would be served by discussing it with Dr Xuma (Dubow 2008:64; Heyns 1995:347). Reporting back to Jan Hofmeyr on the actual 1945 UN Conference in San Francisco Smuts remarked on the "strong humanitarian tendency, finding expression in provisions for equal rights all round and other embarrassing proposals so far as we are concerned" (Hancock & Van der Poel 1973:VI doc. 666). No wonder he referred to his failure at the UN in a 1947 letter to Margaret Gillett as "a bitter experience ... Here is the author of the great preamble of the Charter exposed as a hypocrite and a double-faced time server" (cited in Dubow 2008:68).

Apart from Smuts's own 'humanist' misunderstanding and/or under-estimation of the significance and implications of 'human rights' in the context of the UN Charter there is the larger questions of the historical significance and political functions of the incorporation of the notion of 'human rights' in the UN Charter at the time. Retrospectively this has come to be understood, along with the Universal Declaration of Human Rights in 1948, as the point of departure for the development of an international human rights discourse which had gained unprecedented ascendancy by the closing decades of the 20th century. Mark Mazower has compellingly argued that this is an anachronistic misunderstanding and that the incorporation of human rights in the Preamble of the UN Charter actually served quite different purposes in the great power politics of the time. The relevant context was that of the wartime decision to abandon the interwar system for the protection of minority rights. Entrusted to the League of Nations rather than directly to the Great Powers, the organised protection of group minority rights – not individual human rights – was supposed to have binding legal force. In practice the failures of this system for the protection of minority rights during the interwar years had done a great deal to discredit the League of Nations. Moreover with the prospects of Soviet Russian control over post-war Eastern Europe any revival of an international system for minority rights would evidently be even less practicable. In this context the banner of (individual) human rights offered the Great Powers an attractive and plausible alternative to minority rights – attractive because it promised a morally acceptable alternative to minority rights, and plausible because it was not expected to have any binding legal force (Mazower 2004:387-389).

We may thus conclude that Smuts's contribution to the Preamble of the UN Charter had an altogether different significance and function to that commonly supposed. Smuts understood the incorporation of 'human rights' in the Preamble in line with his 'humanist' commitment to the defence of (European) 'civilisation' threatened by renewed 'barbarism' and was never committed to equal individual human rights in the post-World War II sense. He assumed that the inclusion in the UN Charter of a commitment to human rights in this 'humanist' sense was consistent with traditional doctrines of national sovereignty so that he could still invoke domestic jurisdiction when South Africa was charged with human rights violations. More generally, the function of introducing a non-binding commitment of the UN to (individual) human rights served as a cover for the Great Powers to disentangle themselves from their legal commitments under the previous international regime for the protection of minorities.

Some tentative conclusions

The significance of 'humanist' traditions and figures in South African political and cultural history was by no means marginal. Philip and Smuts were amongst the most influential figures in political developments respectively during the first halves of the 19th and 20th centuries, and their 'humanist' ideas had considerable impact in a variety of ways and contexts. At the same time their particular versions of 'humanism' were bound up with historical configurations that have long since passed away and can no longer possibly be revived or sustained. For better or worse, these versions of 'humanism' in the South African context now primarily belong to history.

A striking feature of both Philip and Smuts's 'humanism' was their ambivalent significance and functions. Thus Philip's evangelical humanitarianism has been celebrated (and also vilified) for its non-racial inclusiveness, but this had a 'dark side', that of a thoroughgoing cultural imperialism in the name of 'Christianity' and 'civilisation'. Moreover, this 'dark side' of evangelical humanitarianism was not a lapse or inconsistency but bound up with its basic 'humanist' assumptions. Similarly it was precisely Smuts's intellectual formation by a classical colonial education and his deep commitment to the ideal of *humanitas* and the art of civilised life which provided the justifications for the exclusion of those perceived as barbarian threats to these civilised values. Smuts's 'classical humanism' may have tempered his white supremacist convictions but 'trusteeship' mainly served to legitimate and mystify the harsher realities of white supremacy.

An equally striking feature in the relation between Philip and Smuts's 'humanisms' are some notable continuities. Philip and Smuts shared a similar discourse of 'civilisation', even if they put this to opposite uses, and they also exhibited a similar paternalism. We should not immediately generalise from this. It would, in fact, be an interesting and possibly significant question to investigate whether, or to what extent, other instances of 'humanism', both in the South African context and elsewhere, involve similar discourses of 'civilisation' and are likewise characterised by paternalist assumptions. Meanwhile, with regard to a possible 'new humanism' we might well consider the question whether we can conceive of a 'humanism' that does not rely on an implicit notion of 'civilisation': what would that look like, and what difference would it make? Similarly, could we conceive of a 'humanism' without paternalist assumptions: what would that look like, and what difference would it make? The crux of these questions is that they should not be posed only in the abstract but concretely in an African context.

Finally, the relation between Philip and Smuts's 'humanisms' also show some striking discontinuities and dissonances. We might even wonder to what extent they would have been prepared to recognise each other's positions as 'humanist' in their own terms. Certainly Smuts is likely to have had a highly critical view of Philip's non-racial humanitarianism while Philip would have been equally critical of Smuts's white supremacist views, even tempered by 'trusteeship', could he have been made aware of these. As we saw, Smuts comprehensively misunderstood and underestimated the significance and implications of the new post-World War II 'human rights' discourse. However, the nature and extent of such comparative misunderstandings is an indication of the lack of any self-reflective consciousness in these 'humanisms'. There is no indication that either Philip or Smuts critically interrogated the assumptions and functions of their respective evangelical humanitarianism or classical humanism or of the notions of 'civilisation' and paternalism with which these were associated. The question must be whether a new and more self-reflective humanism, informed also by the example and outcome of these other 'humanisms' that have gone before, can learn from them and so perhaps manage to avoid these dark sides of humanism.

Reference List

Allen J. 2010. A Competing Discourse on Empire, Nation and Race in Twentieth Century South Africa: Classics and the Political Thought of JH Hofmeyr, TJ Haarhoff and Martin Versfeld. Unpublished paper.

Bank A. 1995. Liberals and Their Enemies: Racial Ideology at the Cape of Good Hope, 1820-1850. PhD dissertation. Cambridge University.

Dubow S. 2008. Smuts, the United Nations and the Rhetoric of Race and Rights. *Journal of Contemporary History* 43:45-74.

— 2010. Human Rights in South Africa: the long and fractured tradition. Unpublished paper.

Evans J *et al.* 2003. *Equal subjects, unequal rights: Indigenous peoples in British settler colonies*. Manchester: Manchester University Press.

Garson N. 2007. Smuts and the Idea of Race. *South African Historical Journal* 57:1,153-178.

Haarhoff TJ. 1970. *Smuts: The Humanist*. Oxford: Basil Blackwell.

Hancock WK. 1968. *Smuts: Vol. 2: The Fields of Force 1919-1950.* Cambridge: Cambridge University Press.

Hancock WK & Van der Poel J (eds). 1966-1973. *Selections from the Smuts Papers*. 7 vols. Cambridge: Cambridge University Press.

Heyns C. 1995. The Preamble of the United Nations Charter: The Contribution of Jan Smuts. *African Journal of International and Comparative Law* 7(2):329-348.

Jenkyns R. 1980. *The Victorians and Ancient Greece*. Oxford: Blackwell.

Keegan T. 1996. *Colonial South Africa and the origins of the Racial Order*. London: Leicester University Press.

Kelsen H. 1946. The preamble of the charter – a critical analysis. *Journal of Politics* 8:134-159.

Lester A. 2001. *Imperial Networks: Creating identities in Nineteenth Century South Africa and Britain*. London: Routledge.

Marks S. 2001. White Masculinity: Jan Smuts, Race and the South African War. *Proceedings of the British Academy* 111:199-223.

Mazower M. 2004. The Strange Triumph of Human Rights. 1933-1950. *The Historical Journal* 47:2,379-398.

Murray G. 1946. Humane Letters and Civilization. *Greek Studies*. Oxford: Clarendon Press.

Nash A. 1978. Dr Philip. The 'Spread of Civilization' and Liberalism in South Africa. Conference on the History of Opposition in Southern Africa. University of Witwatersrand Development Group.

— 1995. The Dark Side of Enlightenment: Social Thought and the Classical Moral Tradition in South Africa, 1795-1910. Unpublished PhD proposal, UCT.

Parker G. 2010. Heraclitus on the Highveld: The universalism (ancient and modern) of TJ Haarhoff. Unpublished paper.

Philip J. 1828. *Researches in South Africa*. London: James Duncan.

Ross A. 1986. *John Philip, 1775-1851: Missions, Race and Politics in South Africa*. Aberdeen: Aberdeen University Press.

Simpson AWB. 2001. *Human Rights and the End of Empire: Britain and the Genesis of the European Convention*. Oxford: Oxford University Press.

Smith H. 1903. *The Autobiography of Sir Harry Smith*. London: Murray.

Smuts JC. 1940. *Greater South Africa: Plans for a Better World*. Johannesburg: Truth Legion.

Stocking G. 1987. *Victorian Anthropology*. New York: Free Press.

Stokes E. 1959. *The English Utilitarians and India*. Oxford: Clarendon Press.

Turner F. 1981. *The Greek Heritage in Victorian Britain*. New Haven: Yale University Press.

SCIENCE, TECHNOLOGY AND HUMANITY

George Ellis

Technology as fundamental to being human

Technology affects all aspects of individual and communal lives; it is an omnipresent feature of our lives that shapes the way we work, play, live, think, and how we interact with each other (Kranzberg & Davenport 1972). Thus it has an enormous impact on daily life, and causes change at an ever increasing rate. Technology has transformed our lives, and is still doing so at an ever increasing pace, reaching every aspect of living (Philbin 2003; Challoner 2009). Consider the following aspects of technology:

- language, writing, printing
- fire, wheel, clothes, shelter, hunting, agriculture
- water, sewerage, electric power, heat, light, engines
- stoves, fridges, washing machines
- tools, hardware, implements, machine tools

- transport, buildings, roads, bridges, dams
- communications: phone, fax, radio, TV, cellphones, Ipods
- medical: medicines, surgery, genetics, neurology
- information technology, computers, the internet

Some animals have quite sophisticated forms of technology (Turner 2000), but it is essentially the advanced nature of our technology and its symbolic foundation that distinguishes humans from other species. We are the `symbolic species' (Deacon 1997), with spoken and written language as our most important abstract technologies because they enable high level thought and planning, and shape the mind through a process of co-evolution and development. However they could not function without fundamentally important social, economic, and political abstract technologies that are embodied in language (such as social roles, the power of money, property rights, and the legal system in a society). Technology not only changes the possibilities open to us, it shapes the way we think. It shapes culture to a major degree, while culture also influences technology, within the limits of what is scientifically and technologically possible.

The key features of technology are firstly its cumulative nature: each further step depends on the one before, and is impossible without it; secondly its dependence on a core of technologically capable people who set up the system and keep it running; and thirdly, its long-lasting international character. Once a discovery is made (fire, agriculture, the wheel, for example), it remains for ever and is adopted by all advanced societies. It outlives all the pomp and ceremony of kings and empires. But technology can be used for good or for ill. The dark side is environmental destruction and mass warfare enabled by technology. There is as a result a widespread fear of technology, often associated with irrationality: a lack of appreciation of its enormous positive side. Key issues are

- What kind of purpose is it used for?
- Who benefits? (haves and have-nots)
- What are its beneficial aspects?
- What are its costs?
- Who controls it, and how?

These issues arise in each domain where technology has a significant impact. There will be commonalities across these domains, as well as differences. We need to regard technology as a positive force in need of direction across all domains. I will discuss this in two parts: first, by considering in more detail the role of technology in society and civilisation; and secondly by considering the conditions for the appropriate development of technology.

Technology and civilisation

Jacob Bronowski in his classic BBC television series *The Ascent of Man* (Bronowski 1976) charted the rise of civilisation as a concomitant of the development of technology. This was in stark contrast to Kenneth Clark's BBC TV series of the same era called *Civilisation* which simply meant Western European art. In order to consider the future of the influence of technology, we must catalogue the major areas where it has had a significant influence, for these are the areas that future planning needs to take into account. I briefly mention them without comment.

Infrastructure of life

Basic to the development of all higher order activity is the infrastructure of civilised life. It includes

- Water supply, waste water disposal, waste disposal
- Electricity supply, other energy supply (e.g. gas)
- Transport: bicycles, cars, buses, lorries, roads, rail, ships, aircraft
- Housing: structure, services, finishes, furnishing, fabrics
- Agriculture and food: farms, ranches, forests, fishing, markets, biotechnology
- Tools, machine tools, construction, manufacturing, industry
- Medical and health systems: medicines, antiseptics, antibiotics, dressings, surgical instruments, CAT scanners, lasers, etc.
- Security: fences, gates, locks, keys, codes, surveillance tools, weapons

These are the basics on which the rest is built.

Technology and daily life

Technology has transformed the drudgery of household and daily life.

- Hot and cold running water, water borne sewerage
- Lighting, heating (fire, electricity)
- Stoves, fridges, canned foods, frozen foods, pots, pans, knives, eating implements, tableware
- Clothes: material (fibres, cloths, colouring agents), design
- Cleaning equipment: soaps, vacuum cleaners, washing machines, dishwashers
- Entertainment: musical instruments, music systems, cinema, TV, theatre
- Leisure: playing cards, board games, balls, bats, sports shoes, playing fields, score cards, video games
- Markets, shops, commerce and advertising

Abstract technology

A key feature of technology is that crucial aspects are abstract, that is while they will eventually be embodied in material entities their key nature is non-physical. They underlie social, economic, political, and legal systems, and centre round symbolic systems (Deacon 1997). They enable sensible organisational structure and control

(Pugh 1975; Handy 1976; Beer 1978), in a way that may or may not be enhancing of humanity (Illich 1973).

- The essential basis is language
- The technological and commercial basis is mathematics
- The basis of economic transactions is money, accounting, auditing
- The basis of planning is theories and models, plans, to-do lists, timetables
- The shape of what is done is embodied in policies and associated indicator systems
- The nature of what is done is regulated by rulebooks, constitutions, laws and regulations

Technology, information, learning

Information technology now permeates all the other aspects of technology, transforming them all, particularly through digital computer systems based in transistors, integrated circuits, CDs, and digital memory systems, enabling information systems to allow sophisticated control of government and business (Anderson 1989), and modelling of environmental systems (Cartwright 1993). Global information and messaging networks lead to a new level of consciousness, because of almost instant awareness of events across the globe and sharing of views and information.

- Writing, paper, pencils/pens, printing, books, e-books
- Money and banking: Credit cards, bar codes, internet banking, ATMs
- Communication: Telex, Radio, Telephones, faxes, cellphones
- Images: Photography, photocopiers, films/movies, TV, global news networks
- Computers (hardware and software), computer networks, e-mail, the world wide web/internet, Google, Wikipedia, Facebook, Youtube
- Global positioning system (GPS)
- Remote imaging from aircraft and satellites: weather, crops, fires, ocean temperature, etc.

These are all becoming integrated into each other so that the boundaries between them are becoming blurred.

Technological usability and design

All technology is designed: houses, offices, cars, planes, computers, roads, cities, etc. are all designed by someone. The way this design is done crucially affects the quality of living in the created environment (Papanek 1974; Faimon & Weigand 2004; Garratt 2004), in particular at home and at the work place, but also for example in whatever form of transport used to get form the one to the other.

It must of course be designed to do well the work it is designed to do. This arises first as regard function, and then as regards appearance. There are a string of constraints on what is possible (Vogel 1998) which must be understood and handled properly. Reliability is crucial, and simplicity should be aimed at. There is a potential tension here between aesthetic design and functionality. Some claim that high level functionality *is* the core of good design, and the technical means should be dominant in design. Others insist on style even to the extent of being dominated by fashion, with the technical aspects being fitted into this aesthetic framework. How this works will vary greatly across all the application areas of technology: in the case of a hammer or screwdriver, function appropriately drives all; in the case of a car or building, other elements enter. There are no reliable rules as to what is good design: there are guidelines and heuristics, but in the end this is where the craft of the designer is crucial. It is interesting here to look at the technology used by animals to attain their needs: what they can do is limited but sophisticated (Gould & Gould 2007).

Two specific features are worth mentioning here. First, there is the issue of the suitable kind of technology to use: when is a low tech approach adequate and when is a high tech approach more suitable? The idea of *appropriate technology* is key here (Schumacher 1999): the right choice is the right level of sophistication to handle the job at hand, as far as possible using local materials and abilities to create and support the technology, rather than importing materials and methods from overseas that will probably fail and fall into disuse (Schumacher 1999; Burdick & Lederer 1958). Political issues will inevitably intrude (Dickson 1974). It is also key to note that any technology has partly a hardware nature (the item itself: a stove, computer, tool, whatever) and partly a behavioural component, that is, how you have to get it to succeed. Hi tech products can be very difficult or very easy to use, depending what they do and how they are designed. There is a trade-off between requiring the user to adapt to the technology, or making the technology adapt to the user. Sometimes the complexity of the user's interaction with it is unavoidable (e.g. a fighter aircraft) but sometimes it is not (e.g. in home computer systems). The designer can make critical choices here, determining how easy it is to adapt to a new technology and make it fulfil what you want it to do.

The issue of the user interface is crucial: the design of the handling or control of the technology. Some devices are notoriously difficult to use, a classic case being home video recorders. So the options made available to the user need to be carefully thought out, and the way decisions are made by the user structured transparently so that use is intuitive and easy. The ideal is that you can use it without needing to read a massive user manual: it should be obvious what to do next, because the options available are presented in a clear transparent way.

Great strides have been made here for example as regards computers, with the transition from a command line system to the use of a desktop with icons allowing selection by pointing and clicking, and drag and drop capabilities as well as clearly structured menus offering alternative ways to achieve the desired aim. The aim is to have largely invisible computers (Norman 1999), with the interface adaptable to individual needs, allowing enough choice but not too much. An advanced system will recognise the need for emotional design (Norman 2004). Our interaction with technology has an important emotional component, and if we are to be comfortable with it, this needs to be handled correctly. The design choices in the end embody an underlying set of values.

Technology and values/purpose/meaning

In the end, the key question regarding technology is what is it all used for? Who will benefit? It has immense powers that can be used for good or for bad. Some technologies are purely destructive (for example weapons production and support) although some will claim that this negative aspect is necessary for a greater good (the just war kind of theory). In the case of napalm that argument is exceedingly thin. However most technologies are neutral: they can be used for good or bad. It is a political and social choice that has to be made, embodying values in technology choice, design, and use.

Access to technology

The first key issue is access to technology: how to make its benefits available to the poor as well as the well off. This is partly a political decision as to how to allocate resources (electricity, water, waterborne sewerage, computer and internet access) but with major economic aspects. So all the usual political debates come up as to who controls resources and how they choose to do so. Perhaps the most enabling thing that has happened in this regard is the spread of cellphone access to impoverished communities worldwide. Projects such as the Grameen bank (Yunus 2001) have the potential to help greatly here, because the access to capital is crucial, as is the understanding of the nature of capital (Hawken, Lovins & Lovins 1999).

But there is also the issue of technological knowledge: how to control it and use it, including how to repair things when they are not working properly. So equity cannot be separated from issues of educational access and quality, particularly as regards mathematics, science and technological subjects. There is the potential for high technology access, particularly computer systems, to help developmental leapfrogging: by making world wide knowledge instantly accessible one has the potential to empower the poor and make individual learning possible for those with initiative. To enable this, computer access must be available in these communities through schools, libraries, or community centres. There is clearly much that can be done in this regard.

Equity is crucial: spreading the benefits and opportunities to create access for all, particularly those in less developed countries. Many issues arise in making this happen, including hardware issues (computers and memory devices, optical fibre lines and broadband communication links), software issues (making access affordable, for example through the open access movement), and capacity issues (training in how to make it all work and to maintain it). Here we need a determination to make it happen, with the privileged countries assisting the less privileged ones.

The second key issue is the effects on employment and livelihoods once IT infrastructure is available: it has good aspects (much improved information access and productivity) and bad ones (in many cases creating unemployment). Each country needs a sensitive engagement with these issues, and the political hot potato: to what degree should this be left to free enterprise and to what degree steered by the state for the communal good. The tendency in most countries is to just let this take its course, particularly as much of the development is powered by multinationals; but it must be possible to design computer applications to support labour intensive employment as well as labour saving systems. Both are needed in the right context; the state can encourage employment creation uses through suitable incentive systems.

Technology and environment

A major issue concerning technology and values is environmental damage due to thoughtless use of technology, including pollution of all kinds, resulting in global warming. There are many innovative options possible as regards energy technology (Lovins 1977). There is plenty of evidence that large scale energy use and associated pollution is leading to drastic climate change (Houghton 2009). This is not the place to go through the details of that debate, but it is my opinion that campaigns carried out under an "environmental" banner against nuclear energy and biotechnology have been positively destructive in their effects. They seem to satisfy the emotional needs of the protagonists rather than truly benefit either the environment or the poor. Certainly some in these campaigns have not hesitated to use untruths to support their agendas, for example labelling GMO foods as dangerous to health – a demonstrably untrue statement. They have not been willing to consider the possibility that nuclear power is a better option than the huge damage caused by coal and oil fired power stations.

What is desperately needed, here is to back off from this kind of environmental fundamentalism and embrace the more moderate kinds of views proposed in Baxter (1974), where one takes into account the employment needs of the poor as well as the welfare of animal species. At present one can state with confidence that whenever any scheme is proposed that will create employment for the poor, there will always be some environmentalist who will say it should not be done. But the greatest threat to the future of South Africa is unemployment. This fact must be seriously taken into account in these decisions. Another example is the way that environmental impact assessments hugely delay making land available for providing adequate housing for the poor. More moderate regulations are needed.

Technology and democracy

On the positive side, there is a major role for technology in terms of enabling democracy: providing information, allowing new efficient voting procedures, allowing efficient public consultation on key issues, and so on. Political will is required to get this right, to provide the environment in which this free information flow can take place. But of course there is also a repressive aspect of technology such as its use to suppress freedom in many coercive ways. Prisons for example are needed, but how should they be designed? How can the technology of the justice system help produce better people, for example by supporting restorative justice?

Technology and education

High technology has the potential to assist learning to take place in a creative way through making all kinds of information available via the internet, and through more specific learning programs and tutorials aimed at specific targets (mathematics, science, learning a language for example). These should carefully take cognisance of the way learning takes place (Vygotsky 1978) and shape the interactions with the learner accordingly. There is of course a good deal of nonsense out there on the internet, as well as good information. What is lacking is an impartial quality assessment system for information on websites. This is a major lacuna, but it would be difficult to implement for obvious reasons. Nevertheless something of the kind should be tried, at least for academic subjects.

Technology and crime

Technology is used by both by criminals and police authorities, and both sides are using increasingly sophisticated technologies. But there is much that can be done on the side of the law to counter criminal activity, for example surveillance systems, and the development of weapon detection systems at a distance for handguns and other small arms. This should certainly be possible if engineers tackle it with determination. The other side of the coin is to set up a regulatory environment that will enable use of such items without abuse. A specific issue of relevance here is the unwillingness of those responsible for the internet to tackle internet crime and spam, as well as virus writing. The phishing and fraudulent prize offers would simply die away if e-mails were charged for on a reasonable basis: say free for the first 300 e-mails per day, a small charge thereafter per e-mail. This is certainly possible. It is a scandal that there are websites that provide virus writing kits for free – limitations on internet abuse should surely be able to ensure that these get closed down as fast as they appear.

Choosing and shaping the technology of the future

In order to shape technology as a positive force in society, one needs to choose what aspects will be encouraged as per all the options above (and more), and then create a technologically enabling environment. I will briefly mention some issues here.

Enabling technological development

Technology has its basis in science, and in particular physics and chemistry, which determines what is possible and what is not (Bloomfield 2008). However, any scientific proposal for a new technology needs a long process of development in order to lead to production. It is a long way from idea to reliable use. One needs to develop and maintain a basic scientific infrastructure but also the technological skills associated with its development to a usable stage. Thus the first *sine qua non* for its successful development is a sound basis in scientific and mathematics education. Probably the best way to go about this is to develop specific technology schools that aim to attract children interested in these areas and develop these skills through suitably skilled, talented and dedicated teachers. This needs to be built on at tertiary institutions which develop specific skills as part of a National System of Innovation encouraging suitable students through scholarships and support right up to the post doctoral level. In principle South Africa has such a system; in practice the real weakness is at the school level. Political determination is needed to tackle entrenched power structures that protect teachers from behaving responsibly.

We need the specific structure that supports technology development. This includes availability of venture capital for good proposals, plus the overall basis of support infrastructure required: tools, equipment, supplies of good quality materials, and above all trained technicians in the relevant areas. It is crucial to recognise here how technological infrastructure is cumulative: one needs high tech measuring and manufacturing instruments that are used to manufacture even more high tech instruments, and the knowledge base in physics, chemistry, computing, biotechnology, and other areas. International involvement and exchange is crucial in keeping up to date with developments in all these areas, so nowadays a really good internet linkage is critical for making this happen. In addition one needs a suitable environment in terms of intellectual property rights: to motivate those who make the most innovative developments, they must know that their ideas will not immediately be taken away form them once they become public.

In developing suitable technology, we need developmental work aimed at specific areas: energy, water, transport, and so on, leading to specific product oriented development. But we also need basic research. The most fundamental technology is a by-product of blue skies research aimed simply at understanding the way things are. Nuclear energy for example came about through Einstein's efforts to understand the nature of space and time – not because he was looking for a new way of providing energy.

Thus we need a sound process of planning and designing involving problem analysis, generating ideas, developing products in consultation with users, and testing the outcome in terms of reliability and user friendliness. Items need to be designed for ease of construction, maintenance, and repair if they are to be of lasting use. Production quality is crucial, so quality checking is vital. Then there is the issue of sales and distribution, and after sales support through a maintenance network with sufficient spare parts and qualified technicians who will handle servicing and repairs. It is a complex system, requiring care and strong support: but the benefits are enormous.

Underlying this we need a developmental process that can handle complexity through an incremental evolutionary process, rather than being based in simplistic domineering visions that attempt to create complex systems in a single step. As in the case of architecture (see Alexander 1979), satisfactory designs evolve over time through development and use with feedback from the users playing a key role in the process. There is no shortcut that can replace painstaking patient attention to detail in design and development, understanding the way complexity arises and can be handled (Simon 2001). Nature took billions of years to achieve the design of living beings, through a series of extraordinary technological innovations (Lane 2009). We can learn from that process.

Control and shaping of technology

So who decides what will be created, and how it is supported and regulated? A delicate balance between government support and individual entrepreneurial development is needed to make an enabling environment and encourages innovation. There needs to be an overall framework that supports sound choices of purpose and values, shaping of technology in a way that brings positive benefits to society. Central control will not achieve this, but central support for individual vision can do so. The tension between private and public control is unavoidable. Government needs to provide support in such a way that the poor benefit as well as the rich. Local Government is key in handling the provision of infrastructure to local communities, and requires capable technical staff who will handle this in a competent way.

The overall intellectual ambience in which this occurs needs to be one where usability and the human interface of high tech equipment are regarded as key priorities. The focus should be on appropriate technology. In South Africa this means that a key requirement should be where possible to increase rather than decrease employment, with unskilled as well as skilled personnel being part of the mix. The National System of Innovation must take the needs of the poor as well as the rich into account. The usual perplexities of how to assist wealth creation abound (De Soto 2000).

Priorities: Possibilities and key issues

As we cannot do everything, we have to select what is most important from the viewpoint of government support. In coming decades, water and energy will be the most pressing issues, as well as access to the worldwide computer network. The greatest opportunities will be in genetics and biotechnology on the one hand, and in developments to do with understanding the brain and neuroscience on the other (Edelman 2006), particularly as regards its educational implications. Generally there is a major information-based transformation of society taking place as regards work, domestic life and leisure: this is where the greatest opportunities will arise.

This requires access to technology such as brain scanners, scanning electron microscopes, X-ray diffractometers, laser systems, and so on: government support for such instruments is crucial. Information and computer systems will underlie this, so developing ability in digital systems and microelectronics is vital.

We dare not neglect the development of abstract technologies that shape the way we think and act. The most important here are the tools and methods we use for transforming the goals of society into the choices we make (Beer 1978). The indicators we use for societal development are critical, for these shape the resource choices we make. Is it adequate for example to use GDP and inflation rates as indicators of successful policy, or can better human development and quality of life indicators be found? Choice and implementation of societal indicators that truly relate to human welfare and development in the framework of sound values may be one of the most important investments we can make. This requires conceptual clarity as well as data collection and analysis of sound quality.

Reference List

Alexander C. 1979. *The timeless way of building*. New York: Oxford University Press.

Anderson RG. 1989. *Business systems*. M&E Handbooks: business and management.

Baxter W. 1974. *People or Penguins: the case for optimal pollution*. New York: Columbia University Press.

Beer S. 1978. *Platform for change*. Chichester: John Wiley.

Bloomfield L. 2008. *How Everything Works: making physics out of the ordinary*. New York: Wiley.

Bronowski J. 1976. *The Ascent of Man: a personal view*. Little Brown & Co.

Burdick E & William LW. 1958, re-issued 1999. *The Ugly American*. W.W. Norton & Co.

Cartwright TJ. 1993. *Modelling the world in a spreadsheet: environmental simulation on a microcomputer*. Baltimore: Johns Hopkins.

Challoner J. 2009. *1001 Inventions that changed the world*. London: Cassell Illustrated.

Deacon T. 1997. *The symbolic species: the co-evolution of language and the human brain*. London: Penguin Books.

De Soto H. 2000. *The mystery of capital: why capitalism triumphs in the west and fails everywhere else*. New York: Basic Books.

Dickson D. 1974. *Alternative technology and the politics of technical change*. Glasgow: Fontana.

Edelman G. 2006. *Second Nature: Brain science and human knowledge*. New Haven: Yale University Press.

Faimon P & Weigand J. 2004. *The Nature of Design: How the principles of design shape our world – from graphics and architecture to interiors and products*. Cincinatti: HOW Design Books.

Garratt J. 2004. *Design and Technology*. Cambridge: Cambridge University Press.

Gould JL & Gould CG. 2007. *Animal Architects: Building and the evolution of intelligence*. New York: Basic Books.

Handy CB. 1976. *Understanding organisations*. Harmandsworth: Penguin.

Hawken P, Lovins A & Lovins LH. 1999. *Natural Capitalism: Creating the next industrial revolution*. Boston: Little Brown.

Houghton J. 2009. *Global Warming: The Complete Briefing*. Cambridge: Cambridge University Press.

Illich I. 1973. *Tools for Conviviality*. New York: Harper & Row.

Kranzberg M & Davenport WH. 1972. *Technology and Culture: An Anthology*. New York: Meridian.

Lane N. 2009. *Life Ascending: The Ten great Inventions of Evolution*. New York: Norton.

Lovins A. 1977. *Soft energy Paths: Towards a durable peace*. London: Penguin Books.

Norman DA. 1999. *The invisible computer: Why good products can fail, the personal computer is so complex, and Information appliances are the solution.* Cambridge, Mass: MIT Press.

— 2004. *Emotional Design: Why we love (or hate) everyday things.* New York: Basic Books.

Papanek V. 1974. *Design for the real world: Human Ecology and Social Change.* St Albans: Paladin.

Philbin T. 2003. *The greatest inventions of all time: A ranking Past to Present.* New York: Citadel Press.

Pugh DS (ed). 1975. *Organization Theory.* Harmandsworth: Penguin.

Schumacher EF. 1999. *Small Is Beautiful: Economics As If People Mattered: 25 Years Later ... With Commentaries.* Vancouver: Hartley & Marks Publishers.

Simon HA. 2001. *The sciences of the artificial.* Cambridge, Mass: MIT Press.

Turner JS. 2000. *The extended organism: The physiology of animal built structures.* Cambridge, Mass: Harvard University Press.

Vogel S. 1998. *Cats' Paws and Catapults: Mechanical worlds of nature and people.* London: Penguin.

Vygotsky LD. 1978. *Mind in Society: The development of higher psychological processes.* Cambridge, Mass: Harvard University Press.

Yunus M. 2001. *Banker to the poor.* Dhaka: The University Press Limited.

CRITICAL ISSUES FOR A NEW HUMANISM

Drucilla Cornell
Kenneth Panfilio

Following the spirit of Charles Baudelaire, captured by the lyrics of his famous poem *Letter to the Reader*, this essay begins with a brazen, self-implicating acknowledgement of our shared culpability in the varied disasters that have unfolded in history as "a demon nation riots in our brains" (Baudelaire 1998:5,7). We often watch "though making no grand gestures, nor great cries" forces of this world that "willingly would devastate the earth" (Baudelaire 1998:5,7). Baudelaire concludes his gripping poem by calling out to the one true figure who stands weighted with the misanthropy of our age; for, "Reader, you know this dainty monster too; -Hypocrite, -fellowman, -my twin!" (Baudelaire 1998:7). Similarly, this essay attempts to ruthlessly stand against any complacency with the varied failures of history and to awaken our selves to a new praxis of being human.

The rhetoric of humanism has become tragically eclipsed by the aggressive, imperialist pursuits of capital accumulation (Chomsky 2003; Kline 2007). That is to say, the ongoing expansion and dominance of neoliberal capitalism has often usurped the language of humanism, bleeding it of any teleological character that would envision a just world. Post-WWII versions of humanism should be rightly critiqued for their unconscious reliance on notions of the human that carry within them a white male bias synonymous with so-called Western society. For the human paradoxically becomes inscribed in a normative framework that has often been used to exclude rather than include indigenous peoples within the reach of humanism, and indeed in its most grotesque manifestations deny that indigenous peoples are human beings. However, unlike those critics who would reject humanism altogether, we think that we are in desperate need of not only a general reconsideration of humanism but more specifically an examination of the intellectual heritage of African humanism.

Ubuntu and its corresponding concepts offer a very different view of personhood than the one we associate with liberal conceptions of the human. Also, *ubuntu* is profoundly rooted in an ethical conception of what it means to be a human being and therefore deserves to be part of any discussion of what constitutes the future of humanism. Further, *ubuntu* should be put into the rich context of African humanism, particularly the modern African humanism that takes seriously questions of social justice and questions of what it means to be an ethical human being. Thus, in a certain sense, African humanism implies a critique of notions of economic organisation that create barriers to the development and the flourishing of each and every human being. Crucial, then, to any integration of African humanism into an exploration of the future of this concept will necessarily involve a prioritisation of questions of justice and indeed socialism.

The human of humanism

Previously, we have written extensively about how there has been a colonisation of critical theory, fitted with prejudices that would reduce varied ways of being-in-the-world to analytic reductions commensurate with so-called Western metaphysics (Cornell & Panfilio 2010). Against such a monolithic force, we defended the work of the oft-neglected German Idealist Ernst Cassirer to unearth his contribution to critical theory via an in-depth understanding of symbolic forms in all their richness and complexity. Such an argument allows an ethical humanism to emerge that grants equal importance and standing both to the intellectual heritage of African humanism – even African spirituality – and to the long-ignored place of black philosophies of existence. All of these provide searing indictments against imperialist domination of the so-called Third World and return such questions of domination to the realm of critical theory against some who would deny that we are still in an age of imperialism.

Such work is relevant for our purposes here in suggesting that any understanding of humanism must be an activity of our being-in-the-world both *ahead of* and *alongside* any conception of the human. All of reality, for Cassirer, comes to us through symbolic forms and is shaped by those symbolic forms. That is to say, reality is not known to us as human beings as a matter of fact, but is actively constituted through our engagement with the varied symbolic forms within our lives. This activity involves the iteration of symbolic forms in a way that is never a mere reproduction of any particular form, precisely because these forms are dynamic, shifting and infinitely complex. Thus, they leave room for reiteration and for the work of the imagination to further develop the meaning of such symbolic forms. Cassirer identifies history, aesthetics, language, myth and science as symbolic forms. However, it is not a matter of necessity that symbolic forms only be perceived through these archetypes.

When discussing the nature of mythic metaphoric thinking in his book *Language and Myth*, Cassirer contends that symbolic forms operate according to a complexity inherent within "the principle of *pars pro toto*" (Cassirer 1953:92). The idea here is that within any symbolic form the utterance of a single symbol initiates the imagination of a symbolic totality conceived of as a constitutive symbolic world. Ceremonies such as rain making involve the power of a particular object like a canteen of water, which when poured out over the parched earth, carries magical force over the symbolic understanding of the elements for those who live in such a symbolic world.

The emphasis by Cassirer on the power of the part to call forth the whole within mythic metaphoric thinking turns the whole of his investigation into one in which a thinking, reflective subject emerges with command over symbolic forms and the production of the symbolic world. As our example of rainmaking suggests, the subject that emerges is not necessarily a product of modernity. Also, on this understanding we are left knowing that language as symbolic form operates in its individual parts within the larger symbolic whole. Each utterance, each gesture, each articulation of symbolic content in our lives does at the same time keynote particular and universal understanding.

From such an understanding of symbolic forms we are able to posit a view of the human that demands radical epistemological openness that can never be cemented to a singular form or a monolithic, totalising conception of the world. A humanism, then, that could speak to such a conception of the human must always take seriously all ways of being-in-the-world and find maturity in its thought by seriously engaging with the infinite complexity and differentiation of symbolic forms throughout the world. Too often, African humanism is either condemned as outdated, dangerous traditionalism or as being so integrally tied to Eurocentric ideas that there is no residue of a living intellectual heritage.

In her essay on "Peace Utopias" Rosa Luxemburg steadfastly argues that the world stands threatened by the militarist enclave both in times of peace and war. For Luxemburg, "bourgeois apostles of peace are relying on the influence of fine words" in their illusionary activities toward peace which "invent all sorts of 'practical' projects for gradually restraining militarism ... [and] consider every outward apparent sign of a tendency toward peace as the genuine article, to take every expression of the ruling diplomacy in this vein at its word, to exaggerate it into a basis for earnest activity" (Luxemburg 2003a:344). The problem with humanism, related to the way Luxemburg critiqued bourgeois peace work, is that we have lost sight of the way in which humanism must function as an activity of our being-in-the-world both *alongside of* and *ahead of* any conception of the human.

Moreover, Luxemburg is clear in her incisive writings on the accumulation of capital that "peasantisation" and modernisation necessitate an ethical shattering of the black world, rending it as mere prey to the larger machinery of capital accumulation that would extract both the natural resources and living labour of peoples for the growth of the capitalist enclave. We follow Rosa Luxemburg here in that capitalist accumulation is inseparable from imperialism and the maintenance of enclaves of *un-free labour* and the perpetuation of otherness in the form of reducing migrant workers to second-class citizens. Moreover, a closed capitalist society cannot simply overcome the core crisis of capitalist accumulation, which inheres in overproduction and/or under-consumption (Luxemburg 2003). These two problems are connected to the drive of capital to ever-increase its profit margins, which in turn depends on the expansion of itself through the creation of not only new markets but the fabrication of cheap labour forces that are denied any of the basic rights we have come to associate with *free labour*. Simply put, capitalism creates an outside to itself that it both needs and destroys at the same time. And, this connects capitalism integrally to political violence and outright oppressions of peoples, nation states and movements that challenge its hegemony.

The challenge of African self-writing

Before turning to a more careful articulation of *ubuntu* as within the realm of any new humanism it is essential to review the challenge of modes of African self-writing. Achille Mbembe offers a searing critique of Afro-radicalism and the metaphysics of difference inherent within nativism. To quote Mbembe:

> The effort to determine the conditions under which the African subject could attain full selfhood, become self-conscious, and be answerable to no one else soon encountered historicist thinking in two forms that led it into a dead end. The first of these is what might be termed *Afro-radicalism*, with its baggage of instrumentalism and political opportunism. The second is the burden of the metaphysics of difference (*nativism*). The first current of thought – which liked to present itself as "democratic", "radical", and "progressive" – used Marxist and nationalist categories to develop an imaginaire of culture and politics in which a manipulation of the rhetoric of autonomy, resistance, and emancipation serves as the sole criterion for determining the legitimacy of an authentic African discourse. The second current of thought developed out of an emphasis on the "native condition". It promoted the idea of a unique African identity founded on membership in the black race. (Mbembe 2002:240-241)

Mbembe's powerful critique argues that African philosophy has nothing comparable to either German philosophy or Jewish Messianism in terms of their aspiration to articulate a universalisable narrative of our being human and an ethics that seeks to justify itself as an embodiment of rightness. For Mbembe, African philosophy, and he would include the intellectual heritage of African humanism, is haunted by four main challenges (Mbembe 2001).

First, modes of African self-writing lack self-reflexivity and as such embrace positive notions of knowledge that have been deployed to silence alternative views of truth other than the one held out by dominant revolutionary parties. Second, there is a reified vision of history in which Africa and its narrative, and certainly the story of African individuals, is rendered as a long series of subjugations and victimisations. The only solution to such a reified history is the uncritical history of the struggle against such "victimage" and subjugation as the only feasible possibility. This leads to a fetishisation of the revolutionary party and at the same time the privatisation of government once the party ascends to power. The third characteristic fault of modes of African self-writing is the destruction of tradition embodied in the idea that the proletariat is the only true class that can represent universal agency. Lastly, for Mbembe, African philosophy relies on a fantasy of the West as the *evil other* that would free Africans themselves from any responsibility for the profound failures of emancipation that have characterised the aftermath of liberation struggles in Africa. How, in light of this powerful critique that we take very seriously, can we defend *ubuntu* as an activist ethic of virtue that must be taken into account for any "new humanism"? We want to argue that at times *ubuntu* has indeed been used in a manner consistent with the four-fold critique issued by Mbembe. However, there are ways in which *ubuntu* can stand against such critiques in the struggle to live by its activist ethic of virtue.

Ubuntu and reparations of redemption

We agree with Mbembe that there are dangers to modes of African self-writing, but we want to argue that in the activist ethic of virtue embodied by *ubuntu* it may be possible to give a complex, coherent voice to the progressive aims of developing a new humanism.[1] For in *ubuntu* human beings are intertwined in a world of ethical relations and obligations with all other people from the time they are born[2] (Cornell & Panfilio 2010:ch.6). The social bond, then, is not imagined as one of separate, atomistic, individuated livelihoods; instead, the ethical, political and moral inscription on each of us by all other people is fundamentally drawn from the fact that we are born into a language, a kinship group, a tribe and a nation. But, this inscription is not something that can be reduced to a mere social fact. We come into the world obligated to others and, in turn, these others are obligated to us. It is a profound misunderstanding of *ubuntu* to confuse it with simple-minded communitarianism or to think that it involves merely forgetting or forgiving the wrongs of the past. It is only through the engagement and support of others that we are able to realise a true individuality and rise above our biological distinctiveness into a fully developed person whose uniqueness is inseparable from the journey to moral and ethical development (Menkiti 2006:326). If the community is committed to individuation and the achievement of a unique destiny for each person, then the person in turn is obligated to enhance their community of mutual support.

We can understand, then, that our ethical relationship to others is inseparable from how we are both embedded and supported by a community that is not outside each one of us, but is inscribed alongside each of us. The inscription of the other also calls the individual out of himself or herself back towards the ancestors, forward

1 During the *Sawyer Seminar Series on Personhood* (28 July to 14 August 2009) at the University of Cape Town, Achille Mbembe participated in several roundtables and panels and showed sympathy to a reading of *ubuntu* similar to the version presented in this essay.

2 The following on *ubuntu* can be found in slightly modified and augmented form in Cornell & Panfilio 2010, Chapter 6.

towards the community and thereby brings about relations of mutual support for the safeguarding and enhancement of the potential inherent within every person. The famous phrase *umuntu ngumuntu ngabantu* literally means "a person is a person by or through other people". Each one of us is called to become our own person and also at the same time to realise and support an ethical quality of humanness in all others. Although other people support me, and an ethical action is by definition ethical because it is an action in relation to other people and their being-in-the-world, it is still up to me to realise my own personal destiny and to become a person. Thus, it is humanity, and not just my community, that is at stake in my ethical action. If I relate to another person in a manner that lives up to *ubuntu*, then there is at least an ethical relationship between the two of us. And, of course, if we relate to others around us in such a way, then we will have helped to create an ethical, and by obvious extension, *human* community.[3]

As a result, doing justice through *ubuntu* does not make a rigid distinction between civil and social-economic rights. Yet, one criticism of *ubuntu* is that it is not specific enough as an ethical or moral ideal to be used as the groundwork of a modern constitution that gives form to the meaning of respect for dignity. But *ubuntu* as an ethical, political and ideological concept is always integral to social bonds. *ubuntu*, in a profound sense, encapsulates the moral relations demanded by human beings who must live together in complex arrangements of sociality. It implies both a fundamental moralisation of social relations, and this moralisation of social relations is forever changing. Thus, the actual demands of *ubuntu* must remain dynamic since *ubuntu* is inseparable from both our present relations to people and also the relations that emerge between all people as societies shift, evolve and transform through the zeniths and nadirs of events in human history. The aspirational aspect of *ubuntu* is that we must strive together to achieve a public good and a shared world so that we can harmonise our individual interests. It is the embeddedness of *ubuntu* in our social reality that makes it a transformative concept at its core. But this transformation can never be far away from the moralisation of social relationships.

In any society there is always conflict, and people are inevitably wounding each other in their engagements. So there can never be any end to the dialogue about what justice means in a given context. In South Africa there has been a traumatic disintegration of the relations between people. The particular devastation of an ongoing double colonialism leaves a gaping wound in the social bond. For restoration or redemption to truly occur, we must acknowledge our inevitable exposure to that wound and the need for entering a healing process. At stake in our own engagement with each other in the new South Africa is our own ethical humanity; for the wound is not abstractly present but buried deep within each one of us. Thus, we become human only in our relationships alongside other people. There is, then, a call to participate in the dialogue of what restorative justice might mean. Indeed, such redemption is always concerned with restoring the fractured ethical relations of the past within the temporality of the present so as to allow for the possibility of a future

---

3 On the different aspects of *ubuntu*, see More 2006:156-157.

life of justice. Such redemption, because by definition it is always "yet to come", cannot be fashioned as an enumerated list of moral and ethical behaviour; rather, it inheres in allowing any community of persons to meaningfully pose questions about the challenges of humanism and dynamically negotiate mediations.

For instance, Sampie Terreblanche, Mahmood Mamdani and Drucilla Cornell have continued to call for the creation of a *Justice and Reconciliation Commission* to "confront the complete failure of supply-side capitalist economics in South Africa – to understand the causes of violence without excusing it".[4] Such a commission aims to take seriously the more than 350 years of racialised capitalism that has rendered the majority black population in South Africa in dire poverty and was institutionalised, yet still functioning, during apartheid. The aim of such a commission was designed in a two-fold manner that would educate "beneficiaries of this exploitative system" and "organize a national effort for a program of reparations, restitution, and, above all, economic measures to grapple effectively with the comprehensively devastating institutional effects of an internal system of colonization".[5] That is to say, an effort such as this aims to bring into national dialogue questions about the insidious nature of racialised capitalism. Corporations were excluded from investigation during the events of the *Truth and Reconciliation Commission* that granted amnesty to those who sought forgiveness for their crimes during apartheid.

What is interesting about such a project, outside of its obvious merits of justice, is that it seeks to mediate the brutality of apartheid, rendering it as a force that does not merely exist statically in some reified history. Rather, the commission argues that apartheid remains present in the lives of people today such that any hope for a future society of justice must manifest in "drawing into a democratic discussion of economic reform all those on-the-ground groups who have worked tirelessly to develop programs of restitution and reparation, as well as consulting with economists who are exploring alternatives to capitalism".[6]

The people in common, the commons of the people

One classic example in South Africa of how the legacy of apartheid yields a difficult situation for the thinking of any new humanism can be found in the conflict between the right of private property[7] and the right to provide adequate housing.[8] Clearly, the conflict between these two rights is not simply a legal matter but is deeply embedded in the horrific inequalities that are the inevitable result of more than 350 years of racialised capitalism. *ubuntu* has played an important role as both a legal and ethical principle for thinking about what this conflict means in terms of

4 Document on file with the authors Sampie Terreblanche, Mahmood Mamdani and Drucilla Cornell, "A Call for a Justice and Reconciliation Commission."

5 *Ibid.*

6 *Ibid.*

7 *Constitution of South Africa* s25.

8 *Constitution of South Africa* s26.

innovative legal solutions toward real justice. In a path-breaking case, Justice Albie Sachs used *ubuntu* to argue that there could be no doing of justice in a situation where there was a demand for eviction unless a process of mediation had taken place between the parties involved.[9] Nor could mediation simply operate as a strategic or cost saving device. Mediation in a profound sense is the demand for doing justice in a specific circumstance. The obligation involves evaluating all of the circumstances that surround a particular eviction. For example, Sachs instructs us to consider: how long the squatters have been on the land; how much of a community they have formed; and, how the city has developed meaningful alternative shelter. To be clear, these are simply factors to be considered and they must be weighted judicially with respect to their specific circumstances.[10] For Sachs, mediation becomes a crucial part of how contending parties come to grapple with the conflict in which they find themselves not as rights-bearing individuals but as people who must live together in a community and must find a just way to resolve any conflict.

Here, we have a classic example of *ubuntu* as a demand to do justice in a way that respects all parties involved in conflict as capable of finding an ethical solution together. This is why there can be no formalistic, legalistic resolution because each case is going to provide us with a unique set of factors that must be considered by the parties themselves in resolving the conflict. We should note, then, anything like a sustainable reconciliation for both parties in this kind of conflicting situation is only possible through direct participatory democracy in which everyone must have a voice and everyone must be heard. Such is the case because participatory democracy is organic to the communities in conflict and it is the actual voices of human beings involved in the conflict that must be heard in order to enable a genuine reconciliation of the parties in which both sides come to accept a resolution as the doing of justice for the purposes of resolving conflict.

In like manner, the Shackdwellers Movement begun in Durban but which has spread throughout South Africa has powerfully argued, using *ubuntu*, that the struggle for housing, education and basic resources integral to life itself is part of a larger struggle for a People's Commons. These struggles are explicitly defined as fighting against the dispossession of resources. Dispossession could only make sense if one assumes that basic resources such as water should belong in the hands of all people and should not be privatised. Only then would it make sense to say that the privatisation of electricity and water is a form of dispossession. What is important for our purposes in these struggles is that *ubuntu* is used to define an ethic of living communism in which people come together as co-producers of alternative ways of sharing resources and indeed as co-producers of a different way of living together by developing a life in common. Living communism for the Shackdwellers Movement involves the struggle to live together in *ubuntu* so that the fight against dispossession is always also a different way of living together as co-producers of an alternative life.

---

9 *Port Elizabeth Municipality v Various Occupiers* 2005 (1) SA 217 (CC).

10 See *Port Elizabeth Municipality v Various Occupiers* at paragraph 32.

We saw earlier that Rosa Luxemburg argued that capital both needs and obliterates its own outside by turning all relations into something that can be captured in the ruthless drive for capitalist accumulation.

S'Bu Zikode, one of the leaders of the Shackdwellers movement, has explicitly connected *ubuntu* with *Abahlali baseMjondolo*, which literally means togetherness; however, the people together in *ubuntu* are creating in their effort to maintain a people's commons and a common life together a living alternative to capitalist relations of production. Thus, here you see another element resonating with an understanding of *ubuntu* as political and ideological and not just ethical. As Zikode powerfully demands:

> Our masses speak volumes; our unity is what will liberate this country. What we have learnt is that the government currently in power cannot understand IsiZulu nor English nor Xhosa. We have written letters, but they cannot understand the language of pen, faxes and telephones ...
>
> So comrades, today, I appeal to you, that what we need to do, is to conquer this capitalist system, because each second you turn your head, the capitalist system is there. We face electricity cut-offs, water disconnections, evictions and so on, because we cannot afford to pay.
>
> Abahlali baseMjondolo has become the home for the homeless, for the hopeless, for the voiceless – in rural areas, in the urban, in the city centre. There are many people who have no home, and nobody in power to speak to. So we are here to stand against the injustices, the inhumane attacks on popular democracy. (Zikode 2007:164-165)

This is not only a movement that makes decisions through participatory democracy and consensus; but it also is a way in which people are treated in union toward building a different life outside of capitalist relations that is in common and demands that resources are held in common.

Conclusion

The development of any new humanism is a worthy endeavour and, indeed, should be the focus of our work despite the mistakes of the past, which has often co-opted or coerced the meaning of humanism for unjust ends. Still, such a new humanism must conceptualise the human through a symbolic formulation respectful and inclusive of all peoples in the world. And we must take seriously the ways in which radicalised capitalist accumulation threaten the progressive, liberatory aims of such a new humanism. Also, one must be wary of the ways in which African modes of self-writing wrongly inscribe reified notions of history, uncritically purport the revolutionary party in monolithic terms, cement the subject in narratives of victimage and subjugation, or function as an apologia releasing Africans from responsibility for failed projects of liberation. Still, *ubuntu*, as a part of the rich intellectual heritage of African humanism, may indeed be a meaningful way to think about the project of new humanism in its activist ethic of virtue. Alongside of struggles such as *Abahlali baseMjondolo* we have an image, to say the least, of human beings thinking, changing and defending a notion of the human that is creatively made in common.

Reference List

Baudelaire C. *Flowers of Evil*. J McGowan (transl). Oxford: Oxford World Classics.

Cassirer E. 1953. *Language and Myth*. New York: Dover Publications.

Chomsky N. 2003. *Hegemony or Survival: America's Quest for Global Dominance*. New York: Metropolitan Books.

Cornell D & Panfilio KM. 2010. *Symbolic Forms for a New Humanity: Cultural and Racial Reconfigurations of Critical Theory*. New York: Fordham University Press.

Kline N. 2007. *The Shock Doctrine: The Rise of Disaster Capitalism*. New York: Metropolitan Books.

Luxemburg R. 2003. Peace Utopias. In: M-A Waters (ed). *Rosa Luxemburg Speaks*. New York: Pathfinder.

— 2003. *The Accumulation of Capital*. A Schwarzschild (transl). New York: Routledge.

Mbembe A. 2001. *On the Postcolony*. Berkeley, CA: University of California Press.

— 2002. African Modes of Self-Writing. *Public Culture* 14(1).

Menkiti I. 2006. On the Normative Conception of a Person. In: K Wiredu (ed). *A Companion to African Philosophy*. Oxford: Blackwell.

More M. 2006. South Africa under and after Apartheid. In: K Wiredu (ed). *A Companion to African Philosophy*. Oxford: Blackwell.

Zikode S. 2007. The Shackdwellers Movement of Durban. In: P Bon, H Chitonge & A Hopfmann (eds). *The Accumulation of Capital in Southern Africa*. Johannesburg, South Africa: The Rosa Luxemburg Foundation.

NEW MUSIC FOR A NEW HUMANISM

Hans Huyssen

Writing from a musician's perspective – more aptly, pronouncing through a musician's *persona* – I want to draw attention to the etymological convention of perceiving the individual human being as 'person', an actor (agent or representative) *through whom* human qualities and characteristics *sound* (speak, emanate or manifest). It is worth probing into this subtle linguistic metaphor as it emphasises the prevailing hiddenness and ambivalence of *being human*. Even though this biological condition is certainly bestowed through birth, *becoming human* in the fullest spiritual sense does not simply happen automatically. It is a state that cannot be achieved passively, but only through the activity of *sounding* (evidencing, proclaiming, ascertaining) one's humanness. Speaking about music and humanism I wish to make an argument for a raised sensitivity towards the underlying deep reference to the role of *resonance* in both instances.

Embarking on a quest to establish criteria for what might justifiably be termed a 'new (appositely contemporary and genuinely sustainable) humanism', is an implicit verdict against the efficacy of previous claims to such an effect. Acknowledging a 'postmodern condition' it is pointless to seek for a 'unifying meta-narrative', which would comprehensively summarise its constituents. Instead it becomes necessary to embrace the given *complexity* as an insolubly *constituent quality* and resist the temptation to reduce it to any seemingly enticing simplification. This implies that the humanism project will remain a dynamically evolving *process*, never an accomplished state; an ongoing endeavour, rather than some kind of established harmonious equilibrium.

This does *not* imply that no meaningful, discerning and qualitative assessments can be made at all. It should rather be understood that any such assessments must be carefully contextualised and delimited and that it might be inappropriate (and hence dangerous) to make general deductions in an essentialist or reductionist manner. However, to avert wilful randomness and chaos, it is as important as ever to gather knowledge, distinguish, organise, order and structure it, albeit acknowledging that there will be various and different ways of doing so – definitely concurrently, possibly antagonistically, probably in the long run mutualistically.

Neither is it necessary to 'reduce' or refer this catalogue of traits and properties to any '-ism' (such as postmodernism, deconstructionism, postcolonialism) and by implication buy into pertaining political ideologies. It proves much more effective to think in terms of systems, in fact to enlist the systems theory as an enabling analytical tool. Since both topics of this reflection, humanism and music, qualify as complex systems of activity, this approach allows for an immediate and intrinsically connected engagement with its subjects.

What kind of humanism?

Any new form of humanism will certainly need to be based on a worldview in which the perceived dualism between humanity and nature as well as that of 'developed' and 'developing' societies or economies has been overcome. While a new humanism must in principle address and account for a "single body of humanity" (Sahtouris 1999:144), this should not be confused with 'globalisation' in the sense of current tendencies of ever increasing standardisation or uniformity at the expense or even loss of diversity. On the contrary, a thriving global body of humanity will depend for its very vitality and resilience on a preferably widely heterogeneous spectrum of constituent characteristics, as they exist in the myriad of cultural, traditional and religious streams, as well as regional economies adapted to local ecologies. This 'holarchy' of a global body of humanity can only be a 'healthy body' (and thus survive) if it is itself embedded "as holon in the Gaian holarchy" (Sahtouris 1999:106). In this terminology *Gaian humanism* would seem an appropriate description for the overarching concept we are trying to grasp.

Gaia theory

Due to its revolutionary approach the Gaia theory has had a somewhat problematic reputation since its very inception. Much of this must be ascribed to spurious New Age notions trading under the same name. I should therefore like to stress, that evoking the name in this context specifically refers to the Gaia hypothesis as developed by James Lovelock and Lynn Margulis based on rigorous scientific principles.

What seemed wildly unimaginable in the late 1970s was Lovelock's proposition to perceive the earth as a "living organism". He arrived at this postulation after comparing the earth's surface and atmosphere with those of Mars and Venus: Whereas the conditions on our two neighbouring planets are in equilibrium and "can be adequately comprehended by physics and chemistry" (Margulis 1997:208), "Earth" boasts a dynamically unstable atmosphere (composed of highly reactive gases in peculiar ratios), which has moreover been regulated and kept within strict temperature limits over vast geological periods of time. He thus concluded, "that the biota ... interacting with the surface materials of the planet maintain these particular anomalies of temperature, chemical composition and alkalinity" (Margulis 1997:208). Lovelock's insight that this planet not only constitutes a lifeless habitat, which living beings inhabit independently, but that these very creatures continuously and actively contribute towards the very conditions that make it habitable (Lovelock 2000), finds its expression in the metaphor that "the planet is not just a home ... but a body" (Margulis 1997:204).

The notion of Gaia refers to this unity of environment and organisms, which are inextricably linked into a single system. As many of the Gaian phenomena couldn't possibly be noticed if studied in isolation, Gaia requires a new methodological approach that cannot be constructed from independently operating specialised and separate sciences. It requires a widely encompassing, interdisciplinary systems approach. Absorbed into a wide array of Earth System Sciences, Gaian ideas now seem far less controversial and have effectively created a unified epistemology allowing for a synthesis of previously disparate theories and findings.

One such contribution is Elizabeth Sahtouris's concept of a "single, globally cooperative body of humanity" (Sahtouris 1999:157). She evokes the concept of *symbiosis*, which, even though present in ancient thinking, has only recently received definite scientific confirmation through the research of microbiologist Lynn Margulis. This adds an extremely important complementary aspect to the previously one-sided emphasis of "selfish competition" as the principal evolutionary agency. Furthermore it effectively extirpates the (biologically defined) notion of "individuality": permeating the complete spectrum of life – from the smallest organic entities to the most complex organisms – it must without exception be replaced by 'mutuality'.

Another important element in Sahtouris's symbiotic vision is the concept of *autopoiesis,* first suggested by the Chilenian biologist Humberto Maturana. Literally translating as "self-making", it originates from Maturana's attempt to arrive at "clear and precise ... definitions of living things" (Maturana 1972:37). In trying to delimitate "life's indispensable aspects", Maturana arrives at a set of principles which he describes as *autopoietic properties* – features that arise from within living organisms, as opposed to the *allopoietic* ('other-made') nature of all non-living things. Given a supply of external raw material and energy, what essentially constitutes a living being according to this proposal is its *identity*, its *integrity*, *self-boundedness* and *self-maintenance* (Margulis 1997:268).

All of these properties relate to physical structures and biochemical processes, foremost to their metabolism, which is seen as "the detectable manifestation [the *sine qua non*] of autopoiesis" (Margulis 1997:269). Thus limited to the material conditions of 'life', the autopoietic definition makes no transcendental references. Rather, it focuses on the constitutive relationship between animate and inanimate matter, emphasising the fact that even organic material is composed of inorganic substances and, more importantly, that every living being is constantly engaged for its 'ongoing survival' in metabolic transactions with lifeless matter. In this sense it overcomes the strict Cartesian dualism between the living and nonliving sphere, suggesting that under certain organisational conditions all matter can be constituent to life. Furthermore it integrates the notions of symbiosis and mutualism and allows for an extended scope of this perspective: "The simplest, smallest known autopoietic entity is the single bacterial cell. The largest is probably Gaia – life and its environment-regulating behaviour at the Earth's surface" (Lovelock 1998, quoted in Margulis 1997:267).

Finally, Sahtouris introduces Koestler's (1978) notion of holons and holarchies, which the latter suggested, are the consistently systemic nature of nature. A holon is always both part and whole, "a whole made of its own parts, yet itself part of a larger whole" and conveys a pertinent image of the continually recursive "embeddedness of natural entities" (Sahtouris 1999:14). In this systemic view an autopoietic holarchy always concurrently constitutes an autopoietic holon on a higher level and these kinds of relationships aptly describe the constitutive embeddedness to be observed throughout all dimensions of the living sphere. In this case the principle is applicable even more widely, allowing for a continuous view from sub-atomic to inter-galactic magnitude. Somewhere on this scale, resulting from and organically embedded into other natural phenomena, resides the holon/holarchy of humanity.

In Sahtouris's view humanity is thus an integral component of a systemic and functionally interconnected global holarchy: "We can – and we must – gain enough perspective to see ourselves as one part of a much greater living system, or being ..." (Sahtouris 1999:168). Assuming the universality of evolutionary principles, including mutualism and symbiosis, she postulates that humanity is on a trajectory of eventually growing into a 'mature body of humanity'. The current state of division, imbalanced competition and war she ascribes to the species' adolescence: As a very recently developed "Gaian organ ... humanity has woefully little experiential intelligence or wisdom". Humanity, she continues:

> ... stands on the brink of maturity in a position to achieve true humanity in the full meaning of that word. Like an adolescent in trouble, we have tended to let our focus on the crisis itself or on our frantic search for particular political, economic, scientific, or spiritual solutions depress us and blind us to the larger picture, to avenues of real assistance. If we humbly seek help instead from the nature that spawned us, we will find biological clues to solving all our biggest problems at once. (Sahtouris 1999:168)

The widespread influence of the predominant "Neo-Darwinian war cries" – competition, mutation, selection, selfish behaviour, survival of the fittest, etc. – on contemporary thinking cannot be doubted. In fact, they probably unconsciously shape modern society's behaviour to a large degree. Sahtouris argues that a different worldview (and here she obviously refers to the *organic* replacing the *mechanistic*, the *symbiotic* the *competitive*, the *autopoietic* the *allopoietic*, embedding *holarchies* replacing power wielding *hierarchies*) will eventually result in a different quality of societal cohesion. It is my conviction that 'musical relations' should in their own right evidence the same principles outlined above.

Introducing music

While music's appeal might lie in its emotional or even "transcendental" qualities, I will concern myself with its more material properties and parameters. This is not to negate such qualities in principle, but they are not conducive to an investigation of the structural relationships between music and humanism. As a basis for the ensuing arguments I posit three basic musical premises:

First I hold that music will always and quite specifically express given characteristics of the society in which they originate. As such they overtly reflect general contemporary or fashionable worldviews, but additionally constitute a valuable means of gathering evidence on often unconscious and otherwise barely tangible preferences, preoccupations or propensities. Music may thus be perceived as a deeply telling indicator of a society's state and – by implication – of its human concerns.

Second, music – in a vast diversity of forms but without exception – has been and is present in every known human society. Opposing current (pragmatic and economically motivated) iterations of music as a dispensable luxury, this is evidence of *music as a desideratum of humanness*, an activity resonating with a deeply ingrained and apparently universal human need. Making and responding to music may thus be understood as a core component amongst the activities constituting humankind's humanness.

Third, music has no immanent *a priori* meaning. However, and in spite of its transient nature, it constitutes an extraordinary evocative medium, which may be used as carrier or signifier in just about any context. Hence music is employed throughout the spectrum of human emanations – from the sublime to the profane. It is suited to conveying religious or political messages equally well, as serving the entertainment or marketing industry. Its position with regard to the emanation of humanist qualities is thus open; it would be naïve to associate music in principle with sublime or positive properties. As a human activity and extension of human behaviour it is just as fragile and multivalent as the condition of its protagonists and may well be practiced inappropriately, unethically or in artistically unsound ways. The Renaissance humanist notion of music as divine or celestial art *per se* is a historically contingent one.

Music never sounds without agency: while it can depict or express anything, it cannot express nothing. Each performer, by virtue of being a person and existing in given political relations, has an agenda, even if she herself would be unaware of it. In the same way that every human action has certain ethical dimensions, so has music; it is never "innocent".

'Folk music'

There is a qualitative distinction between 'folk music' – meaning the collective, anonymously and unconsciously created occasional music of traditional communities – and all other deliberately exercised and purposefully developed musical practices. Folk music is primarily functional – a means to ensure collective cohesion and formalise important societal occasions. It is the origin of all human 'musicking' and the genesis of that reciprocally constitutive union of *musical* and concurrently *human* expression, which remains so fascinating to this very day. In its incognisant original instance this simultaneousness would have guaranteed a procedural innocence, comparable to that of other functional practices, like breathing or walking, which all consciously knowing engagements with music would subsequent loose. This then describes the second category of 'deliberate music', born in the moment where its dualistic constituency would have been perceived, freeing the musician from a merely functional task and enabling him to intentionally negotiate between the musical and the human aspects of his trade. This constitutes the transition from "culture" to "Culture" (see Eagleton 2000:44) where a consciously held worldview would replace unconscious instincts in determining behavioural and artistic decisions.

Only remnants of this phenomenon exist today, as historical developments – culminating in globalisation – severely imperil previously independent and locally rooted and restricted musical practices. Moreover, in analogy with the sociological notion of specific ethnicities becoming increasingly blurred, the musical category of 'folk music' grows similarly vague. Postcolonial musicology therefore altogether dismisses the term as untenable. However, this position ignores the factual, albeit marginal perseverance of musical instantiations of this kind all over the world, and potentially allows for the loss of the music-immanent definitions of its constitutive elements. These could however, act as important catalytic principles in the reorganisation of sustainable musical practices.

Folk music – as the primary sphere of intrinsically human musical instantiations – connotes a field with an extremely 'rich identity'. By dissolving or 'categorically' dismissing it on the grounds of contentions arising from the potential abuse of power relations in the encounter with the 'different Other', postcolonial ideology – in an ironic perversion of its stated intentions – jeopardises its very mandate of representing marginalised voices.

Described in complexity terms, folk music systems with "rich identities" are also "richly constrained, ... specific, nuanced ... and [therefore] resilient". They "operate in a state far from equilibrium and have the capacity to self-organise ..." (Cilliers 2010:61). With regard to the huge variety displayed in the global cultural diversity, different systems of 'folk-music' retain their *meaning* – and in this sense, their *identity* – due to the relatively strict constraints (which might manifest in very specific conventions and idioms). Furthermore identity should be understood as "an emergent property resulting from the diversity in the system" (Cilliers 2010:61) and "from the way in which the boundaries and the hierarchies of [the system] are simultaneously maintained and transformed" (Cilliers 2001:146). Boundaries, in turn, are not to be seen as rigid delimitations or partitions, but rather as "a function of the activity of the system itself ... something that constitutes that which is bounded ... enabling, rather than confining" (Cilliers 2001:141). As even this cursory exploration shows, the systems view offers an intriguing perspective on a field of research, which ideological dissent has largely obscured.

Folk music defined as a self-regulatory, autopoietic entity falls beyond the realm of ethical considerations. All other music – like all conscious behaviour – must be subjected to normative standards – especially if they are to serve a mutual goal, such as the establishment of an ecologically sustainable global co-existence of humanity and nature, which would be the prerequisite for a new humanism.

'Deliberate music'

For the overwhelming majority of citizens of contemporary civilisation the notion of 'music' is synonymous with the genre of 'pop music'. While such mass consumption reaffirms the universal craving for music, it concurrently demonstrates the cynical workings of capitalist demand-supply mechanisms: a banally simplistic product is found in response to a complex need, whereby the certainty that this kind of response will in no way be satisfactory, guarantees the protracted demand for more 'Ersatz' – for which a perfect market has thus been established.

It is not my intent to denigrate an element of entertainment in any musical activity, but it should be equally clear that the complexity of music as a phenomenon, as well as that of its appreciation cannot, at the cost of all other constituents, be reduced to this single aspect. Yet, in the inference that only entertainment sells, this is the sole purpose and reason for the popular music industry. It commodifies music by fragmentising it into marketable and consumable units. By implication it systematically and tragically supplants the individual and personal act of making music. Such commodification follows the logic of a consumer society and is not unique to the music industry. Yet, in this instance the reduction of content and quality is especially severe. However, a monotonous, drum-computer generated loop is not the same as a pulsating rhythm; ear-deafening artificial amplitude will never produce greatness. Reverb is but a preposterously technological counterfeit of the magic of resonance and the unendingly superficial entreatment of romantic love as the exclusive topic of the whole genre can only be explained by Sahtouris's interpretation of humanity as a "new, experimental and brash, young species" currently "in its adolescent crisis" (Sahtouris 1999:1,105).

The aggressively expanding activities of the commercial music industry pose a real threat to the global diversity of musical voices and cultures. Being effortlessly reproducible and fit for passive consumption – thereby sidestepping the patience and skill required to actively make music – yet promising of voguish participation in a universal movement, the ubiquitous accessibility of pop music presents a temptation too great to be resisted. Sadly, inside the sophisticatedly packaged lure, the artificial, high-tech dependant products fearfully, closely resemble the state of processed food – having lost all nutritional value at the expense of overindulgent manufacturing procedures. In this game vociferous marketing hype compensates for the deprivation of genuine musical qualities. What sells as a universal commodity must already account for a catastrophic impoverishment of musical tradition and skills on a global scale.

Classical music

Classical music has – in shameless imitation of the marketing principles of its popular counterpart – recently been built up or subsumed as a 'brand', symbolising a sophisticated lifestyle and taste, elegance, luxury and a certain slickness of approach and appearance. A certain type of classical musician has all too eagerly embraced this image, sensing that the association with the kind of clientele attracted by such a brand would potentially yield the kind of offshoots necessary to gain personal access to those very sought-after commodities. What trades under the name of 'classical music' today – but mostly consists of 19th century works in modernist renditions – is a highly problematic construct of anachronistic conservatism paired with pretentious 'cultured-ness'.

The problem might be traced to the phenomenon of canonisation, a principle that epitomises the quest of the Romantic movement. By this is meant the elevation of certain 'classical' works and masterpieces into a sacrosanct pantheon representing the not-to-be-negotiated core values of the profession. This marks a significant shift in musical culture: previously self-evidently and even somewhat carelessly concerned *only* with contemporary and context-related creations, the 19th century conjured up the notion of 'autonomous' music, elevating it from craft to art. Henceforth a normative repertoire was established as canon and, through its ominous presence, began to exert a strong influence on musical practice. Canonical institutions were founded, such as symphony orchestras, reputable publishing houses and conservatories guarding over the canon with "almost scriptural awe" (Haynes 2007:6). Predictably time has rendered the canon and its guardian institutions anachronistic, as can be gauged for instance by the almost full expulsion of contemporary music from its forums. In many ways these resemble museums with concerts as ritually attended re-enactments of historical scenes.

Having lost touch with the primal realm of folk music, with historical developments, with locally pertaining contextual questions, even with the dynamics of contemporary challenges, classical music keeps on making its dated offers of presenting historical masterpieces in technically spotless, predictably repetitious renditions. The only viable option of still making sales is to employ stars and superstars as performers, engage a massive promotional machinery and perpetuate the vague notion of the importance of the canon to safeguard 'Cultural' integrity.

Neither symbiotic nor mutualistic characteristics feature strongly in this system. The idea of the *musical ensemble* would be a perfect example of *symbiosis* and certainly is a constitutive principle for most classical genres. However, the notion of competition currently prevails by far – the close relation to the 19th century Darwinian perceptions is no coincidence – and veritably permeates the professional engagement with classical music. Exam passes, auditions, bursaries, prizes, concert engagements, appointments, even artistic prestige are allotted only to the fittest in the Darwinian sense. It is therefore hardly surprising that quantifiable, material features, such as measurable technical abilities and virtuosic display hold far stronger currency than the less tangible but intrinsically more musical qualities.

Fortunately music as a system with complex interactions eventually displays resilience against abusive practices. Amidst all romantic and modernist errancies, novel approaches as self-correctional tendencies have gradually been emerging, very much in the manner of an autocatalytic process. I refer here to the advent of *historically informed performance practice*.

Historically informed performance practice

Currently trading under the acronym of HIPP, this approach has developed from unsung beginnings in the 1950s to become a revolutionary method of dealing with the anachronism problem in the performance of historical music. In contrast to prevailing conventions of classical music's mainstream practice, HIPP does not deny the historical nature of its subject. On the contrary – focussing on the inseparable correlation of compositional and performance conventions mutually tied into their constitutive historical context – it has introduced an ethic into the profession of observing this notion as a key feature of any performance practice. The physical use of period instruments has empirically demonstrated that *no musical work can be perceived in separation from its specific emanation in a historically determined performance style*.

Hinging on the fact that any performance, by virtue of its momentarily transient nature, is always a currently present, contemporary act, HIPP has succeeded in 'unscrambling' or decoding Early Music in a manner that would at once do justice to the historical source, as well as to its pertaining interpretation in a fully different – present – context. It manifests as an undeniably rejuvenating influence on the perception of classical music. The rigid canon is being transformed into a pool of accessible repertoire, which is once again growing and now contains works from previously excluded historical and geographical origins.

HIPP has rediscovered a previously self-evident instance of mutualism: Contemporary music reflecting its contemporary context performed on contemporary instruments for a contemporary audience. On another level it has shown how *current* and *historical* elements may be indispensably complementary components in a mature system, thereby fully discharging the modernist belief of 'progress' as always being synonymous with improvement.

Yet another mutualistic relationship – of prime importance in Renaissance humanist perception but subsequently de-emphasised – has once again been brought to the fore: that of *music* and *speech*. HIPP strongly emphasises the rhetorical, communicative, responsive, reflective, signifying propensities of music, substantiating the ancient notion of music as a language, and as such an explicitly *affective* medium. In this approach the *human* and not necessarily the *professional* musician stands in the fore. Finally the ultimate mutualism of music as an essentially human activity comes into perspective again.

Many 'professional' musicians still belittle HIPP as insignificantly nerdish expertise, but I suggest that its far-reaching consequences will eventually amount to nothing less than a full shift of musical paradigms. Already its track record is that of a much more open, interesting, human, speaking, emotive, conspicuous, diverse and lively – in short a "hipper"(!) musical landscape.

As is evidenced by the terminology of 'performance practice' the performative act is central to this approach, also in the sense that it should "carry" the music to its listener, not intimidate him or her. Whereas many late romantic works serve the sole purpose of displaying the technical proficiency of the performing virtuoso, the opposite applies in earlier music: instrumental technique always serves the musical intent; empty technical display would be seen as musically immoral. Whereas dazzling 19th-century virtuosity seems instrumental in upholding the structural segregation between artist and audience – genius and disciple – the primal purpose of Baroque music is the stirring of affects, in other words a direct communication with the audience – 'creeping into his soul and up his spine' as it were. These images might ultimately over-emphasise the notion of symbiosis, but the point of purposeful and immediate human interaction should be clear. The fact that even contemporary performances of Baroque music attract an especially interested kind of audience and often evoke immediate and very personal reactions, speaks for the symbiotic quality of this music and its appropriate performance.

Local indigenous music from a HIPP perspective

In the heterogeneous South African musical landscape traditional indigenous African idioms must certainly count as the oldest – in some cases probably linking current to prehistoric practices – but also the most marginalised. In the light of the political coinage of an 'African Renaissance', the proclaimed new estimation of the nation's 'cultural heritage' and the tourism trump card of 'cultural diversity', this is ironic; with regard to the quest for humanism it is tragic. In the light of my discussion it should be clear that I regard the extant instantiations of indigenous African musical practice as an all-important cultural asset of the country and the continent. Experiencing such practices conveys a quality of ancient human expression, which at once radiates grandeur and humbleness. The former derives from the – real or imagined? – evocation of primeval ancientness and spaciousness, the latter emanates from the unassuming manner of rendition with which these grand testimonies of time enduring traditions are usually rendered.

How can we as contemporary musicians and listeners engage with these rare musical instances? Since the cultural environments for the originally embedded emanations of such practices are continuously eroding, their disappearance as authentic forms of expression is imminent. Neither the efforts of ethnologists or archivists, recording and documenting, nor those of composers, transcribing or arranging material, can prevent this. What is more, the items thus procured remain separated from the actual practice; at best they constitute 'material', but can never replace a living 'practice'.

Adding a new dimension to the notion of 'archive', the method of historically informed performance practice suggests a promising approach. Confronted with the problem of lost performance traditions, it does not seek to conserve, nor preserve 'authenticity'. Its concern is a living practice, not embalmed traditions. To a certain degree it must even consciously *fail*[1] the literal traditions to arrive at viable substitutes. Yet, it very deliberately seeks to connect the novel with the ancient and not to act randomly. Once again, it follows the model of an autopoietic process as a kind of healing.

Another way of describing the process once again evokes the notion of resonance, introduced at the beginning of this essay. *Resonance* is vitally important during any performance. It is the phenomenon of echo, agreement, acclaim, reverberation – of returning something of what a performer emits. It is not the same as the source, not the performer's own any more; something has been taken, something added. It constitutes the essentially needed participation and involvement of audience and environment in a performance; it guarantees the mutualism of performance and response. It is the most powerfully energising and inspirational force for a musician, to continue making music and thereby catalysing the responsive cycle anew. It makes for the richness of sound, not only in the acoustic sense, but also in that of added soul, warmth, understanding, attention and consensus. I can think of no better metaphor for a human and humanising condition, individual utterances being acknowledged, reflected and returned, creating – and thus being in – community. Resonance may, in its 'historical dimension', be translated as *tradition*, pertaining to such an experience on the level of the body of humanity. Perhaps this then is the best description or ultimate task of conscious performances: to facilitate historical resonance and thereby contribute to the weaving of the web of a resilient and sustainable humanism.

1 A good example of such a 'failure' is the famous 17th-century attempt of the Camerata Fiorentine to revive the art of ancient Greek Tragedy. The attempt at a revival of Greek Tragedy was futile, yet, in the event the genre of 'opera' was invented!

Reference List

Cilliers P. 1998. *Complexity & Postmodernism. Understanding complex systems*. London: Routledge.

— 2001. Boundaries, Hierarchies and Networks in Complex Systems. *International Journal of Innovation Management* 5(2):135-147. London: Imperial College Press.

— 2010. Difference, Identity and Complexity. In: P Cilliers & R Preiser (eds). *Complexity, Difference and Identity. An Ethical Perspective.* New York: Springer.

Eagleton T. 2000. *The Idea of Culture*. Oxford: Blackwell Publishers.

Haynes B. 2007. *The End of Early Music. A Period Performer's History of Music for the Twenty-First Century*. Oxford: Oxford University Press.

Koestler A. 1978. *Janus: A Summing Up.* London: Pan Books.

Lovelock J. 1988. *The Ages of Gaia. A Biography of our living Earth.* New York: Oxford University Press.

Margulis L & Sagan D. 1997. *Slanted Truths. Essays on GAIA, Symbiosis, and Evolution*. New York: Springer-Verlag.

Maturana HR & Varela FJ. 1972. *Autopoieses and Cognition. The Realization of the Living*. Dordrecht (NL): D. Reidel Publishing Company.

Sahtouris E. 1999. Earthdance: Living Systems in Evolution. (Updated 1999.) [Retrieved 03 May 2010] http://www.ratical.com/LifeWeb/Erthdnce/

INDIGENOUS HUMANISM

Manifestations of interconnectedness

Antjie Krog

Through a set of quotes I want to open up a space in which one can begin to consider that there had always been manifestations of a particular kind of humanity in this part of the world which profoundly influenced its indigenous inhabitants.[1] The worldview of being interconnected at several simultaneous levels could have its roots in the belief and cultural systems of the San (as the click sounds survived in the indigenous languages, so could some belief systems?). This (indigenous) humanity felt and still feels itself affronted by the humanities brought to the continent by those who are described as the "latecomers".

---

[1] In assembling and commenting on this series of quotations subsequent to the symposia, Antjie Krog helps connect the "New Humanism Project" to a much older humanist tradition deeply rooted in our southern African context. While distinct in some ways, these insights about being human resonate with much that is said elsewhere in the book. Yet, they have a character and lineage that adds depth to our reflections and also corrects misperceptions about our shared past.

"As Fellow Humans"

Vasco da Gama came ashore on the coast of south-east Africa around 1497 to repair a vessel. Somewhere between the current border of South Africa and Mozambique the Portuguese sailors met indigenous black people. The kindness, assistance and generosity of the local people led the foreigners to call the area "Terra da boa gente" meaning "The land of the Good People" (Axelson 1973:24).

Martin Prozesky

This striking but little-known episode of great moral goodness of Africans towards outsiders should be seen as a powerful indication of the importance of Africa's ancient moral wisdom and practice in today's globalising and all too uncaring world (in Murove 2009:3).

The Lusiads (1572) based on the voyage of Vasco da Gama, describes an earlier meeting.

Luis de Camões

62 The people who owned the country here[2]
Though they were likewise Ethiopians,[3]
Were cordial and humane, ...
They came towards us on the sandy beach
With dancing and an air of festival

...

64 These, as their smiling faces promised,
Dealt with us as fellow humans,

With the Universe

Bushman informant, Díä!kwãin's culture, which had already existed for thousands of years, suggested an interconnectedness with the universe:

The star does it in this manner, at the time when our heart falls down, that is the time when the star falls down; while the star feels that our heart ( ) falls over ... For the stars know the time at which we die. The star tells the other people who do not ( ) know that we have died (Bleek 1911:389) ... The hammerkop acts in this manner, when a star has fallen, it comes; when it flies over us, it cries: ɣák ɣääk, ɣák ɣääk. The people say: Did you not hear the hammerkop when the star fell? ( ) It came to tell us that our person is dead. (Bleek 1911:391)

/Han≠kassó

The Wind (i.e. the wind's son) was formerly a man. He became a bird. And he was flying, while he no longer walked, as he used to do ... (Bleek 1911:107)

---

2 Near Mosselbay where Vasco da Gama landed in 1497.

3 The term then for all Africans south of the Sahara, although they must have been Khoi.

/Han≠kassó

They (a commando) shoot at us in the mist. We make clouds. Our blood is smoking. ... The mist did this: when the people went away and left us, it also went because it felt that our blood had flowed out. That is why our mist went away; it felt our blood, which had been making clouds there, had flowed. (Lewis-Williams 2000:121)

Díä!kwãin

Baboons speak Bushman ... When we hear them talking there, we are apt to think that other people are to be found there, though we did not know of them. ... My father was the one who told me that baboons speak Bushman. My grandfather *!xu:gen-diken* also told me that baboons speak Bushman. (Hollmann 2004:10)

Eugène Marais

The learned German Dr Bleek, who studied the Bushman language and literature in the Cape about fifty years ago – a literature without letters! – and made a large collection of Bushman tales and poems for the Cape Library, tells how his investigation was made difficult by a surprising discovery he made early on. He found that in the animal stories each animal spoke its own, distinct language! (Marais 2007:1)

Roger Hewitt

A most curious feature in Bushmen folklore is formed by the speeches of various animals, recited in modes of pronouncing Bushman, said to be peculiar to the animals in whose mouths they are placed. ... (the clicks) are either converted into other consonants, as labials (in the language of the Tortoise), or into palatals and compound dentals and sibilants (as in the language of the Ichneumon) or into clicks unheard in Bushmen (as far as our present experience goes), – as in the language of the Jackal, who is introduced as making use of a strange labial click, which bears to the ordinary labial click ʘ, a relation in sound similar to that which the palatal click ≠ bears to the cerebral !. Again, the moon – and it seems also the Hare and Anteater – substitute a most unpronounceable click in place of all others, excepting the lip click ... Another animal, the Blue Crane, differs in its speech from ordinary Bushsmen, mainly by the insertion of a tt at the end of the first syllable of almost every word. (Hewitt 2008:38)

Blue Crane

Ng kang ka ng se //na hi u,u se //a twaja ke
Ng k*itten* ka*tt* ng se*tt* //na*tt* hi u*tut* se*tt* //a*t* twa*tatt* ke*tt*
(I wish I could be with you so that you could louse me)

Díä!kwãin

If we (Mother and I) are sitting in the shade when the place is not particularly warm, and we feel that the summer seems as if it would be hot ... I will sit a little while in the shade: (then) we make clouds, our liver goes out from the place where we are sitting in the shade, if the place is not hot. Therefore, we make clouds on account of it. For, when it is really summer, then we (may) sit in the shade. (Bleek 1911:399)

//Kabbo

We have a sensation in our feet as the Springbok come rustling the bushes. In the same way we have a sensation in our heads when we are about to chop the Springbok's horns. We have a sensation in our face because of the blackness of the stripe on the face of the Springbok. (Bleek 1911:334)

Jeremy Hollmann

In a real sense, game animals were extensions of people's senses; by observing the behaviour of animals, the /Xam transcended the limitations of their own sense perceptions and tapped into those of other species. The eland, hartebeest, gemsbok and springbok "have such acute senses that people not familiar with scientific thinking may believe that these animals have extra-sensory perception. 'Antelope often seem to be in a continual state of nervous tension because their senses are so acute that they respond noticeably to stimuli too faint for most humans to detect. Their sensory abilities allow non-human mammals to communicate, navigate, find food and avoid enemies by signals that humans cannot even detect. (Hollmann 2004:66)

//Kabbo

The Bushmen's letters are in their bodies. They (the letters) speak, they move, they make their (the Bushmen's) bodies move. They (the Bushmen) order the others to be silent; a man is altogether still, when he feels that ( ) his body is tapping (inside). ... The Bushmen perceive people coming by means of it. ... He feels a tapping (at) his ribs; he says to the children: ( ) 'The springbok seems to be coming, for I feel the black hair (on the side of the springbok). Climb ye the Brinkkop standing yonder, that ye may look around at all the places. For I feel the springbok sensation.' ... I feel a sensation in the calves of my legs when the springbok's blood is going to run down them ... when I am carrying the springbok. (Bleek 1911:331)

(The most famous poems produced by the /Xam informant, Díä!kwãin describes how the occupation of the land where the /Xam hunted and lived for centuries has destroyed their culture. The string, used to make music and call the rain, or used in a bow to hunt, was no longer making a sound (ringing through the air) and this changed their whole relationship to the cosmos and made them feel displaced. Central to the lament is the fact that it was "people" who did this destruction.)

the broken string

People were those who
Broke for me the string.
Therefore,
The place ( ) became like this for me
On account of it,
Because the string was that which broke for me.[4]
Therefore,
The place does not feel to me,
As the place used to feel to me,
On account of it.

4 Now that "the string is broken", the former "ringing sound in the sky" is no longer heard by the singer, as it had been in the magician's (!Diakwain's father) life time (Bleek 1911:237).

For,
The place feels as if it stood open before me,
( ) Because the string has broken for me.
Therefore,
The place does not feel pleasant to me,
On account of it.

Ali Mazrui

Traditional African culture had started from the premise that the whole universe, not merely man, had been created in the image of God. And so many African societies made some trees sacred, some hills holy, some animals totemic siblings, some forests the abode of ancestors. African cultures made no sharp distinction between the human race and other species. While some monkeys were sacred, some humans were evil. (Murove 2009:326)

Father Placide Tempels

Nothing moves in this universe of forces without influencing other forces by its movement. The world of forces is held like a spider's web of which no single thread can be caused to vibrate without shaking the whole network. (Mosley 1995:72-73)

Birago Diop

Those who are dead have never gone away.
They are at the breast of the wife.
They are the child's cry of dismay
And the firebrand bursting into life.
The dead are not under the ground.
They are in the fire that burns low
They are in the grass with tears to shed,
In the rock where whining winds blow
They are in the forest, they are in the homestead.
The dead are never dead.
(transl. Reed and Wake, Diop 1964:26)

Augustine Shutte

The ancestors are also part of the extended family. ... When one dies one does not leave the earth but moves deeper towards the centre. So the earth is one's eternal home. Because of this it is also the common property of all people. No one can own part of it simply for themselves. ... (Murove 2009:96)

Kwesi Dickson

The sense of community is a characteristic of African life to which attention had been drawn again and again by both African and non-African writers on Africa. Indeed, to many this characteristic defines Africanness. (Gyekye 1987:36)

The 'Latecomers'

R.L. Ndlovu uses a Venda phrase to describe whites:

Latecomers who soiled the water as they were grabbing everything for themselves (Nga mulandu wa nyeni dzo dzhavhulaho vhune ha danga / Dzi si fune tshisima tshi tshi vha tsha madilutshele). (Ndlovu 1991:145)

Dividing the stars among nations, S.E.K. Mqhayi (recorded live by H. Tracey circa 1943, published by Jeff Opland in 1977), characterised white people as follows:

You from Brittan, take Venus,
And share it with the Germans and the Boers.
You whites-with-an-inability-to-share-anything
Learn to share it with the Boers and the Germans.
(Nina baseBritani thathan' iKhwezi,
Niya kubambana namaJamani namaBhulu,
Noko nibantu bangakwaziy' ukwabelana
Nisuke nenz' imfazwe yamaBhulu neyamaJamani)

Describing the Prince of Wales visiting King Williamstown in 1925, S.E.K. Mqhayi wrote:

'Trasher-with-the-feet, trashing us for a long time already" (*Nyashaz' ekad' inyashaza*!)'
'The-one-who-feasts-on-our-inheritance (*Ndlalifa yelakowethu*)'. (Mqhayi 1931:60,61)

Praise poet Yali-Manisi encouraged Nelson Mandela before the Treason Trial not to be scared of the whites:

Do not fear those-with-the-red-stomachs,
Their indecencies are now in the open.
Everybody sees their (mean) secrets,
They-who-cut-out-glands-from-meat-but-do-not-realize-that-it's-the-truth-that's-so-bitter-on-their-tongues,
It stings as bitter as aloes;
They beam with arrogance and undermine rudely.
Maz' ungaboyik' ooSiswana-sibomvana,
OoSobindeka nooQhinga-libhentsile.
Bonga bakubon' amadlala,
Kanti kukrakr' inyaniso;
Kuba kamb' ihlaba ngokwekhala,
Budul' ububhengega nobunggwanganggwili.
(Yali-Manisi 1954:66)

H.M.L. Lentsoeane describing the Soweto uprising against Afrikaans in terms of the language itself:

The red-beards were spreading in the township,
Posting themselves at the meeting-places of men.
They spoke a language only spoken by its masters,
A language spoken as if others were dirty linen,
A language spoken as if others were bundles of paper,
A language spoken as if the lips were sewn together.
A phatlalala le metsemeso,
A ipala ka magorogoro.
Polelo a boletše ya go tsebja ke beng,
Polelo ya go bolelwa ke mašela,
Polelo ya go bolelwa ke dipampiri,
Polelo ya go bolelwa o rokile molomo. (Lentsoeane 1981:177)

Reconciliation

Wole Soyinka

There is a deep lesson for the world in the black race's capacity to forgive, one which, I often think, has much to do with the ethical precepts which spring from their world view and authentic religions, none which is ever totally eradicated by the accretions of foreign faiths and their implicit ethnocentrism. (Bell 2002:87)

Pumla Gobodo-Madikizela

We are induced to empathy because there is something in the other that is felt to be part of the self, and something in the self that is felt to belong to the other.

The victim needs forgiveness as part of the process of becoming rehumanized. The victim needs it in order to complete himself and wrest away from the perpetrator the fiat power to destroy. Far from being an unnerving proposition and a burdensome moral sacrifice, compassion, for many, is deeply therapeutic and restorative. (Gobodo-Madikizela 2003:127,132)

Cynthia Ngewu, one of the Gugulethu mothers whose children were killed by Apartheid Security Forces:

> This thing called reconciliation ... if I am understanding it correctly ... if it means this perpetrator, this man who has killed Christopher Piet, if it means he becomes human again, this man, so that I, so that all of us, get our humanity back ... then I agree, then I support it all. (Krog 1998:109)

Ethics of Interconnectedness

Gabriel Setiloane

The greatest of all evils according to African Traditional Religion is to live in 'careless disregard of others'. (Brand 2002:98; also see Setiloane unpublished)

Kwame Gyekye

Communitarian logic 'assumes a great concern for communal values, for the good of the wider society as such. ... (it) deeply cherishes the social values of peace, harmony, stability, solidarity and mutual reciprocities and sympathy'. (Gyekye 1987:65)

Augustine Shutte

The goal of morality according to this ethical vision is fullness of humanity; the moral life is seen as a process of personal growth. And just as participation in community with others is the essential means to personal growth, so participation in community with others is the motive and fulfilment of the process. Everything that promotes personal growth and participation in community is good, everything that prevents it is bad. (Murove 2009:30)

Keith Fernado

... sin in many African cultures is defined not so much in terms of the nature of the act itself, but rather of its consequences ... Thus to say that 'sin' disrupts harmony and causes suffering is tautologous ... An act that disrupts the harmony of the cosmos in a way harmful to the interests of man, is ipso facto evil; if no harmful consequences are entailed it is therefore probably inaccurate to speak in terms of 'offence' or 'sin'. (Brand 2002:83)

Ifeanyi Menkiti

As far as Africans are concerned, the reality of the communal world takes precedence over the reality of the individual life histories and therefore comes to three conclusions: 'the community defines the individual; personhood is not bestowed on somebody simply through birth, but is something to be acquired; personhood is something at which an individual could fail.' (Gyekye 1987:37)

Augustine Shutte

I am a potential person. ... So I must see my life as a process of becoming a person. It is not just that I change and grow. I am being built up, constructed. My life is a progressive increase in vital force. That depends on the moral quality of my life. (in Murove 2009:92)

Desmond Tutu

One consequence of *ubuntu* is that we recognize that we all need to live our lives in ways that ensure that others may live well. (Tutu 2010:47)

Kwame Gyekye

It is also possible to derive a conception of human dignity ... not from theism but from reflections on human nature, particularly on the qualities that will dispose the human being to function at his best in human society and realize his potentials to the full. (Gyekye 1987:63)

David Cranmer Theko Bereng (1931) wrote a lament on the death of the Basotho king, Moshoeshoe, who lived during the nineteenth century. In it he describes how Moshoeshoe 'built' his personhood through actions which benefited the community.

He distributed to everybody with a hand used to giving.
His heart was the bearer of the weak.
Bohle ka tsoho le fanang a ba abela.
Pelo ea hae, lere la ba fokolang. (Bereng:43)
He went away, our Great Soldier
The one who broke Shaka's assegai
And bound it to the others
O ile ea matla mohale,
Moroba rumo la Chaka a b'a le khomeletse (Bereng 1931:35)
...
Never before had a king been so loved by his people
E mo hlōlisitseng ka ho ratoa, (Bereng 1931:37)
...
Here he rests, our Great-Binder-together
Mona ho phomotse Thesel'a Matlama (Bereng 1931:43)

Desmond Tutu

In the African *Weltanschauung* a person is not basically an independent, solitary entity. A person is human precisely in being enveloped in the community of other human beings, in being caught up in the bundle of life. To be ... is to participate. (Hulley 1996:105)

Kwame Gyekye

If one were to look for a pervasive and fundamental concept in African socio-ethical thought generally – a concept that animates other intellectual activities and forms of behaviour, including religious behaviour, and provides continuity, resilience, nourishment, and meaning to life – that concept would most probably be humanism: a philosophy that sees human needs, interests, and dignity as of fundamental importance and concern. (Gyekye 1987:70)

Mark Sanders

In the context of Soga's essay, ukuvimba is an attitude specifically towards the traveller or stranger (umhambi). This makes of *ubuntu* a relation to the stranger, to the one not one's own, to the one not *of* one's own, to the one who has come to be treated as one not one's own. Hospitality is called for when the ties that make an other one's own do not exist or have fallen away. Hospitality is a way of owning – in a limited sense, through artifice of convention – the one who is not one's own, the one through whom one owned oneself and became who one is. ... If the disasters of the past are to be avoided, the figure of the stranger must be continually invented. (Sanders 2002:125,129)

Nelson Mandela

To the extent to which I was able to achieve anything, I know this is because I am a product of the people of South Africa. I am a product of the rural masses who inspired in me the pride in our past and the spirit of resistance. I am the product of the workers of South Africa, who in mines, factories, fields and offices of our country have pursued the principle that the interests of each are founded in the common interest of all. (Krog 2003:220)

JM Coetzee

Because blood is precious, more precious than gold or diamonds. Because blood is one: a pool of life dispersed among us in separate existences, but belonging by nature together: lent, not given: held in common, in trust, to be preserved: seeming to live in us, but only seeming, for in truth we live in it. (Coetzee 1990:58)

Conclusion

I agree with MH Prozesky:

In the light of its historical context, African ethics must thus be seen as a moral cluster that is immensely old, deeply embedded in the cultures of the continent, still strong, and the survivor of massively powerful, disruptive, outside influences. That indicates a resilience and inner strength which non-Africans need to know about. (Murove 2009:8)

At the same time one is keenly aware how this multilayered interconnectedness has grown many permutations. When interconnectedness imagines and moves towards a humane wholeness, it elicits actions like building, caring, helping, etc. But if the community and/or its ecological setting have been disrupted and disconnected through slavery, colonialism, urbanisation, displacements, apartheid and Aids, to name a few, interconnectedness becomes severely disturbed and distorted. If a community is distraught or brutalised, the self has little to connect to in order to build a personhood. A common replacement for a multilayered interconnectedness is to conflate interconnectedness with race and build solidarity through skin colour. It may also mean that for indigenous people to accommodate "black" in this part of the world, ultimately means to accommodate the "stranger".

Reference List

Axelson E. 1973. *Portuguese in South-East Africa 1488-1600*. Johannesburg: Struik.

Bell RH. 2002. *Understanding African Philosophy. A cross-cultural approach to classical and contemporary issues in Africa*. New York: Routledge.

Bereng DCT. 1931, reprinted 1991. *Lithothokiso ta Moshoeshoe, le tse ling.* Morija: Sesotho Book Depot.

Bleek WHI & Lloyd LC. 1911. *Specimens of Bushman Folklore.* London: George Allen & Company, Ltd. Ruskin House.

Brand G. 2002. Speaking of a Fabulous Ghost – In search of Theological Criteria, with special reference to the Debate on Salvation in African Christian Theology. *Contributions to Philosophical Theology* 7. Frankfurt am Main: Peter Lang.

Coetzee JM. 1990. *Age of Iron.* London: Secker & Warburg.

De Camões LV. 1997. *The Lusiads.* L White (transl). Oxford: Oxford University Press.

Diop B. 1960/1964. *Breath – A Book of African Verse.* John Reed & Clive Wake (eds). London: Heinemann Educational Books Ltd. PK. 26. (This poem by Diop first appeared in *Lueurres et Lueurs* in Heinemann's series of French African Verse.)

Gobodo-Madikizela P. 2003. *A Human being died that night – a Story of Forgiveness.* Cape Town: David Philip.

Gyekye K. 1987. *An Essay on African Philosophical Thought. The Akan Conceptual Scheme.* Cambridge: Cambridge University Press.

Hewitt R. 2008. *Structure, Meaning & Ritual: In the Narratives of the Southern San.* Johannesburg: Wits University Press.

Hollmann JC. 2004. *Customs & Beliefs of the /Xam Bushmen.* Johannesburg: Wits University Press.

Hulley LK, Kretschmar L & Pato LL. 1996. *Archbishop Tutu – Prophetic Witness in South Africa.* Cape Town: Human & Rousseau.

Krog A. 1998. *Country of my Skull.* Johannesburg: Random House.

— 2003. *A Change of Tongue.* Johannesburg: Random House.

Lentsoeane HML. 1981. *Ihlo la Moreti.* Pretoria: Van Schaik.

Lewis-Williams JD (ed). 2000. *Stories that float from afar.* Cape Town: David Philip.

Marais E. 1921/2007. *The Rain Bull and Other Tales from the San.* J Coetzee (transl). Cape Town: Human & Rousseau.

Mosley AG (ed). 1995. *African Philosophy: Selected Readings.* Upper Saddle River, NJ: Prentice Hall.

Mqhayi SEK. 1931. *Ityala Lamawele.* Alice: Lovedale Press.

— 1943. *Inzuzo.* Johannesburg: Wits University Press.

Murove MF. 2009. *African Ethics – an Anthology of Comparative and Applied Ethics.* Pietermaritzburg: University of KwaZulu-Natal Press.

Ndlovu RL. 1991. *Mulisa.* Johannesburg: Out of Africa. (Title of poem: "Mukapi wa tshimsima".)

Opland J. 1977. Two unpublished Poems by SEK Mqhayi. *Research in African Literatures* 8:27-53.

Sanders M. 2002. *Complicities – The Intellectual and Apartheid.* Durham & London: Duke University Press.

Setiloane GM. n.d. How the traditional World-View persists in the Christianity of the Sotho Tswana. Unpublished.

Soyinka W. 1999. *The Burden of Memory, The Muse of Forgiveness.* New York & Oxford: Oxford University Press.

Tutu D & Tutu M. 2010. *Made for Goodness: and why this makes all the difference.* New York: HarperCollins.

Yali-Manisi DLP. 1954. *Izibongo zeenkosi zamaXhosa.* Alice: Lovedale Press.

TOWARDS A NEW HUMANISM IN AFRICA

Njabulo Ndebele

I have a great interest in a set of trends observable across Africa in the last ten years or so. First is the pattern of democratically elected governments across the continent. The second is the marked decline in the number of transnational conflicts across the continent. Third is the steady growth of market economies across the continent, in which the spirit of entrepreneurship seems to thrive promising more goods and services to Africa's people over the coming years. These are largely positive trends.

Taken together, these trends suggest the following: they point to the imperative for increased public accountability based on electoral mandates; they suggest a transnational politics based on mutual needs and the recognition of legitimate differences recognised and respected within a frame-work of bilateral or multilateral agreements; they strongly suggest conflict prevention and conflict resolution as behaviour attributes of the future; they promise greater intra-continental trading and greater movement of people and goods across the continent; they point to the beginning of a process of social experimentation (within individual countries and transnationally), in many areas of public and private life. The resulting societies will not be lacking in tension, but the high quantum of human energies released should interact within an environment subject to value-driven as well as legal regulation.

These trends will yield their full promise on the premise that they demand from us a greater understanding of human motivation in which people interact as free and active agents with equally predictable and unpredictable consequences. Solutions or answers to questions will not emerge from pre-packaged offerings, overarching explanatory theories, or heroic leaders. They will emerge from the interactions of sturdy, open-minded agents. The group as the defining attribute of identity should progressively give way to the needs of individuals forming lasting or temporary collectives, within or across groups, which result in shifting or ever widening personal identities. This trend will not eliminate the group, but will render it more porous and more inclusive, qualities that may be a new source of group strength. Counterintuitively, freer individuals will result in stronger groups and communities.

For South Africa such a process could represent a fundamental shift from a past of predetermined group based identities, towards a future of groups re-energised and re-humanised by free individuals.

The historic trends alluded suggest that they are an enabling framework at the heart of which are the people of Africa. How can we work with these historical trends to meet the deep-seated needs of Africa's people? What indeed are the deep-seated human needs and can these trends meet? These thoughts suggest that any 'new humanism' in Africa may have to begin there, that whatever that humanism will be, it could promise to be one viable basis on which Africa can interact with itself and with the rest of the world on an equal and mutually beneficial basis.

RELATIONAL HUMANISM

Jan-Hendrik S Hofmeyr

I am biologist with a passion for understanding the phenomenon of life itself. From this broad perspective I find it difficult to conceive of the human species as something deserving of its own "ism". That said, I have no doubt that we need a re-assessment both of ourselves and our species as living organisms and of our place in the planetary "physiology", in Gaia, if I may use James Lovelock's more poetic term (Lovelock 2000). I am deeply concerned, however, that any effort to develop a "new" humanism will not be able to shed the baggage of old and current humanisms, whether religious or secular, which always seem to be wedded to a limited and overwhelmingly anthropocentric point of view. Despite the lofty ideals of these humanisms we as a species have managed to land ourselves and our planetary home in a royal mess.

Any form of humanism or whatever we want to call it must inevitably be based on a conception, a model, a view of what it is to be a human being in a complex and inherently unpredictable world. If our starting point is the human being as a special creation of some god or gods who in the end will bail us out of the disasters we create, we are going to end up with a different humanism than if we assume that humans are just animals, albeit rather special ones, that have evolved through natural selection and are therefore in the same boat as the rest of the biosphere, with no deities to throw us lifelines. Although there are many softer versions of these two extremes I find myself very close to the latter stance. Just like all other extant organisms we carry with us an evolutionary past from which we cannot escape. With brains adapted to consider our own typical lifespan of somewhat more than half a century we clearly find it very difficult to plan for the long-term. We are hard-wired to think locally and, when the crunch comes, to take responsibility only for ourselves, our kin and our livestock. We tend to look inward, not outward. We tend to ascribe that which we do not understand to some metaphysical being; in Carl Sagan's (1997) words, we live in a demon-haunted world. Despite the many wonderful things we have accomplished – science, art, music, literature, to name the obvious ones – we have still managed, in the words of my colleague Paul Cilliers (personal communication), to "reduce humanity to an instrumentalised, commodified, superficial thing, isolated in a very real sense from the rest of life on earth".

I do not profess to know how we can transcend our natures, how we can bootstrap ourselves from what we have become to what we should be, how to stop being a disruptive cog in the physiology of our planet, how to discard the arrogant notion that we are caretakers or custodians of this planet, or, worse, that the planet is ours to exploit. I suspect, however, that we will be required to understand deeply our place in the complex web of life, not only in the social, political and economic webs that we have created, but in the planetary web itself. For that we need a new perspective, a new worldview, a new science perhaps, that transcends the boundaries that we have created between disciplines, between bodies of thought, and between ourselves and the rest of our world. We need to regard the relations between things as more important than the things themselves, ourselves of course being a part of those things. We need to emphasise the whole rather than the parts, connections rather than objects, organisation rather than material structure. We need, in short, to cultivate a relational view of the world and our place in it.

Rather than describing the details of such a relational view – of which excellent accounts can be found in works such as Laszlo (1997), Cilliers (1998) and Meadows (2008) – I want to reflect on why it does not seem to be our natural inclination to adopt such a view. It has become fashionable to blame our apparent inability to think relationally or systemically on the reductionistic and deterministic heritage of Newtonian science, but I believe the problem goes much deeper than this and that it is another result of our evolutionary heritage.

I want to suggest that the current, predominant worldview, especially that of the Western world, has its origins in the way we perceive things. Spencer-Brown (1979), in his *Laws of Form*, identifies the drawing of a distinction, distinguishing a "this" from "everything else but this", as the root of cognition. This extrapolates naturally to our perceiving ourselves and the world around us as discrete entities that can be grouped or subdivided. We naturally classify things: dangerous or not dangerous, us or them, human or non-human, black or white, Christian or Moslem, etc. Ervin Laszlo (1996), in his wonderful little book *The Systems View of the World*, makes a similar point when he argues that what he calls the classical worldview is atomistic and individualistic: objects are viewed as separate from each other and from their environments.

Consider that most human of natural sciences, mathematics. It is telling that the mathematics that we have developed since Newton mirrors this apparent imperative to group things into classes. Modern mathematics is grounded in set theory, in which the most fundamental attribute of an object is membership of a set. Given a set, set theory uses the notion of equivalence classes to construct new sets using an equivalence relation that groups together objects that share some common property. For example, given the set of all humans the equivalence relation "belongs to the same sex" divides humanity into two equivalence classes: male and female.

I therefore argue that our propensity for perceiving and classifying objects, seeing the world in, for want of a better word, an "atomistic" way, is an innate propensity of humankind, one which we cannot escape and one which is apparently stronger than our innate propensity for perceiving relations among objects. A relational view of the world therefore does not come naturally and must be actively cultivated. Again this is mirrored in mathematics. It is only in the last half of the 20th century that we have seen the development of an alternative foundation for mathematics, called category theory, where the most fundamental concept is that of a mapping or morphism, which describes a relationship between two objects (Lawvere & Schanuel 2009). In category theory it is even possible to do away with elements of sets completely, casting everything in terms of mappings. In a real sense, category theory provides a calculus of organisation, and, thereby, a formal basis for understanding systems in relational terms. It has already escaped the confines of pure mathematics and is being applied in physics, computer science and biology.

In biology we find the same trend as in mathematics. Biology started as an exercise in classification, whether of organisms or, much later, of their molecular constituents. Modern molecular biology is still essentially reductionistic in that it devolves understanding of the behaviour of organisms solely to the properties of their parts. It is only very recently, with the rise of systems biology (Noble 2006), relational biology (Rosen 1991) and biosemiotics (Hoffmeyer 2008), that the web of interactions and communications between the parts has become an essential part of the story. From the perspective of process ecology (Ulanowicz 2009) has developed what he calls a "third window" on nature to complement and counterbalance the first and second windows of Newton and Darwin.

My reflection therefore ends on a cautiously optimistic note. The recent development of the sciences of systems and complexity in the domains of both the natural and human sciences shows that not only do we realise the need for a relational view of the world but that we are actively striving towards it, despite our predilection for atomistic thinking. Nonetheless, much remains to be done and it is my belief that it is only when such a view forms the basis of all education that we shall find a way of being human in harmony with the rest of our world.

Reference List

Cilliers P. 1998. *Complexity and Postmodernism: Understanding Complex Systems*. London: Routledge.

Hoffmeyer J. 2008. *Biosemiotics: Signs of Life and Life of Signs*. Scranton: University of Scranton Press.

Laszlo E. 1996. The *Systems View of the World: A Holistic Vision for our Time*. Creskill: Hampton Press.

Lawvere FW & Schanuel SH. 2009. *Conceptual Mathematics: A First Introduction to Categories*. 2nd Ed. Cambridge: Cambridge University Press.

Lovelock J. 2000. *Gaia: A New Look at Life on Earth*. Oxford: Oxford University Press.

Meadows D. 2008. *Thinking in Systems: A Primer*. London: Earthscan.

Morin E. 1999. Organization and Complexity. *Ann. NY Acad. Sci.* 879: 115-121.

Noble D. 2006. *The Music of Life: Biology beyond the Genome*. Oxford: Oxford University Press.

Rosen R. 1991. *Life Itself. A Comprehensive Enquiry into the Nature, Origin, and Fabrication of Life*. New York: Columbia University Press.

Sagan C. 1997. *The Demon-Haunted World: Science as a Candle in the Dark*. New York: Ballantine Books.

Spencer-Brown G. 1979. *Laws of Form*. New York: EP Dutton.

Ulanowicz R. 2009. *A Third Window: Natural Life beyond Newton and Darwin*. West Conshohocken: Templeton Foundation Press.

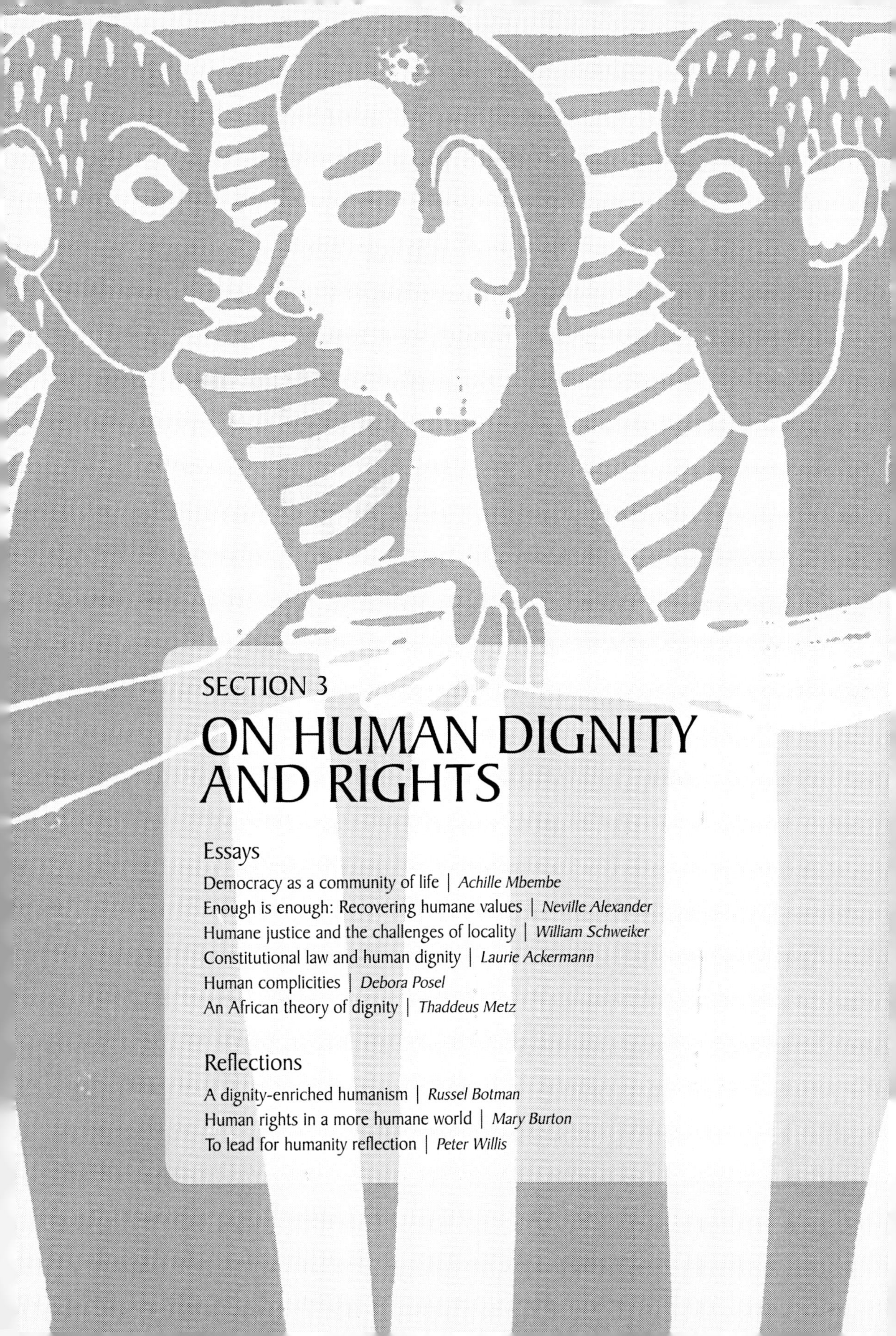

SECTION 3

ON HUMAN DIGNITY AND RIGHTS

Essays

Democracy as a community of life | *Achille Mbembe*

Enough is enough: Recovering humane values | *Neville Alexander*

Humane justice and the challenges of locality | *William Schweiker*

Constitutional law and human dignity | *Laurie Ackermann*

Human complicities | *Debora Posel*

An African theory of dignity | *Thaddeus Metz*

Reflections

A dignity-enriched humanism | *Russel Botman*

Human rights in a more humane world | *Mary Burton*

To lead for humanity reflection | *Peter Willis*

DEMOCRACY AS A COMMUNITY OF LIFE

Achille Mbembe

Preliminary observations

During the last quarter of the twentieth century we have witnessed the development of modes of ethical reasoning which dealt with the difficult question: what is 'the human' – or what remains of 'the human' or even of 'humanism' – in an age of violence, fear and torture; war, terror and vulnerability. Propelled by the repetition of violent events and human-made catastrophes and disasters, this critique has profoundly shifted the manner in which we used to define law and life, sovereignty and the political. It is now understood that if life itself has become the prime medium for exerting power, power in turn is fundamentally the capacity to control and redistribute the means of human survival and ecological sustainability.

Some of these forms of political and cultural critique are not simply paying incidental attention to the religious. In most instances, they have explicitly and deliberately engaged with theology itself. A number of secular intellectuals have moved beyond a time, not so long ago, when generation after generation of leftist revolutionaries denounced religion as a force of alienation which threatened human freedom. To a large extent, this new critique has also taken the form of *witnessing*. As has long been the case in black radical intellectual traditions, to witness is the attempt to disrupt and destabilise the prevalent order of things. The task of the witness is to reopen the emancipatory possibilities which, as a consequence of the structured blindness and collective self-deception of the age, are in danger of foreclosing the future. Propelled by the belief that history can be made possible again, late 20th-century forms of critique have posited the pursuit of truth as a form of struggle in and of itself. Furthermore, the turn to the politico-theological has been the cornerstone of a renewed drive to expand our definition of "the human" and to re-imagine democracy as a community of life – life itself understood as a relentlessly regenerative force and possibility.

The emergence of late 20th-century forms of theologico-political critique has coincided with our disjointed world experiencing a radical uncertainty. This sense of uncertainty particularly affects three domains of social life: (1) the nature of historical praxis; (2) the categorical foundations of experience; (3) and the moral economies of signification. We no longer have ready-made answers to such fundamental questions as: Who am I? Who is my neighbour? What should we do with our (former) enemies? How should we treat the migrant, the asylum seeker, the stranger or the prisoner, the widow and the orphan? Can we forgive the unforgivable? What is the relationship between the quality of persons on the one hand and material wealth, poverty, hunger and disease on the other? Is there anything that can be considered to be so priceless as to be immune from sacrifice? If the possibilities of utopian thinking have receded, what are the conditions of a radical, future-oriented politics in this world and in these times?

Africa is a particularly revealing site from which to reframe these renewed interrogations of 'the human', of 'life' and of 'possibility'. Here, under conditions of slavery, colonisation and apartheid, brutal forms of dehumanisation have raised, in the starkest terms possible, the political and moral dilemmas of human difference. A racially exclusive ideological discourse in the heyday of conquest and occupation, 'humanism' was predicated on the belief that a difference of colour was a difference of species. Race in particular did not simply become a crucial, pervasive dimension of colonial domination and capitalist exploitation. Turned into law, it was also used as a privileged mechanism for turning black life into *waste* – a race doomed to wretchedness, degradation, abjection and servitude.

This is why, in their effort to vindicate their race, black intellectuals devoted most of their energies drawing complex portraits of themselves as actors in the history of humankind. As a result, two perspectives have historically dominated modern African discourses on 'the human'. The first – a substantivist perspective that used blackness as a strategic concept in a broader economy of self-affirmation and reinvention – ended up giving priority to an ontology of difference. To the colonial negation of black humanity, it substituted a narrative of black collective identity born of a common historical experience of subjugation and suffering. But even in the most radical forms of black self-assertion, race consciousness was always a transitional move on the way to universal or planetary humanism. Although always keen to provide a full account of 'the lived experience of the black' (Fanon), the second – a political and future-oriented perspective – sought to move away from racialism and toward seeing each human being as only a human being in a future shared community. Such a community was usually envisaged as a community of life, freedom and possibility. It included everyone equally and was produced through struggle.

Today, questions concerning the place of race in capitalism and capitalism's intrinsic capacity to generate *'the human' as waste* are being raised anew, at a time when radical shifts can be observed in the way neo-liberalism operates. In many places, the Continent is witnessing the consolidation of rapacious and predatory modes of wealth extraction. As Jean Comaroff writes, a new scramble for Africa is underway. Many of the investments currently being made flirt with forms of deregulation that pave the way for criminal economic transactions – trade in blood diamonds, contraband substances, protected species, sex workers, toxic dumping. Privatisation is being carried out in the midst of acute levels of material deprivation. Both the logic of privatisation and that of extraction are underpinned and buttressed by various processes of militarisation. In order to raise profitability levels, capital and power manufacture wars and disasters, feeding off situations of extremity which then allow for 'indirect forms of private government' of which 'humanitarian interventions' are but the most visible. Where access to wage labor is still a – remote – possibility, it is more and more embedded in a logic of disposability.

The 'human' in the South African context

Whether there is anything which is still to be rediscovered or to be reanimated from the term 'the human' takes on a paradoxical resonance in contemporary South Africa. With the end of apartheid, South African culture and society was confronted with the urgency of engaging in *affirmative politics* in lieu of the politics of destruction of the years of racial segregation. Affirmative politics entailed the production of social horizons of hope. At the same time, it meant resisting both the inertia of the present and the nostalgia of the past. To reconstruct what centuries of racial brutality had destroyed, a balance had to be found between the mobilisation, actualisation and deployment of cognitive, affective and creative possibilities which had not so far been activated, along with a necessary dose of oppositional consciousness.

Critical humanism in this new context would have meant a persistent commitment to the possibilities and powers of life. There is substantial evidence that a return to the question of the possibilities and powers of life as a precondition for the reconstitution of 'the human' in politics and culture was recognised as a matter of ethical and political urgency during the first decade of democracy. During this decade, South Africa became a model of how to dismantle a racial mode of rule, strike down race-based frameworks of citizenship and the law while striving to create racial equality through positive State action. The post-apartheid State fostered a normative project with the aim of achieving justice through reconciliation, equality through economic redress, democracy through the transformation of the law and the restoration of a variety of rights, including the right to a dignified life. This normative project was enshrined in a utopian Constitution that attempts to establish a new relationship between law and society on the one hand and law and life on the other, while equating democracy and the political itself with the ethical and the just. This Constitution's underlying principle is *ubuntu* or *human mutuality*. It promises a transcendence of the old politics of racial difference and an affirmation of a *shared humanity*. Underpinning the Constitution is the hope that, after centuries of attempts by white power to contain blacks, South Africa could become the speech-act of a certain way of *being-in-common* rather than *side by side*.

This drive to 're-humanise' society and culture and to institutionalise a new political community that defines itself as an ethical community is nevertheless unfolding against various odds. Perhaps to a degree hardly achieved in the rest of the Continent, the human has consistently taken on the form of *waste* within the peculiar trajectory race and capitalism espoused in South Africa. Traditionally, we speak of 'waste' as something produced bodily or socially by humans. In this sense, 'waste' is that which is *other than* the human. Traditionally, too, we speak of the intrinsic capacity of capitalism to waste human lives. We speak of how workers are wasted under capitalism in comparable fashion to natural resources. Marx in particular characterises capitalist production as thoroughly wasteful with what he calls 'human material' just as it is with 'material resources'. It squanders 'human beings, living labour', 'squandering not only flesh and blood, but nerves and brain, life and health as well', he writes. In order to grasp the particular drama of the human in the history of South Africa, we should broaden this traditional definition of 'waste' and consider the human itself *as* a waste product at the interface of race and capitalism. Squandering and wasting black lives has been an intrinsic part of the logic of capitalism, especially in those contexts in which race is central to the simultaneous production of wealth and of superfluous people.

Today, this logic of waste is particularly dramatised by the dilemmas of unemployment and disposability, survival and subsistence, and the expansion in every arena of everyday life of spaces of vulnerability. Despite the emergence of a solid black middle class, a rising superfluous population is becoming a permanent fixture of the South African social landscape with little possibility of ever being exploited by capital. Only a dwindling number of individuals can now claim to be workers in the traditional sense of the term. How to govern the poor has therefore become one of the biggest moral questions facing the nascent democracy. Behind policy debates on 'welfare' and 'service delivery' loom fundamental ethical choices that will determine the nature of the South African experiment in democracy – questions of how to right historical wrongs; what is the relationship between personal or collective injury and larger problems of equality, justice and the law; hunger and morality; owning and sharing; or even truth, hope and reconciliation. The urgency of these new moral dilemmas is such that, for the democratic project to have any future at all, it should necessarily take the form of a conscious *attempt to retrieve life and 'the human' from a history of waste.*

Wealth and property

Meanwhile, wealth and property have acquired a new salience in public debate. They have become the key, central idioms to framing and naming ongoing social struggles – from imagining the relationship between 'the good life' to redefining value itself; from claims of citizenship, rights and entitlements to the definition of the forms of property and the economy itself (whether we should nationalise or not); from matters of morality to those of lifestyle and accountability.

The centrality of wealth in the moral discourse concerning the 'human' is not new. In various parts of pre-colonial Africa, discourses on 'the human', or, on 'humanity' almost always took the shape and content of discourses about 'wealth', 'personhood' and 'social multiplicity'. Traditional definitions of wealth usually encompassed 'people', 'things' and 'knowledge'.

'People', that is, other human beings, were not only the most important unit of measurement of ultimate value. They also formed the material basis or *infrastructure* of human life. 'People' consisted of interpersonal dependents of all kinds – wives, children, clients and slaves. As Jane Guyer argues in a striking study of forms of wealth in pre-colonial Equatorial Africa, they were sought, valued, and at times paid for at considerable expense in material terms. Kinship and marriage especially were critical components of accumulative strategies. But wealth also covered traded goods, including the imported goods brought from elsewhere. Things could be personalised objects. Goods could be functionally interchangeable with human beings who in turn could in certain respects be 'objectified' or converted into clients or followers.

Wealth – embodied in rights in people – remained a persistent principle of African social and moral life even in the midst of the various shifts induced by the slave trade and colonialism. Knowledge on the other hand was understood as an ever shifting spectrum of possibility. Jane Guyer makes it clear that it was highly valued, complexly organised and plural by definition. There was no social organisation of kinship and material life that did not depend, to some extent, on a regime of distribution of knowledge – the arts, music, dance, rhetoric, spiritual life, hunting, gathering, fishing, cultivation, wood-carving, metallurgy. If certain forms of knowledge were specialised, controlled and monopolised by a small cadre of experts or a secret society hierarchy, other forms of knowledge were conceptualised as an open and unbounded repertoire. This unboundedness made it possible for such forms of knowledge to be widely distributed throughout the society and among many adepts on the basis of *personal capacity or potentiality*.

Indeed, African pre-colonial discourses on the 'human' allowed for personal differentiation or *singularity*. It was believed that certain qualities lived in the individual from his or her birth; which he or she had no need for 'magic' to arouse although there was always the indispensable need for magical rites to conserve these. Personal abilities could be augmented, conserved and actualised within the person, making that person a 'real person', recognised as such by the community. Each individual person's power was itself a composition.

That some of these old tropes might still be at work in current controversies on wealth and property should not be entirely excluded. But that wealth, poverty and property have become essential to the self-understanding of South African society after liberation should also be read against a long history of black dispossession. In the new phase of 'frontier accumulation' made possible by the 1994 negotiated settlement, they have become the new idioms for political and normative arguments about what should be the proper relation of people to things; what should be the proper relation of people to each other with respect to things; how much property is enough for one person and how much is too much; how much enjoyment is justifiable especially for the opulent in an environment where hunger and debasement are all too real for many. It is this tension between what looks like an unstoppable logic of unproductive excess on the one hand and on the other, a logic of scarcity and depletion that is turning wealth and property into dramatic sites of contestation.

Wealth and property also operate as means of regulating access to resources that are scarce for some and plentiful for others. They are the main means by which life chances are assigned to different kinds of persons at a time when pockets of wealth and privilege are proving hard not only to account for and even less so to control, but also hard to subject to some form of accountability and redistribution. Furthermore, as Arjun Appadurai observes, the life of the poor has become a strenuous effort to produce, if not a sense of stability, then something like permanence in the face of the temporariness or volatility of almost all the arrangements of social existence. Indeed, one of the most brutal effects of neo-liberalism in South Africa has been the generalisation and radicalisation of a condition of temporariness for the poor. For many people, the struggle to be alive has taken the form of a struggle against the constant corrosion of the present, both by change and by uncertainty.

In order to reanimate the idea of 'the human' in contemporary South African politics and culture, there is therefore no escape from the need to reflect on the thoroughly political and historical character of wealth and property and the extent to which wealth and property have come to be linked with bodily life. If what distinguishes the South African experiment from other such experiments elsewhere in the world is the attempt to establish a new relationship between law and life while equating democracy and the political itself with the ethical and the just, then we have to ask under what conditions can this project of human mutuality result in a broader and more ethical *commensality*.

Race and difference

Another major challenge to any re-imagination of 'the human' in contemporary conditions is race. South Africa's democracy asserts the equality of all human beings and seeks to derive powers of government from the consent of the governed. Yet, this is a democracy founded on deep and entrenched forms of racial dispossession and inequality inherited from a past of racial brutality. The country's entire modern history is spliced around and fractured by the question of the relationship between its *parts* – whether they should exist alone, *separate*, or whether they should exist *with* other parts, *together*. This dialectic between *with* and *without* played itself out dramatically during the years of apartheid. It is being played out again, in no less dramatic fashion, between *those with and those without property*. The end of apartheid has not resolved the old question of difference. It has simply shifted the terms of the difference and of the dispute. In order to make decisions about issues of distribution and sharing in such a way that the social body does not turn against itself, the new democracy must find an adequate language of claims, liabilities, or debts – a proper language to keep putting forth the demand for justice, compensation, redress, restitution and reparation our history places before us.

To these challenges must be added yet another, represented by the stranger in our midst. In contemporary South Africa, 'undocumented' or 'illegal migrants' are people whose fundamental rights are in jeopardy. They are halfheartedly protected in the confines of the national territory where they reside. Post-apartheid South Africa has inherited a long tradition of a 'politics of separation'. For centuries, this country was ruled according to that principle – to physically separate itself from all kinds of 'other humans'; the refusal to share the same space with these 'other humans' or to live with them.

Worldwide, a global regime of walling is fast contributing to *the manufacturing of entire categories of unwanted people* of which the illegal migrant, the undocumented worker, and more and more the refugee and the asylum seeker, are the prototypes. This global regime is characterised by the differential treatment of individuals, groups or communities with respect to movement or circulation. This differential treatment raises, at a deeper level, questions about the way in which the '*quality of being human*' as such is instituted in a globalised society; the way in which the quality of being human becomes once again categorised and hierarchised so that its selective reproduction can be controlled; so that some human beings can be hunted by the police of certain States and their freedom of circulation subjected to massive controls and restrictions.

The gigantic inequality with regard to the right of circulation and the mobility of persons nowadays constitutes a transnational social relationship in and of itself. It is fuelled by an anthropological crisis of the category of 'the human person' as a 'universal' category. It is also at the roots of new, global forms of racialisation, in the name of security.

The category of the future

The 'human' is another name for the future. In the political history of South Africa, the future has always been the term by which the struggle to produce a meaningful life has been named. What gave the category of the future its power was the hope that we might bring into being – as a concrete social possibility – a radically different temporal experience; that a systemic transformation in the logic of our social life and in the logic of our being-in-common as human beings might happen as a result of historical praxis.

For many, the process of producing life now tends to take the form of a struggle to make it from today to tomorrow, and to cross the boundary from today to tomorrow can no longer be taken for granted. In fact, it has become eminently hazardous, risky. To be alive is to constantly be at risk; to constantly have to take risks because the penalty for not taking risks is to not be able to make it from today to tomorrow. As the possibility of the Event recedes, South Africa is faced with the 'liquid' character both of the present and of the future, their dizziness, their mirage-like qualities, the weakness in our grip on the future.

We should wonder whether there is a direct relationship between the liquidity of the present and the overwhelming feeling of the elusiveness of the future – and therefore the apparent foreclosure of any plausible form of radical politics. In fact, many live as if the present, democracy, the law and the Constitution, had unexpectedly betrayed them. What consequences this feeling of betrayal entails for our imagination of the future is far from having been properly assessed. On the one hand, it manifests itself via the constant re-apparition of the past in almost every single act that aims at bringing a different future into being. On the other hand, it is as if for many people too much has changed and yet not enough has changed. There is a feeling (especially among the poor) that they are now not merely deprived of wealth and power, but even of life possibilities as such. Throughout the entire society, there is a widely shared belief that in order to further one's claims, it might be better and more efficient to resort to violence rather than to invoke the law. This accelerated turn to an *everyday politics of expediency* rather than a demanding, *disciplined politics of principle* is fuelled by the inability to open freedom onto the un-chartered territories of the future.

Many have the feeling that they might never really fulfil their lives; that their lives will always be somewhat truncated; that these lives will never achieve the status of lives that are accounted for, inhabited as they are by a 'ghost'. Beyond the repetition of dead paradigms, any new form of radical politics will have to deal with this ghost in life, the pain of disappointment and the sharp experience of defeat, of palpable powerlessness and dashed hopes.

The period after apartheid is a period of 'reconstruction' and 'redesign'. The challenge ahead is nothing less than the re-foundation of democracy as a community of life. The end of apartheid, just as decolonisation in other parts of Africa, has opened the door to internal partition. It has not entirely resolved the question of difference; of how to make decisions about issues of redistribution and sharing. Yet, the need to experiment with new forms of ethical relations has never been as acute as now. The question this country is therefore facing today as yesterday is under what conditions can South Africa re-imagine democracy not only as a form of human mutuality and freedom, but also as a community of life. In order to confront the ghost in the life of so many, the concepts of 'the human', or of 'humanism', inherited from the West will not suffice. We will have to take seriously the anthropological embeddedness of such terms in long histories of 'the human' as waste.

ENOUGH IS ENOUGH
Recovering humane values

Neville Alexander

A time of multiple crises

In South Africa at the time of writing, we seem to be hovering in an emotional zone between a *fin de siècle* sense of decay and dead ends on the one side, a nd an almost desperate search for signs of millenarian renewal on the other side. We are faced with multiple interconnected crises that, in the mode of the four horsemen of the apocalypse, threaten the entire globe and can only be countered if humanity as a whole finds the mechanisms to cooperate in the interest of our survival on the planet. The most critical and obvious crises are manifest in the impending ecological collapse, the terminal hallucinations of the world capitalist system, which produces both superfluous wealth and an ever-growing army of unemployed, the massively destructive international as well as national civil wars, under the cloak of which the most unspeakable brutalisation and abuse, especially of women and children, are actively encouraged by criminal politicians and 'leaders', the all-pervasive social pathologies linked to the drug cartels, the breakdown of health services for the poor which exacerbates the spread of HIV/AIDS, TB, malaria and so many other preventable diseases. Towering above all of these is an unprecedented moral crisis of the elites across the globe, a crisis that manifests itself physically in the fact of gross inequalities of access to basic resources, including quality education for all.

Whether we take as our point of departure the ecological, the global economic or the worldwide socio-ethical crisis associated with the pathologies I have referred to, it has become an unavoidable obligation on activist scholars, organic intellectuals of the working classes, if you wish, to speak up and to point to the all-too-obvious alternatives to the current world order. Almost daily, one or other Cassandra raises her voice on the issue of the imminent collapse into anarchy and barbarism of the existing order. Recently, for example, the *Cape Argus* published a very relevant article by Vivien Horler on the views of the Chinese scholar, Tu Wei Ming, in which, among other things, he says that "... the world is at a crossroads, with one way leading to irreversible destruction and the disintegration of the world order, the other leading to *a rethinking of what it is to be human*" (my italics) (Horler 2010). In another very illuminating contribution on the ecological disasters that human action in the epoch of capitalism has produced, John Bellamy Foster goes as far as stating the paradoxical view that we are fast reaching the end of the anthropocene, i.e. the era of human beings' domination of the planet. "Human actions are generating environmental changes that threaten the extermination of most species on the planet, along with civilization, and conceivably our own species as well" (Foster 2010).

Our image of the human being today

This subtitle derives from the German *das Menschenbild*. It conjures up immediately all the nuances of the philosophical frame of reference within which one interacts with other human beings. In Africa, we would like to believe that all of us are, for example, at the very least influenced by *ubuntu*, the notion that I am a person through other persons, a very particular way of expressing the universal commonality of the sense of fellow feeling all of us have when particular personal or social contradictions do not supervene.

It is, therefore, of some interest to note that the somatic projection of the human being, the human body, is itself changing as the result of all kinds of transplants, implants and other medical interventions. In a recent article in *Le monde diplomatique* by Mateo Cueva, the author foresees, perhaps somewhat melodramatically, with reference to the dangers and possible unintended consequences of nanotechnology, a Frankenstein future as a real possibility. His view is that great danger lurks in the intersection of nanotechnologies, genetics and robotics and he refers, among other things, to the fact that "... a report by UNESCO suggests that, in the long term, nanomedicine could allow people to modify themselves so much it would no longer be possible to talk about 'human beings' new age would dawn of 'posthumans' with enhanced physical and intellectual attributes living alongside ordinary second-class humans, marginalized by their own humanity ..." (Cueva 2009).

These seemingly far-fetched thoughts lead me to recount the well known story about the five most influential Jewish philosophers in history, all of whom allegedly based their understanding of the 'essence' of the human being on a particular organ of the body (in descending order). In the version of this parabolic story as told to me, Moses believed that the brain is the most important part of the body, a view that led him to propagate the message of monotheism. Jesus, the second of the five philosophers, believed that the heart is determining; hence his injunction to "love thy neighbour as thyself". Karl Marx, as everyone knows, proclaimed the doctrine of the stomach: in Brecht's phrase, "first comes the belly, then morality". Freud, however, took things right down to the genitalia and thought we could understand ourselves best by interpreting our dreams, until Einstein made the quantum leap and declared that it is all "relative".

This humorous story has an obvious point in the present context, i.e. reductionism of any kind is a trap that will not let us get to a proper understanding of 'the essence' of being human; indeed, the search for 'essences' is a futile endeavour since, in Hegel's words, "the truth is the whole" and, as I see it, in spite of the mega-enlargement of our brains through ICTs, there is no way that we will ever get to encompass "the whole". Our search is bound to be asymptotic in character and it is precisely this fact that sustains our humanity, i.e. our creativity, our imagination and our refusal to be satisfied with anything 'given'.

Enough is as good as a feast

These thoughts should obviously be explored further and they remain a challenge to all who are concerned about the human condition in the 21st century. However, I want to get to the immediate purpose of my contribution to this volume. As my point of departure, I take Marx and Engels's deceptively simple statement in *The German Ideology* that "[...] in general, people cannot be liberated as long as they are unable to obtain food and drink, housing and clothing in adequate quality and quantity" (Marx & Engels 1976:38). As will become clear presently, the operative word in this quotation is 'adequate'.

Before I elaborate on this, however, it is necessary to clarify a few other things. To begin with, the sincere, indeed the naïve, belief in the values of freedom, equality, solidarity and democracy, which drove all of us involved in the struggle for national liberation in South Africa especially in the decade of the 1980s, has been systematically eroded by the irruption of the narcissistic, dog-eat-dog virus that is spreading across the globe in the current era of the hegemony of neo-liberal capitalism. The critical question we are faced with as social activists is what we can and should do to change the situation towards one where other, more humane values will prevail. There are probably as many answers to this question as there are activists. However, we have, in philosophical terms, to navigate carefully between the Scylla of voluntarism and the Charybdis of political paralysis. Today, we would deal with the question in terms of the relationship between structure and agency. In simpler terms, the question is whether, and if so, how it is possible in the era of neo-liberal barbarism to implant a different set of values among especially the younger people in South Africa and elsewhere, in spite of the many structural constraints that determine their individual existential projects and the massive bombardment of negative and self-destructive ethical messages emanating from the media and other ideological state and non-state apparatuses. It is clear, certainly to me, that this is the challenge that faces all thinking South Africans, and people on the Left specifically, if we are to have any hope of turning our society to head once again in a direction that can lead to the post-apartheid and even post-capitalist situation we had envisaged before 1996, more or less.

We know, of course, that it is a combination of ideas, organisation and political-economic developments at the macro-level that brings about fundamental social shifts at any given time and place. It would, therefore, be a mistake to think that by harking back to a concept such as psychological liberation, I want to suggest that we focus all our energies on the moral education of the youth, as important as that activity is. Marx and Engels, incidentally, in the same paragraph I cited above, state that "'Liberation' is a historical and not a mental act", something which the Black Consciousness generation knew only too well. The real question behind these reflections is how we can tap back into the power that actually exists in many different social spaces and instantiations but which we have made ourselves believe is vested only in and, indeed, *belongs to*, 'the government'. If the Black Consciousness Movement and other movements, especially in the 1970s and 1980s, taught us anything, it is that we always have access to power, as long as we know how it is distributed.

The Biko generation inculcated positive values of self-respect, self-esteem and self-consciousness into the young people at schools and at higher education institutions as well as older people in communities and in workplaces. They did so because they understood that the slave mentality is the proximate source of the sense of disempowerment, despair and political apathy that keeps the oppressed in thrall. Above all, they understood intuitively that power is not simply the control of armed force, legitimate or otherwise. Hence, they undertook community development programmes and mobilised people at the grassroots in order that they might survive in the menacing environments of apartheid South Africa. Under the banner of the slogan *You are your own liberators*! the Black Community Programmes empowered whole communities across the country. Together with the evolving modern labour movement inside the country, it was this war of position that eventually put an end to the apparently linear curve on which the apartheid regime thought itself to be proceeding ever upwards. There is no doubt, of course, that the struggle against racial oppression in all its reprehensible forms compelled everyone to focus on the overriding objective of throwing off the yoke of racism. The mistake that many made was to assume that the end of apartheid would bring about the end of class exploitation which, in South Africa because of the peculiar historical dynamics, continues to perpetuate racial inequality.

What does the picture look like today? Let me begin to answer this question by referring to the fact that when Evo Morales became President of Bolivia a few years ago, one of his first official acts was to get a law passed that reduced his presidential salary by 57%. In post-apartheid South Africa, the very opposite occurred. The recommendations of the Melamet Commission of 1994 and of the subsequent annual increases recommended by the Independent Commission for the Remuneration of Public Office Bearers, based on the principles of remuneration of the apartheid dispensation, were accepted without much soul searching among the new elite. This, in my view, was the first sign that we were headed in the wrong direction. It sent entirely the wrong message to the youth of a poor, 'third-world' country, South Africa, to the effect that successful black people are people who earn in these brackets and who own fancy cars and houses. The role model effect of this kind of lifestyle and value system which, today, 15 years later, has become the accepted thing, will take many years and many alternative models of success to turn around. I cite the effect of the acceptance of the salary packages recommended by the Melamet Commission in its different instantiations as the first of a series of lifestyle signposts for the youth. Add to this the fact that during the struggle against the apartheid regime, everyone, including your 'Comtsotsi', was seen to be and treated as an equal, whereas after 1994, there was this sudden and very visible divide between those who were deemed to have been 'successful', on the one side, and the Great Unwashed, on the other side, the veritable underclass, victims of apartheid before 1996 and of neo-liberalism thereafter. One does not need any special analytical powers to work out the socio-psychological results of this situation. The thousands of 'service delivery protests' – a euphemism for localised mini-uprisings – the vandalism that accompanies them as well as 'ordinary' crimes such as hijackings, cash heists, kidnappings, armed robberies, etc.: all of these horrendous manifestations of barbarism induced by the logic of capitalism in the 21st century, are payback acts of entitlement. "If you who, yesterday, were in the trenches with us or with our parents can now drive around in a Mercedes Benz or a BMW, live in a mansion or even a palace in the leafy suburbs, and generally live it up, why should I continue to be mired in poverty and filth in so-called informal settlements with pit latrines, no garbage removal and no proper educational and health facilities"? This is the logic that is playing itself out on the streets of South Africa. The simple fact is that if young people in the townships and in the rural areas are unemployed, hungry, frustrated and angry, they will, under these circumstances, resort to theft and even murder in order to live like those few others who, by grace of birth or because of political connections and patronage, belong to the new elite. Given the retreat of all the moral and political censors that kept things 'looking good' during the period after 1945, one can hardly 'blame' this youth for behaving in such a reactionary manner. Drugs and Americanised TV are increasingly added to this lethal syndrome of social pathologies.

There have been many more or less sophisticated attempts at explaining the sociology of the current disaster and it is unnecessary to add another such attempt to this list. What is clear, however, is that if we fail to address the question of values with even a modicum of success, we will inevitably arrive at the edge of the abyss, pushed there by this logic of capitalism. The intelligentsia in particular have a moral obligation to help the entire nation to find and accept the alternative. Today, when we are witnessing the collapse of the global financial system which reflects the terminal condition of the system of capitalism as a whole, the Thatcherite mantra: *There is no alternative*, which in any case never had any basis in fact, is no more and no less than an expression of social dementia and denialism of the most self-destructive kind. For, not only are there alternatives, they are staring us in the face if we have the boldness and the imagination to explore them.

How do we re-establish a culture of positive values, one that is socially critical but not destructive in its modalities? What is the foundational value that should inform everything else we believe in and do? I am here referring to the kind of value system that can inspire an entire generation of young people to take on to themselves the task and to forge the instruments of social mobilisation on a large scale and for decades, rather than just a few years, knowing full well that the realisation of their 'dream' will change everything from the bottom up and shape social structures and processes that will be very different in form and effect from those of the neo-liberal imperialist agencies that now disfigure their lives and ruin our societies. In the previous dispensation, anti-racism and anti-apartheid for most, as well as anti-capitalism for some, were such a set of beliefs that not only fostered solidarity and unity but also charged the imagination of young people with a vision of the 'non-racial, non-sexist and democratic' alternative to apartheid.

The answer is to be found in, among other places, the ecological economics of scholars such as André Gorz (Gorz 1987), whose work has been foundational in this area. It has taken global climatic disasters and the collapse of the tyrannical political structures in Africa, Latin America, Asia, Eastern Europe and elsewhere to make us understand the full significance of the present stage of bourgeois rule. Today, we know that political diversity is as important for a humane society as are bio- and cultural diversity. For some years now, it has dawned on me that a humanism of the 21st century will have to be based on what Gorz calls the *principle of sufficiency* which, for the sake of a broader understanding of what this concept entails, I have transliterated as *Enough is as good as a feast*.[1] It should be clear, however, that I am not at all suggesting that the approach outlined here is directly related to the wider concerns of Gorz's work.

Besides other considerations, against the background of the ecological imperative, it ought to be obvious that if the structures and processes of modern industrial societies were informed and shaped by this view of life, most of the currently existing social modalities, human desires, dispositions and activities in most contemporary states would forthwith become antiquated and counter-productive. The hegemony of the world view that proclaims, among many other things, that 'more is better', that in terms of the much-vaunted 'intellectual property rights', I deserve all the fruits of what I have initiated, and that the ideal is to be the 'world champion' in all spheres of life: in short, that the good life is to be had by competing and fighting against other human beings who, in the extreme case, have to be dehumanised so that I am not constrained by any fellow-feeling from killing them.

---

1 This is not an arbitrary act on my part; Gorz in fact derives the principle from the same pre-industrial period in which this aphorism originated.

Through class struggle: from *uhuru* to *ubuntu*

I can do no more here than to suggest some of the consequences of applying the principle of sufficiency as the major moral force shaping post-apartheid South Africa. To begin with, in the domain of education, where the state and other public institutions can legitimately intervene, the content, orientation and delivery of the curriculum at all levels of the system would be changed fundamentally. The psychological, pedagogical, ideological and emotional revolution implied by an approach that does *not* glorify individual or group domination while allowing for the full development and flowering of the potential inherent in each and every human being can be imagined and extrapolated very easily. Individual brilliance expressed and deployed on behalf and for the benefit of democratically legitimated groups at different levels of society will continue to be one of the drivers of all social progress, including economic development. In the domain of the media and especially advertising, we would be rid of the brutalities and socially disreputable messages which subject us to the domination of capital. Adverts like one that is currently popular in South Africa which claims that everyone wants to be a 'winner' and in the 'first team', rather than a 'deputy-chairperson' or a 'benchwarmer' – or words to that effect – would become as absurd and counter-productive as they are from the point of view of a more humane social order. The glorification of the ostentatious consumption and high life of so-called celebrities in politics, culture, sport and even religion would cease to be the supposedly inspiring models of 'the good life' that they are marketed as being in programmes such as *Top Billing* and others. All domains of life would be affected in the most profound possible way.

Is this too drab and boring a vision to inspire our young people? I have no doubt that some will think so. I believe, however, that the challenge of constructing a new, humane order that is based on respect for and valuing of others will have the very opposite effect on the youth of South Africa. Artists, designers, architects, urban planners, in fact all creative individuals and agencies will be faced with the challenge of finding the optimal ways of expressing and realising the entire range of possibilities in every domain of life. This will be the terrain of competition, not for individual glory and unequal reward but precisely for the common good, the old-fashioned commonwealth!

How do we begin to initiate and incrementally realise this vision and this set of values? Besides the ongoing political and economic class struggles, in which we are willy-nilly involved and by means of which we attempt to create and to consolidate more democratic space in the short to medium term, we have to go back to the community development tasks that the BCM initiated so successfully, if not always sustainably, owing to the ravages of the apartheid system. We have to rebuild our communities and our neighbourhoods by means of establishing, as far as possible on a voluntary basis, all manner of community projects which bring visible short-term benefit to the people and which initiate at the same time the trajectories of fundamental social transformation, which I have been referring to. These could range from relatively simple programmes such as keeping the streets and the public toilets clean, preferably in liaison with the local authority, whether or not it is 'delivering' at this level, to more complex programmes such as bulk buying clubs, community reading clubs, enrichment programmes for students preparing for exams, teachers' resource groups at local level, and, of course, sports activities on a more convivial basis. It is important that I stress that, wherever possible, the relevant democratic authority should be asked to support the initiative. On the other hand, the community and its community-based organisations must remain in control of what they are doing. This is the difference between South Africa today and South Africa yesterday. As long as, and to the extent that, we have a democratic system, there is no reason why any of these programmes have to be initiated as anti-government initiatives. Any representative democratic government would welcome and vigorously support such initiatives, since they are pro-people and, in the current context, pro-poor initiatives.

There are already many of these initiatives and programmes in existence. They will, if they are conducted with integrity and not simply for party-political gain, inevitably gravitate towards one another, converge and network. In this way, the fabric of civil society non-government organisations that was the real matrix of the anti-apartheid movement will be refreshed and we will once again have that sense of a safety net of communities inspired by the spirit and the real practices of *ubuntu* that saved so many of us from being destroyed by the racist system. Today, the struggle is much more obviously being conducted as a class struggle against exploitation and unconscionable as well as totally unnecessary and unjustifiable social inequality, manifest in the miserable lives of the vast majority and the vulgar parading of wealth and comfort of the few.

I have kept this statement deliberately simple and direct. It would have been easier for me to have formulated yet another analysis of 'the global crisis of the capitalist system' but there are more than enough of these, I think. Here, too, enough is as good as a feast. It may suffice for the moment, if we began a national discussion on the subject: *what is 'enough' in post-apartheid South Africa and in what kind of society can this be realised?* It has been more difficult and challenging for me to return to the source, to reflect on the first principles that motivate us in our struggle for a humane world order, one where every child and every person has more than an outside chance of fulfilling his or her human potential. Today, we have to formulate these principles in a new language, one that will find readier access among the youth, to whom, as we say so beautifully but so ineffectually, the future belongs.

Reference List

Cueva M. 2009. Nanotechnology: Towards a new age of 'posthumans'. *Le monde diplomatique*. December.

Foster JB. 2010. Ecological revolution? http://sociologias-com.blogspot.com/2010/01why-ecological-revolution.html

Gorz A. 1987. *Ecology as Politics*. London: Pluto Press.

— 1989. *Critique of Economic Reason*. London & New York: Verso.

Horler V. 2010. The quest for a common humanity. *Cape Argus*. 9 October.

Marx K & Engels F. 1976. *Collected Works, Vol. 5 Marx and Engels 1845-1847*. London: Lawrence and Wishart.

HUMANE JUSTICE AND THE CHALLENGES OF LOCALITY

William Schweiker

What follows are ruminations on justice from the perspective of a particular sort of Christian humanist. My topic is humane justice rather than (say) divine or perfect justice. In brief, this means that I understand my Christian convictions as a way to respect and enhance the integrity of life and thus an affirmation of the special responsibility human beings bear for social peace and justice. I want us to consider the question of justice from this perspective.

One often finds in religious and philosophical thinking either the attempt to establish abstract principles of justice grounded in reason, discourse, or the social contract, or, conversely, appeals to specific religious or cultural authorities as the standard of justice. While important, these strategies usually fail to achieve consensus and often elide the struggle for humane forms of justice. My strategy departs from these options. I seek to isolate certain goods and norms implicit within the structure of lived reality, the localities of life as I will call them. Justice, we can say, is the central good of social life. An unjust society is failing morally: it thwarts human flourishing and dignity, endangers its neighbours, and exploits its natural environment and resources.

But what are the components of justice, especially in societies as diverse as South Africa? Paying attention to the localities of life help us to grasp the components of justice and thereby help people labour for a good social order. I want to isolate three such 'localities' (social, historical, natural) and show how reflection on these enables us to grasp features of a conception of justice needed for the reconstruction of common life. The question of whether or not people will orient their social lives by a conception of justice is one that thought alone cannot answer.

Social locality

The first challenge to a just society is about the social locality of human life, that is, the fact that we live in particular places and within distinctive sets of relationships and communities. The focus of this book is being human "in" South Africa and so reflection arises out of and is meant to contribute to a specific social locality. That location is the wonderful and yet troubling, the complex and yet too often divided, reality of this nation with its diverse cultures, languages and, of course, the staggering beauty of its land, seas and creaturely life as well as grinding poverty and horrific disease.

I have been lucky to visit South Africa a few times, most recently in July 2009 for a meeting at STIAS just as the stadiums were being built for the World Cup. Those stadiums became concert halls for vuvuzelas and also venues for human struggle and excellence. My son, Paul, who travelled with me, and I would take walks under the African sky, past guinea fowl and along streets where houses and schools were ringed by wire fences. John de Gruchy was kind enough to invite us to his home and to visit the community of which he is a member. The deep piety, the constant outreach and the faithfulness of the community stood like the surrounding mountains against counter-forces – those during the apartheid times and those which still beset human life.

However, that is the first challenge: to reflect from within this social locality about current life in South Africa is something I cannot properly do. I am not African; I have never lived for an extended period here; I do not speak one of the indigenous languages. More pointedly, I am part of the so-called First World (and in that designation the shameful need to order peoples and lands) and even the pinnacle of that world, namely the USA. The legacy of 'Western' colonialism, the spread of the global market system and the historic reality of slavery scar my land and our world. The current military might and conflicts that beset our age are factors this nation and my nation experience in powerfully different ways. To be human "in" South Africa must mean, if it is to mean anything at all, the attempt to live and to think about the value of individual and social life beyond patterns of Western thought and value. It is to think deeply within the values, aspirations and forces in South Africa for the sake of current social life.

My only recourse in response to the challenge of 'social locality' is to accept the gift of tolerance. Tolerance is justice without vindictiveness. 'Tolerant justice' acknowledges the contextual nature of human life and the realisation that some ideas, some values, arising out of the context of so-called Western history are not germane to being human "in" South Africa. It is also to grant that 'Western' forces have been present here for a very long time and with a profoundly ambiguous legacy. Tolerance is that part of justice which enables the inclusion of others in a shared social project in response to diversity, brokenness and legacies of violence within social life. One task now facing diverse and complex societies – here and elsewhere – is to identify within their social life and memory, resources both to acknowledge the deeply 'located' nature of social existence and so to work to respect and to enhance local forms of social life, while also developing habits and policies of tolerance and respect in the quest for social justice. Without acknowledging the fact of social locality, tolerance and justice are abstract ideals; without an abiding commitment to form just and tolerant communities, human localities harden into battle lines. Tolerance without social locality is empty; social locality without tolerance becomes violent.

Of course, there are limits on tolerance. Some actions and policies are morally intolerable and must be resisted. But those cases cannot circumvent the demand for respect and tolerance. To think about being human "in" South Africa today, means, then, addressing the challenge of justice and how it can be lived in ways that further cultures of respect and tolerance.

Historical locality

Now it happens that 'humanists', and I am one, have always believed that tolerance, properly understood, is a virtue and not a failure. This commitment flows from a deep understanding of human fallibility and limitation. But the commitment to tolerance poses the next challenge to these reflections signalled by a central theme of this book. We are asked to reflect on being human in South Africa "today" and thereby the historical locality of life. Just like social locality, the fact of historical locality challenges the possibility of affirming human commonalities, our being human.

The conviction that there is a basic 'human' commonality is partly indebted to Western civilisation, broadly defined. Yet, how does one counter the historic betrayal of humanistic values by those powers, colonial and otherwise, that have brutalised the African continent? Relatedly, humanistic thinkers have traditionally asserted that human beings are 'makers of history' and thus history is not fully understandable when it is reduced to the working of massive social processes, or, religiously speaking, to divine action or some religious structure (e.g. Predestination; Karma). But human beings have 'made history' with chains, rape camps, war and brutal regimes. Today non-human and supra-personal forces (economics, political orders, media, etc.) are in fact shaping the structure of lived reality – often in dangerous and life-threatening ways – and are thus historical forces. How can and ought we to conceive of human beings as historical agents?

The idea and reality of *ubuntu* provides some hints for reflection to that question. *Ubuntu*, if I understand it correctly, is a form of self-assurance that arises from affirming oneself as part of a larger community and thus also the awareness that the demeaning and destroying of anyone in that community is a loss for one's own being. If a possible response to the reality of social locality was an attitude of respect for and enhancement of specific forms of social life infused with abiding tolerance, then the challenge of 'historical locality' demands a related but different response found in the meanings of *ubuntu*. How is human commonality to be thought of?

Typically Western thinkers have spoken about rationality or the free will or bonds of sympathy to get at what human beings share. Christian thinkers, for their part, often appeal to the belief that human beings are created in the image of God. Perhaps more than ever, we need, given the reality of the injustices of history, to develop an ethos of genuine 'humility' in thinking about justice, and in the root sense of the term. Humility comes from 'humus', the earth and human beings as creatures of the earth. To be human is to be mortal, to bear the remembrance of death in one's being, and yet also to hope and dream that the innocent will no longer suffer. This shifts the idea of human commonality from reason, will, or feeling and even from claims about the human as the image of God. Human commonality is of the earth and yet also the capacity to hope. We are creatures that bridge dust and dreams, finitude and infinite desire. It has rightly been said that religious consciousness is the awareness both that we are finite, imperfect, and yet also an awareness of some perfection, something infinite. This dual awareness is basic to our humanity. The flight from finitude too often seen in religious and secular forms is just as destructive of human life as reducing human life to the finite, the death-bound.

Humility, I am suggesting, is the expression of our shared 'being human' which both affirms finite life (dust) and yet also recognises perfection beyond our bounds for which we seek (dreams). Genuine humility is what backs the courage to face historical injustice with the demand of restorative justice while always remembering that justice was made for human beings and not human beings for justice. Retribution for unjust actions unmoored from restorative justice is neither humane nor good. Justice must build up and guide actions towards a more perfect future ever mindful of proper humility that bespeaks our shared mortal condition.

Natural locality

The two challenges of human locality noted, one about history and the other about social life, are deeply connected to a third, 'natural locality'. This form of human locality is about the meaning and worth of human existence and our relation to and interdependence with the rest of the living world. In our time, not only are natural environments endangered, but so, too, the idea that there is a shared and stable human 'nature'. Many speak of a 'post-human' future and the 'end of nature' meaning that the limits inscribed in an entity's 'nature' have been transgressed by the advance of technological powers. This poses the question about the worth of existence. Is the worth of a human being derived from membership in some (racial, tribal, religious, political, ethnic) community? Is it something intrinsic to the nature of being a member of this species – say, the capacity for language or the possession of 'reason'? Does human value depend on a relation to some divine reality, a God, or some sacred truth? Is our worth something we make?

Pressed to its extreme, too much humanism endorses a thoroughgoing anthropocentrism wherein human beings and humans alone have intrinsic worth. In this perspective, other forms of life are accorded worth in terms of instrumental value to human flourishing. Further, it seems that humanism must, per definition, be atheistic or 'secularist' since no being or reality, including a deity, can claim supremacy over human worth. Yet, in an age of environmental endangerment and also increasing religious sensibility, strident and otherwise, one must conceive of human worth in relation to other forms of life and in the terms of specific religions. While insisting on a humanistic outlook, there is also a conception of worth with and for other forms of life inscribed in the structures of lived reality. It is related to humane responsibility for the integrity of life. A deep challenge people face is the conception of life's worth at the root of every appeal to justice.

I have intimated that *ubuntu* connects to other ideas and beliefs about tolerance and humility necessary to sustain human life and the struggle for justice in South Africa today, or, for that matter, anywhere on this planet. And to be sure, *ubuntu*, again if I understand rightly, means that to be human is to be deeply connected to other forms of life. Yet, the pressing challenge is how to conceive of that 'connection' and also, as indicated, how it relates to the worth of a human being. The connection among forms of life and also human worth can be conceived in social terms – and so, I am who I am in connection with a specific community in time and space. That conception returns to social locality and would limit justice to respect and tolerance. Perhaps we could conceive of the 'connection' and human worth historically insofar as memory, lineage and tradition fashion and sustain human identities, for good and for ill. This idea would express historical locality, as I have called it, but focus justice on humility in the face of finitude and hope. The connection might be conceived 'ontologically', that is, in terms of something about the 'being' of humans that designates how we are bound together with other creatures but also have distinct worth. Yet, in that case, the question is left open about how we can and ought to orient human life. Finally, one might think about the connection among peoples and other forms of life as well as human value in distinctly religious terms, say, that we are all created by God, or that human beings are the vice-regents of Allah, or that, as Buddhists and Hindus in South Africa might say, we are beings that suffer and therefore need compassion. The question then arises, must we adopt one specific religious outlook in order to affirm the deep connections among forms of life and also the dignity and worth of human beings? Is it realistic to believe that one religion can obtain for every human society?

Each of these ways of conceiving the connections among people and other forms of life have been and are being used to speak to current social questions. My strategy in these reflections has been to isolate within the challenges posed by the fact of locality elements for humane justice: tolerance rather than strident divisions and humility rather than hardened ethnocentrism or anthropocentricism in a conception of justice. I have tried to suggest that from within my own historical and social context, these ideas are analogous to what I understand to be designated by *ubuntu*. Further, the distinctive worth of being human, I suggest, is manifest, comes to light, when we undertake responsibility with and for others. Justice takes humane form in the responsible use of power. A failure of responsibility is in some deep sense a betrayal of humanity and human worth.

To be human in South Africa today – or, for that matter, anywhere on this planet – must mean assuming the task of respecting and enhancing the integrity of life. This responsibility requires careful and diligent reflection on the imbalances of power so that human life might be enriched and planetary life sustained. Such reflection and diligence can only take some place in some time among some particular people. Reconstructing the social order in South Africa in ways marked by tolerance, humility and responsibility as aspects of a humane conception of justice is related to but different from the labour I must assume in my place and time to reconstruct the social order. Yet, it is hoped that the task of social reconstruction "in South Africa today" is one that affirms and discloses our shared humanity.

A new universalism?

My task has been to outline – and only to outline – a humane account of justice for the reconstruction of social life around *tolerance* in the face of diversity, *humility* as a response to our finitude and also hope, and *responsibility* as the way to live out the meaning and worth of being human with and for others. Justice can take various forms (retributive, distributive, restorative, etc.) and some speak of divine or perfect justice, but whatever form it takes, justice, humanely conceived, must entail respect for and the enhancement of the integrity of life marked by tolerance, humility and responsibility. And we now reach an ironic insight. This insight is dependent neither on abstract principles nor on the authority of a specific religious or cultural tradition. It arises from close attention to features of locality and the vulnerabilities of lived reality. While this moral outlook – like every set of moral convictions – can only be lived locally, its meaning and validity must be trans-local. The peoples of the world are too intertwined, too connected and too vulnerable to the works of wanton power and legacies of oppression to imagine that what one means by tolerance, humility, or responsibility – and so justice itself – is defined only by our local communities, traditions and practices. Nor can the truth of this ethics be grounded in local communities and traditions because what we seek is a just reconstruction of the (global) social order in ways that sustain life and enhance human flourishing.

In our age, we need a trans-local, or global ethics for the integrity of life. This trans-locality cannot be the old universalism of Western Values imposed on others as if those values were obviously True and Real. It cannot be the old universalism built on colonial, economic, or missionary power: Roman, Ottoman, European, Christian, Muslim, American, Global Markets, etc. Rather this trans-local or global ethics is a new universalism that roots the claim of responsibility in the awareness of the vulnerability of human and non-human life to unjust destruction. The claim to responsibility in our world today, the call for people to the task of being human, is sensed in the vulnerabilities of life that come to expression in respect and tolerance, humility and responsibility. An urgent task is also to fashion communities of *perceptiveness*. This means working to overcome forces in local communities, specific histories, and a shared world that deaden peoples' abilities to sense the claim of vulnerable life as the origin of justice that is also joy in life.

Arguably the most profound moral crisis in societies is a crisis of human perception: people do not see or sense the claims to justice that arise within the vulnerabilities of lived reality. Moral awareness and perception are endangered by cultural, religious, ethnic and technological forms which deaden and restrict that awareness. We must, accordingly, take the time to attend to the vulnerabilities of life and so, too, the roots of tolerance, humility and responsibility. People must learn to live freely within religious, cultural, ethnic and racial heritages in ways that enable them to use those resources to sharpen and to enliven moral awareness and perception. Oddly enough, we must become consciously responsible for the forces that are shaping human consciousness. Here, I believe, religious resources are crucial to a humane form of justice. Christian convictions about care for the outcast, the poor and the widow, the demands of neighbour love and even love of enemy can be used to tutor moral perception in ways that enable people to perceive the claims of justice on their own lives. The same is true of the resources of other religious communities in South Africa and around the world today. But those resources are themselves defined and determined in light of the claims of justice and the integrity of life.

To put the matter otherwise, what we mean by justice today as the central social good must be marked by the acknowledgement of human difference tempered by tolerance, human finitude with humility, human power lived responsibly, and human worth sensed and recognised in its vulnerability. These are, I suggest, the components of justice for the reconstruction of social life today and tomorrow if we are committed to forging a humane future in the various localities of our lives. That commitment, one must admit, lies at both the origin and the end of the work of social transformation. To be human in our world today is to sense the claim to justice and joy in life as the meaning of one's humanity.

Reference List

Appiah KA. 2007. *Cosmopolitanism: Ethics in a World of Strangers*. New York: W.W. Norton.

Behabib S. 2002. *The Claims of Culture: Equality and Diversity in the Global Era*. Princeton: Princeton University Press.

Browning DS. 2010. *Reviving Christian Humanism: The New Conversation on Spirituality, Theology and Psychology*. Philadelphia: Fortress Press.

De Gruchy J. 2006. *Confessions of a Christian Humanist*. Minneapolis: Fortress Press.

Klemm DE & Schweiker W. 2008. *Religion and the Human Future: An Essay on Theological Humanism*. Oxford: Wiley-Blackwell.

Nussbaum M. 2000. *Sex and Social Justice*. Oxford: Oxford University Press.

Ricoeur P. 2003. *The Just*. Chicago: Chicago University Press.

Said E. 2004. *Humanism and Democratic Crisis*. New York: Columbia University Press.

Schweiker W. 2010. *Dust That Breathes: Christian Faith and the New Humanism*. Oxford: Wiley-Blackwell.

CONSTITUTIONAL LAW AND HUMAN DIGNITY

Laurie Ackermann

The modern constitutional law concept of inherent human dignity or human worth – particularly as developed in Germany and South Africa – makes an important contribution to understanding what it means to be human in South Africa today. Conversely, an enquiry into what it means to be human in South Africa today will stimulate and guide constitutional law development in this area.

The concept of human dignity

The concept of human worth (dignity) does not belong to the 'vocabulary' of the classic human rights declarations and catalogues of rights prior to World War II. It is only afterwards that it features, not merely as an appended right, but as a core right, in the founding documents of the United Nations; in the Charter and in the 1948 Universal Declaration of Human Rights. Soon after, it found its way into the first German *Länder* (State) Constitutions and, in 1949, into the *Grundgesetz or* German Basic Law (GBL). Much later, it was embodied in the 1994 South African Interim Constitution and the 1996 Constitution.

The preamble to the 1948 Universal Declaration powerfully proclaims that the "inherent dignity" and the equality of "all members of the human family" belong to those values and human rights that constitute "the foundation of freedom, justice and peace in the world"; and whose contemptuous disregard has "resulted in barbarous acts which have outraged the conscience of mankind". We ought all to respond to the Declaration's appeal for the mandatory protection of these rights by the rule of law – which includes the concept of the constitutional state if humans are not "to be compelled to have recourse, as a last resort, to rebellion against tyranny and oppression". Human societies throughout the world have, in the more than sixty years since the Universal Declaration, failed lamentably to turn this appeal into a reality. A greater global understanding of and a real commitment to human dignity (worth) will contribute to eliminating 'barbarous acts which ... outrag[e] the conscience of mankind'. It will also, one hopes, counteract the negative influence of culture when it serves in any community to undermine human dignity. Hence the importance of continuously re-examining the questions of what it means to be human.

Human dignity in law

The constitutional provisions proclaiming and entrenching human dignity in the German Basic Law (GBL) and the 1996 South African Constitution are remarkably similar. Art. 1(1) GBL provides:

> Human dignity is inviolable. To respect and protect it is the duty of all state authority.

Section 10 of the SA Constitution is to the following effect:

> Everyone has inherent dignity and the right to have their dignity respected and protected.

In both, human dignity is a supra-constitutional categorical imperative. The above Constitutions do not create or confer human dignity. It already exists and both Constitutions make it the duty of all state authority to '*respect*' and '*protect*' it.[1] The value and the right of human dignity are given special protection by these Constitutions. Under the GBL no amendment of Art.1(1) which deals with the inviolability of human dignity, is possible.[2] In South Africa, human dignity is, according to section 1 of the Constitution, one of the values on which the South African state is founded. This provision enjoys the highest protection under the Constitution, requiring, inter alia, a 75% majority of the National Assembly to be amended.

Since 1951 we have had sixty years of human worth (dignity) jurisprudence from the German Federal Constitutional Court and extensive commentaries on it. The depth of such scholarship is remarkable and a great source of knowledge and inspiration

---

1 Unlike the GBL, Section 10 of the SA Constitution does not itself place this obligation on all state authority, but section 7(2) does, providing that the 'state must respect, protect, promote and fulfil the rights in the Bill of Rights', while section 8(1) provides that the 'Bill of Rights ... binds the legislature, the executive, the judiciary and all organs of state'.

2 Art. 79(3) GBL.

for anyone interested in the protection of human dignity. In the seventeen years of its existence the South African Constitutional Court has drawn, both directly and indirectly, on such scholarship. By comparison the protection of human dignity is not expressly provided for in the Constitution of the United States of America. More surprisingly, since it came into existence as late as 1982, the Canadian Charter of Rights and Freedoms also does not have an express provision guaranteeing human dignity.

There is debate about human dignity in Germany, but all critique is premised on the acceptance that human dignity is a core right and concept of the GBL and that its essential components have, in broad terms, been well established. What the precise parameters of human dignity are, is a matter of ongoing enquiry. The real debate concerns the outer limits of human dignity – when precisely does human dignity start and end, and whether it should, quite literally, be an absolute right and subject to no limitation whatsoever. There are of course critics, most often from the Anglo-Saxon legal systems, who – without reference to German jurisprudence – challenge (or are at the very least highly skeptical of) the basic value and use of human dignity as a legal concept (Botha 2009:172, fn. 4 & 5; Easterbrook 1990:29; Berger 1992:134; Davis 1999:143).

I have previously suggested (Ackermann 2006:602), a preliminary description of the 'human dignity (worth) of each and every person' as:

> ... the capacity for and the right to respect as a human being that arise from all those aspects of the human personality that flow from human intellectual and moral capacity; which in turn separate humans from the impersonality of nature, enables them to exercise their own judgment, to have self-awareness and a sense of self-worth, to exercise self-determination, to shape themselves and nature, to develop their personalities and to strive for self-fulfilment in their lives.

This description has been closely modelled on the formulation by Günter Dürig (Dürig 1956:125), widely accepted in Germany as the 'classic' formulation of human dignity. I have somewhat broadened Dürig's exposition by introducing the *desire for self-fulfilment*, and by adding the individual's *own sense of self-worth*, as components of human personality and dignity. I stress that my formulation is not a definition but merely a preliminary description. It is moreover implicit in such descriptions that humans are also able, in a unique way, and for a variety of unique reasons, to enter into relationships with other human being, and that such relationships are vital for the full blossoming of the human personality.

The concept human dignity, as understood and elaborated by Dürig, and by a considerable body of German scholars and the German courts, has a powerful Kantian basis. Kant's work establishes a universal basis for the fundamental recognition and protection of dignity, particularly through the categorical imperatives, their different formulations and their applications. In the first place Kant regards freedom (independence from being constrained by another's choice), insofar as it can coexist with the freedom of every other in accordance with a general law, as "the ground of the dignity of human nature and of every rational creature" (Gregor 1996:85). In the second place Kant enjoins one so to act "that you use humanity, whether in your own person or in the person of any other, always at the same time as an end, never merely as a means ..." (Gregor 1996:80-81) and states that

> [i]n the kingdom of ends everything has either a *price* or a *dignity*. What has a price can be replaced by something else as its *equivalent*; what on the other hand is raised above all price and therefore admits of no equivalent has a dignity. (Gregor 1996:84)

Kant supplies one of the most powerful rational bases for the constitutional value (and right) of human dignity. The importance of Kant in this regard has been recognised by scholars from different backgrounds. Thus Arieli, writing as an historian on the 1948 Universal Declaration of Human Rights, and considering an underpinning for the principles contained in the Declaration, suggests Kant as a guide

> ... as his philosophy presents a feasible link between a possible metaphysic and secularism which is the existential dimension of modernity and of modern history ... his basic assumption is man's capacity to shape his individual and collective existence according to the highest ideals implied in the concept of the dignity of man and his existential autonomy and freedom. (Arieli 2002:7)

The renewal of the Abrahamic theological concept of human dignity in secular form through the Enlightenment tradition generally, and in Kant's philosophy in particular, is pointedly commented on by Bernard Williams in his celebrated essay "The Idea of Equality" as follows:

> This strain of thought has found many types of religious expression; but in philosophy is to be found in its purest form in Kant ... The ground of the respect owed to each man thus emerges in the Kantian theory as a kind of secular analogue of the Christian conception of the respect owed to all men as equally children of God. Though secular, it is equally metaphysical: in neither case is it anything empirical *about* men that constitutes the ground of equal respect. (Williams 1967:115-116)

Concerning the Christian conception, this is correct as far as it goes. It omits to mention, however, the further basis in Christian theology (as in others) for the innate dignity of human beings – of which Kant's theory is equally a secular analogue – and that is the belief that all humans are created in the image of God.

In seeking to describe human dignity, I deliberately refrain from using the word *definition*, since this conveys the idea of having neatly and comprehensively captured all the essential components of a concept. As German jurisprudence makes plain, the meaning or content of human worth cannot be fully captured at one given moment. Our understanding of human dignity will be extended as our knowledge of the human being increases, and as we view the human being in the context of the development of the modern natural sciences. The human dignity challenges posed by the genetic, embryo, stem-cell and similar branches of the natural sciences, will challenge us continuously to reflect on our understanding of the human being and her protection. Hence the importance of the other contributions to this book in reflecting critically on what it means to be human in South Africa today. It is well recognised that an understanding of human dignity often arises negatively, i.e. by considering instances of its denial, a phenomenon accepted by German scholars (Huber 1996:10; Böckenförde 2006:382).

The South African Constitutional Court and human dignity

The South African Constitutional Court and other courts have, since 1995 proceeded along very much these lines in developing, on a case by case basis, a coherent concept of human dignity. The Court has understood human dignity (worth) in unmistakable (though not always explicit) Kantian terms and has regarded the concepts of *human dignity* and *human worth* as synonymous. It has repeatedly emphasised that human worth is impaired when persons are treated as mere objects. In the case of *Ferreira vs Levin (1)*[3] the following was said with regard to the nature of human dignity and its close relationship with freedom:

> Human dignity cannot be fully valued or respected unless individuals are able to develop their humanity, their "humanness", to the full extent of its potential. Each human being is uniquely talented. Part of the dignity of every human being is the fact and awareness of this uniqueness. An individual's human dignity cannot be fully respected or valued unless the individual is permitted to develop his or her talents optimally. *Human dignity has little value without freedom; for without freedom personal development and fulfilment is not possible. Without freedom human dignity is little more than an abstraction. Freedom and dignity are inseparably linked. To deny people their freedom is to deny them their dignity.* (Emphasis supplied)

In the same case[4] express reference is made to Kant's view that freedom is an essential part of human dignity, as pointed out and quoted above. The South African courts have pointed out that contractual autonomy is part of freedom and also informs human dignity. Individual moral agency has been held to form part of the concept of human worth. The importance of work for the development of the human personality and for human self-fulfilment has been recognised as forming part of one's identity and constitutive of one's dignity. Self-esteem and self-identification have been included in the concept of dignity. A component of human worth (dignity) is the ability to form human relationships, to find personal meaning in such relationships and to determine personal identity in and through such relationships. In fleshing out the concept of human dignity the courts have not seen the individual as an isolated and unencumbered being.

The Constitutional Court in the *Second Certification* case[5] accorded full recognition under the Constitution to the communal nature of human beings (and hence of human dignity) and its protection by means of, *inter alia*, the 'associational individual rights' of the Constitution.[6] The Court defines such *associational individual rights* as 'those

---

3 *Ferreira v Levin NO and Others; Vryenhoek and Others v Powell NO and Others* 1996 (1) SA 984 (CC); 1996 (1) BCLR 1 (CC) par. 49.

4 Id par. 52.

5 *Chairperson of the National Assembly, Ex Parte: In re Certification of the Amended Text of the Constitution of the Republic of South Africa,* 1996 1997 (2) SA 97 (CC); 1997 (1) BCLR 1 (CC).

6 Id par. 22-27.

rights which cannot be fully or properly exercised by individuals otherwise than in association with others of like disposition'.[7]

The African indigenous concept of *ubuntu*, has been proffered as an aid to the proper contextual understanding of the value of dignity under the Constitution and has been referred to in many judgments. Shutte regards *ubuntu* as 'the idea of community, that persons depend on other persons to be persons' (Shutte 2001:10-11). He contends that *ubuntu* is an ethical concept and that 'the understanding and vision of humanity embodied in *ubuntu* is of vital importance to the contemporary world, not just to contemporary South Africa but to all the rest of the nations as well, developed or undeveloped'. *Ubuntu* has been referred to, somewhat cursorily, in a number of Constitutional Court judgments but without mention of any literature on its meaning.

After referring to the maxim or aphorism *umuntu ngumuntu nga bantu (motho ke motho ka batho)*, Ramose states the following:

> Although the English language does not exhaust the meaning of this maxim or aphorism, it may nonetheless be construed to mean that to be a human being is to affirm one's humanity by recognizing the humanity of others and, on that basis, establish humane relations with them. *Ubuntu*, understood as be-ing human (human-ness); a humane, respectful, and polite attitude towards others constitutes the core meaning of this aphorism. (Ramose 2003:231)

In the *Makwanyane* (the death penalty) case[8] Justice Langa himself pointed out that 'references to *ubuntu* have already been made in various texts, but largely without explanation of the concept'. Later, in the same case, after pointing out that the concept of *ubuntu* is not defined in the Constitution, he observes as follows:

> [224] ... It is a culture which places some emphasis on communality and on the interdependence of the members of a community. It recognizes a person's status as a human being, entitled to unconditional respect, dignity, value and acceptance from the members of the community such person happens to be part of. It also entails the converse, however. The person has a corresponding duty to give the same respect, dignity, value and acceptance to each member of that community. More importantly, it regulates the exercise of rights by the emphasis it lays on sharing and co-responsibility and the mutual enjoyment of rights by all ...
>
> [225] An outstanding feature of *ubuntu* in a community sense is the value it puts on life and human dignity. The dominant theme of the culture is that the life of one person is at least as valuable as one's own. Respect for the dignity of every person is integral to this concept ...

I consider that the exploration, elucidation and appropriate application of the ideas inherent in the concept of *ubuntu* are of great importance. There is nothing strange about such incorporation into our common law, or these values being used to inform our Constitution and legislation. Our common law is extremely adaptable, itself being the result (in large measure) of the reception of the Roman Law into Europe, and one of the products of this, in the form of the Roman-Dutch law, being the subject

7 Id par. 24.

8 *S v Makwanyane and Another* 1995 (3) SA 391 (CC); 1995 (6) BCLR 665 (CC) par. 227.

of a later (and second) reception in Southern Africa. There is no reason why concepts such as *ubuntu* cannot form the subject of a third and post-constitutional reception.

Equality, relationality and the environment

It is impossible to make sense of concepts such as legal equality, equality before the law and unlawful discrimination without reference to human worth (dignity). These concepts only make sense if human dignity is used as the *tertium comparationis*, i.e. the respect in which all human beings (despite their enormous empirical differences) are equal and in respect whereof they cannot be discriminated against. Any concept of humanism should take account of this.

Although trespassing on the theological field, I would simply point to the fact that the *imago Dei* concept of creation in the Abrahamic religions has played an influential role in the secular and constitutional development of dignity and equality. The reasoning underlying this offers much scope for achieving an "overlapping consensus" with regard to human dignity and equality.[9] In the present context I understand this to mean that in order to build a universal consensus on the nature of human worth and the fact that equality means equality of human worth (human worth being beyond price), it is legitimate to refer to religious views despite the fact that some would not subscribe to their relevance or persuasiveness, but would reach the same 'political' conclusion via another line of reasoning. It is for this reason also that theological perspectives are relevant in a discussion of constitutional values and rights in a constitutional state. The best and most legitimate way of doing so is by appealing to values that command universal respect whether derived from religious or secular ethics or cultural norms.

I fully subscribe to the crucial importance of relationality and concern for the environment in exploring what it means to be human in South Africa today. In passing I would mention that the South African Constitution makes clear provision for the so-called "associational individual rights",[10] relating to – amongst others – religion, belief, opinion, the broad rights of association and assembly themselves, labour relations, education, language, and culture; and also makes specific provision[11] for the protection of the environment for the benefit of 'present and future generations'. It is also beyond the purview of this note to address the issue of basic socio-economic rights[12] for full human dignity. I do not underestimate their importance. I have elsewhere emphasised the following:

> As a transforming constitution, [the South African Constitution] has extended established ideas regarding enforceable fundamental rights to socio-economic and environmental spheres. Without entrenching socio-economic and environmental

9 The political philosopher John Rawls (1973:387) developed a concept of 'overlapping consensus' which is relevant to the use of theological ethics. This idea is discussed more fully in Rawls (1993:133-172).

10 Sections 15, 17, 18, 23, 29, 30, 31 of the Constitution.

11 Section 24.

12 See sections 22, 23, 25, 26, 27, 28, 29 of the Constitution.

rights, the Constitution may very well have little or no credibility for the dispossessed, the poor, and the socially marginalised. By entrenching them, the Constitution has highlighted the greatest challenge facing South African society at large in the decades to come. ... The most sophisticated tools have been fashioned for the courts to enforce, promote, and protect the Constitution and its values. But the ultimate fate of the Constitution, a bridge with a very long span, will not be decided by the jurisprudence of its courts alone, however devoted and inspired that might prove to be. A transforming constitution such as ours will only succeed if everyone, in government as well as in civil society at all levels, embraces and lives out its values and its demands. It will only succeed if restitutionary equality becomes a reality and basic material needs are met, because it borders on the obscene to preach human dignity to the homeless and the starving. This must, however, be achieved in a manner consonant with the human dignity of all. (Ackermann 2004:678-9)

It is as inescapable for us, as it was for Kant and Dürig, to determine what the full nature of the human being is and what her/his full image is, in order to determine the scope of human worth (dignity). It is similarly impossible, in my view, to understand what being fully human means without addressing these or very similar questions. A multi- and interdisciplinary dialogue on human worth (dignity) is essential for understanding what it means to be human in South Africa today. It is important not only for informing ourselves directly as to what human dignity (worth) embraces, but what facts about human beings might be relevant to so informing ourselves.

Reference List

Ackermann LWH. 2004. The Legal Nature of the South African Constitutional Revolution. *NZ Law Review*:633-679.

— 2006. Equality and Non-Discrimination: Some Analytical Thoughts. *South African Journal on Human Rights* 22:597.

Arieli Y. 2002. On the Necessary and Sufficient Conditions for the Emergence of the Doctrine of the Dignity of Man and His Rights. In: D Kretzmer & E Klein (eds). *The Concept of Human Dignity in Human Rights Discourse*. 1.

Baer JA (ed). 1990. *Politics and the Constitution: the nature and extent of interpretation*. Washington DC: National Legal Centre for the Public Interest: American Studies Centre.

Berger R. 1992. Justice Brennan, human dignity, and constitutional interpretation. In: MJ Meyer & WA Parent. *The constitution of rights: human dignity and human values*. 130 note 2.

Böckenförde E-W. 2006. *Recht, Staat, Freiheit*. Expanded edition. Frankfurt am Main: Suhrkamp.

Botha H. 2009. Human Dignity in Comparative Perspective. *Stellenbosch Law Review* (2):171.

Coetzee PH & Roux AJP. 2003. *The African Philosophy Reader*. 2nd Ed. London: Routledge; Cape Town: Oxford University Press.

Danieli Y *et al* (eds). 1999. *The Universal Declaration of Human Rights: Fifty Years and Beyond*. New York: Baywood.

Davis DM. 1999. Equality: The Majesty of Legoland Jurisprudence. *South African Law Journal* 116:398.

Dürig G. 1956. Der Grundrechtssatz von der Menschenwürde. *Archiv des öffentlichen Rechts* 81:117.

Easterbrook FH. 1990. Approaches to judicial review. *Baer*:29.

Glaeser WS. 1997. In Memoriam Günter Dürig. *Archiv des öffentlichen Rechts* 122:134.

Gregor MJ (ed). 1996. *Immanuel Kant: Practical* Philosophy. Cambridge: Cambridge University Press.

Häberle P. 1997. Günter Dürig. *Neue Juristische Wochenschrift* (5):306.

Huber W. 1996. *Violence: The Unrelenting Assault on Human Dignity*. RCL Gritsch. Minneapolis: Fortress Press.

Isensee J. 2006. Menschenwürde: die säkulare Gesellschaft auf der Suche nach dem Absoluten. *Archiv des öffentlichen Rechts* 131:173.

Kretzmer D & Klein E (eds). 2002. *The Concept of Human Dignity in Human Rights Discourse*. The Hague: Kluwer International.

Meyer MJ & Parent WA. 1992. *The constitution of rights: human dignity and human values.* Ithaca & London: Cornell University Press.

Ramose MB. 2003. The Philosophy of *ubuntu* and the *ubuntu* of philosophy. In: PH Coetzee & AJP Roux (eds). *The African Philosophy Reader.* 2nd Ed.

Rawls J. 1973. *A Theory of Justice.* Oxford: Oxford University Press Paperbacks.

— 1993. *Political Liberalism*. New York: Columbia University Press.

Shutte A. 2001. *Ubuntu: An ethic for a New South Africa*. Pietermaritzburg: Cluster Publications.

Williams B. 1967. The Idea of Equality. In: P Laslett & WG Runciman (eds). *Philosophy, Politics and Society*. Second Series. Oxford: Basil Blackwell.

HUMAN COMPLICITIES

Deborah Posel

Our humanity implicates us in the lives of others, in different ways at different times, for good and for bad, whether we know and like it or not. This is the condition of our ethical community, a productive basis of connection and empathy; it also entails that we cannot altogether distance ourselves from the suffering of others if our lives have been implicated in producing it. Complicity is crucial then, to how we should think about our human expectations of, and accountability to, others.

Many elements of this argument are not new. There are different literatures on, and varying genealogies of, the idea of complicity. In South Africa, among the most provocative is the philosophy of Black Consciousness, drawing in turn on Fanon's diagnosis of the psychological complicities that characterise the colonial condition. More recently, Mark Sanders (2002) has written powerfully on the subject. This essay does not engage substantially with these bodies of work; it is a personal reflection on the subject, inspired and informed by the contributions of these others, and drawing on my own work on apartheid and its aftermath.

At the outset, let me clarify my understanding of the term 'complicity'. Some colloquial uses of the term are overly attenuated: complicity is taken to mean being a knowing accomplice directly involved in an act of wrong-doing. I use the term to cover a broader range of possibilities. Complicity entails being implicated in wrong-doing, with varying degrees of knowledge and volition. In my usage, there are degrees and types of complicity, depending on the extent to which an individual directly consents to and comprehends the processes that have morally harmful effects.

"We live in a morally flawed world," writes legal scholar Christopher Kutz. "Our lives are complicated by what other people do, and by the harms that flow from our social, economic and political institutions. Our relations as individuals to these collective harms constitute the domain of complicity" (Kutz 2000:1). How implicated any individual is in collective harms, will depend on the particular institutional and social milieu, and the terms of that person's inclusion – all of which will be historically and socially specific. So, putting the concept of complicity at the foreground of an ethics of legitimate expectation and accountability grounds such philosophical issues in the concrete realities of living in particular places and times; different societies and historical periods will produce different orders and modes of complicity.

As a South African and a scholar of its history, this is where I want to bed down the bigger question of the humanity of complicity. My starting point is a reflection on South Africa's project of constitutional democracy and in particular on the major theoretical texts undergirding this project: the Constitution, the TRC, their enabling legislation, and the landmark early Constitutional Court rulings. These are texts that in the aggregate theorise the normative foundations of the new democracy in the light of a reading of the human condition. They took us to the brink of a powerful encounter with our human complicity, but ultimately retreated – probably under pressure from the *realpolitik* of the negotiated political compromise and its aftermath. I want to retrace our steps to that brink and consider how we might have confronted the question of complicity with a blighted past, and the implications thereof.

Living in apartheid South Africa produced – *entailed* – a keen awareness of difference. This was primarily, but not exclusively, a racial difference, borne of the tenacious and pernicious power of race categories that came to constitute the moulds of everyday life. These categories retain some – perhaps much – of their original purchase, despite the formal abolition of apartheid legislation. So it would be naïve and misleading to start any reflection in South Africa on what it means to be human without acknowledging a profoundly formative history of difference and differentiation – to the point that for some people, questions about what we might share, what connects us as human beings, are not the primary questions to be asking.

For me, however, one of the most hopeful aspects of the demise of apartheid was the opening up of a space to think again about what connects us as human beings: an invitation to think about our human sociality in the midst of our differences, and to ponder the ethical consequences thereof. Indeed, a version of our shared humanity, and the humanism it enjoins, underpinned the new constitution and its enabling legislation, as well as the TRC, and often quite explicitly informed the judgments of the Constitutional Court. The question of being human was a central preoccupation.

This theoretical opening, moreover, connects the South African experience to wider international currents and concerns. The South African theoretical inquiry was one version of a more general, and more global, theoretical challenge of how to raise questions about what it means to be human without reinventing old Enlightenment chauvinisms that simultaneously heralded a universal human nature and then invoked it to judge those other than white western males as inferior.

On being human

The key theoretical texts that shaped South Africa's embrace of democracy raised the question of being human in a primarily ethical register, in two different ways: the first, by way of a discussion of human rights, associated with a notion of human dignity, and the second, by invoking the notion of *ubuntu*, as an ethic of human interconnectedness. At first sight, these two lines of inquiry might seem to some to pull in opposite directions. The idea of human rights, with its long liberal pedigree, speaks to the ethical entitlements that accrue to all individuals on the grounds of their being human, but in acknowledgement of their individuality and plurality. The doctrine of human rights – invoked in South Africa in so-called first and second generation modes – sets out to adjudicate legitimate individual freedoms and their limits, as well as the legitimate claims that individuals can make on the state to guarantee the minimum requirements of a humane and dignified existence. Rights acknowledge, and protect, individual autonomy and plurality: they guarantee the possibility of diversity, disagreement and spaces of individual choice.

Ubuntu, on the other hand, marks the limits of individual separateness and autonomy by embedding such claims in a version of ethical community that precedes any individual's values or entitlements. In terms of the version of the human condition theorised by the South African constitution, the concept of human interdependence *precedes* that of the individual. Being a person – an individual human being – is only intelligible on the strength of the prior recognition of the many others in relation to whom one person exists.

Sociality, then, *is* the human condition. And this has powerful ethical consequences: to be humane is to recognise our human mutuality, to acknowledge and respect the humanity of the other. This is the locus of *ubuntu*, typically defined by way of the claim: 'a person can only be a person through others'. We are human through our recognition of the humanity of others; this is the kernel of our sociality as well as our ethical community. *Ubuntu* is primarily an ethical idea, a prescriptive evocation. But it becomes plausible on the strength of a tacit ontology, a version of the human condition as irrevocably social and interconnected. Taking inspiration from indigenous African ethical thinking, organic intellectuals of South Africa's constitutional transition found in *ubuntu* 'a new analytical framework of human interdependence', as Constitutional Court judge Albie Sachs put it (*Soobramoney vs Minister of Health, KwaZulu Natal*, par.54).

Justice Yvonne Mokgoro, one of the most dedicated exponents of the concept, explicitly grappled with the question of how the ethics of human rights and *ubuntu* linked up during the constitution-making process, from the Interim Constitution through to the final text.

> Not only is the notion of *ubuntu* expressly provided for in the epilogue of the [Interim] Constitution, the underlying idea and its accompanying values are also expressed in the Preamble. These values underlie, first and foremost, the whole idea of adopting a Bill of Fundamental Rights and Freedoms in a new legal order. They are central to the coherence of all the rights entrenched in Chapter 3 – where the right to life and the right to respect for and the protection of human dignity are embodied in sections 9 and 10 respectively. (*S vs Makwanyane* 1995:par.307)

So possible tension between the individualising imperative of rights reasoning, and the more communitarian ethos of *ubuntu*, is resolved in favour of the primacy of the latter, but affirming rather than overriding the former. *Ubuntu* 'regulates the exercise of rights by the emphasis it lays on sharing and co-responsibility and the mutual enjoyment of rights by all' (Justice Langa, in *S vs Makwanyane*, 1995, par.224). But this also means that the theoretical underpinnings of South Africa's constitutional democracy are a communitarianism of a particular type: with a strong acknowledgement of, and commitment to, the ethical claims of individuals and their differences. With human sociality, goes a keen recognition of human plurality, and carefully calibrated claims to degrees and types of individual autonomy and choice.

The interconnectedness of life under apartheid

I find this an appealing combination, both in its ethics and in the version of the human condition that informs it. Nor is the latter an abstract existential proposition. In this country, it resonates powerfully with the apartheid past, as much as the post-apartheid present. Indeed, the idea of connectedness in difference makes sense of a long history of authorised disconnection and differentiation under apartheid that simultaneously generated distorted forms of exactly the opposite (see also Sanders 2002:16,19). Black Consciousness thinkers recognised these paradoxical inversions in the experiences of black people subjected to apartheid, understanding that while race produced different modes of being-in-the-world (Manganyi 1973), these worlds were ultimately inseparable: being black made no sense other than in relation to being white. Apartheid fashioned race as simultaneously a point of relation and disconnection (see Biko 1987:27; Sanders 2002:ch.5). A similar logic applied to whites: inhabiting a social fabric that knitted them into unsettling dependencies on blacks, patterned too by fault-lines of class, gender and generation. If a regime hell-bent on separation and segregation also produced proximity and interdependence – distorted and oppressive though these were under apartheid – then it is that much more convincing and appropriate to ground South Africa's efforts to grapple with its past, and fashion a democratic polity, in our irrevocable human sociality, as simultaneously a condition of plurality.

The first fulcrum of the (distorted and unwitting) interconnectedness of life under apartheid was the primary motor of its separateness: the system of racial classification, fundamental to the aspirations to keep each race in its proper place. Every South African was required, by law, to submit to a process of racial classification; to refuse or fail to do so was an act of defiance that rendered a person invisible, officially non-existent. Being classified as a member of one of the four officially recognised races, or 'population groups', then informed the allocation of all opportunities, resources, penalties and strictures. Race became the basis of where people lived, worked, travelled, studied, worshipped, shopped, drank, ate, swam, picnicked and played. Some transgressed racial boundaries, of course; but the racial matrix defined the very terms of these transgressions. It was difficult, if not altogether impossible, to inhabit South Africa outside the rubric of apartheid categories. The 'fact' of race was insinuated into popular common sense, across the racial spectrum – to the extent that few disputed the centrality of race in the making of subjective and inter-subjective experience, even if many protested its consequences vehemently. All South Africans were ensnared in – and therefore connected by – a shared framework of everyday life, a common set of categories in terms of which people defined at least one dimension of who they were in relation to others (Posel 2001).

The ambitions of apartheid's practitioners produced similarly paradoxical loci of connectedness. If the discourse of apartheid was pre-eminently one of the need to keep races apart, to maintain their 'purity' and cultural integrity, then the apartheid mode of being-in-the-world – as Manganyi puts it (1973:28) – was a dialectic of distance and proximity, of strangeness and intimacy. As a system of governance, apartheid was predicated on the realisation, reluctant though this was, that white people were as dependent on black people as they were threatened by, and fearful of, them. This dualism persisted throughout the life of apartheid, at the very core of the project. The practitioners of apartheid were as set on driving people apart as they were on pulling them together – in particular, by creating supplies of cheap black labour as the fount of white economic prosperity. As more and more black people were drawn into the modernising economy and its wider milieu, so, too, this dependency deepened. And this in turn stoked the anxiety that fuelled ever more fervent desires to remain separate.

The simultaneity of strident differentiation and everyday interdependence was perhaps most striking, and strange, in the homes of white families employing black domestic workers: typically housed in slum-like conditions on the property outside the white home, restricted to eating on tin plates so as not to contaminate the family's china – daily reminders of a servitude justified by fiercely fortified racial privilege and distance – domestic workers were nevertheless privy to intimate family encounters and entrusted with caring for those most precious in the home.

In short, the history of apartheid was one of interdependence as much as separation; the moral distortions and oppressiveness of apartheid were vested in this dialectical nexus. The theme of interconnectedness in the midst of separation is fundamental, too, for South Africa's philosophical and ethical 'transition' – albeit with the aim of transcending apartheid's distortions. Thus, the idea of human mutuality pervades the Constitution and the TRC. And their enabling legislation made it clear that this was not merely a philosophical abstraction, but an embedded, contextual idea.

In the 1990s, as the transition was unfolding, its theorists emphasised that what South Africans shared – what bound them together – was our past: a past that had brutalised and damaged all. We had been in it together, whether we liked it or not.

The TRC and the mutuality of damage

The TRC was a process of bearing witness to that past, with a view to producing, among other things, recognition of the mutuality of violation and suffering under apartheid. One of the most remarkable features of the TRC – the feature that rendered the Commission so offensive in the eyes of Thabo Mbeki and others, prompting the ANC's (unsuccessful) legal injunction to bar the publication of the TRC Report – was the insistence that the country bear witness to gross human rights violations across the board, from those committed within the apartheid regime to those of the liberation struggle.

This was in no way to render all these violations morally comparable. On the contrary, the TRC was emphatic that they were not: apartheid was judged far more heinous, as a crime against humanity. Still, the TRC identified and witnessed wrongdoing across the board, which was then linked to a claim about the historical *mutuality of damage*: the inhumanity of apartheid had damaged all who had grown up in it. In the words of the TRC's chairperson Archbishop Tutu, in his address to the first gathering of the TRC on 16 December1995: "We are wounded people ... all stand in need of healing ... Every South African has to some extent or other been traumatized."[1] The TRC Report quoted President Nelson Mandela in similar vein:

> All of us, as a nation that has newly found itself, share in the shame at the capacity of human beings of any race or language to be inhumane to other human beings. (TRC Report, vol.1, ch.5, par.109)

And later, the Report cited Constitutional Court judge, Pius Langa, to similar effect:

> We have all been affected in one way or another by the "strife, untold suffering and injustice" of the recent past ... [of] violence on human beings by human beings. (TRC Report, vol.6, ch.5, par.86)

What then, was the damage? Again let me stress: this was not homogenous damage and there was no ethical equivalence imputed to the different orders of wrongdoing symptomatic of the damage.

The first element of the mutuality of apartheid's damage was that *all*, in some or other way, were victims: victims of the apartheid system. This was explicit, and central to the thinking of Tutu and Mandela, as charismatic theoreticians of the transition to democracy. And this went hand in hand with the recognition of different types of victimhood, associated with varying degrees of trauma and suffering. Thus family members of someone who had been the victim of a gross human rights violation were also victims, albeit at some remove. And the society at large was the victim of a systematic dehumanisation – albeit with varying effects on the individuals inhabiting it.

---

[1] www.justice.gov.za/trc/media/pr/1995/p9512a.htm

Less visibly and less consistently – certainly, more controversially – *all* were perpetrators, too. The TRC's mandate, established in the enabling legislation, required the commission to conduct its proceedings and reach conclusions within the dyadic categories of 'victims' and 'perpetrators', assuming that these were readily separable and well-bounded. And the object of the TRC's inquiry was gross human rights violations (murder, abduction, torture, rape and other modes of "severe ill treatment"), which produced – as the TRC Report put it – "a focus on the outrageous" (TRC Report vol.5, ch.6, par.108). That the commission struggled with the strictures of this focus and the conceptual opposition linked to it, is evident in the Report's recourse to *a typology of complicity*, which complicates and unsettles the apparently clear boundary between victim and perpetrator, and ventures well beyond the terrain of those directly and immediately responsible for gross human rights violations (GHRVs). This was not an explicit or systematic exercise in the Report; it is not named in these terms or with this purpose. Yet, the Report goes a long way in delineating types and degrees of complicity, as distinct from direct and immediate responsibility for GHRVs. And in so doing, the Report ventures to the brink of naming all South Africans as perpetrators.

Those found to be direct perpetrators of GHRVS – which included many institutions of the apartheid state from the late 1970s to early 1990s, homeland governments, liberation movements (including the ANC and PAC), the UDF, IFP and several right-wing Afrikaner organisations – were those who 'knowingly planned, undertook, condoned and covered up' GHRVs of one kind or another (TRC Report, vol.5, ch.6, par.77). But the Report also recognised a range of more indirect ways in which GHRVs were perpetrated, with varying degrees of proximity to, and knowledge of, the direct violation.

The first was named as *collusion:* less direct than plotting to kill or pulling a trigger, but entailing a knowing involvement in acts of wrongdoing, aiding and abetting these outcomes, an 'active contribution' (vol.5, ch.6, par.158) to heinous ends. Thus, members of the legal profession, for example, were judged to have 'knowingly colluded with police' (vol.5, ch.6, par.158). The second was *collaboration* with GHRVs, defined by lesser orders of knowledge and active involvement than in the case of collusion. In the main, the Report depicts collaboration as 'acts of omission':

> It would be misleading and wrong to assign blame for the gross violation of human rights only to those who confronted each other on the political and military battlefields, engaged in acts of commission. Others, like the church or faith groups, the media, the legal profession, the judiciary, the magistracy, the medical/health, educational and business sectors, are found by the Commission to have been guilty of acts of omission in that they failed to adhere or live up to the ethics of their profession and to accepted codes of conduct. (TRC Report, vol.5, ch.6, par.74)

Theirs was a "failure to oppose the injustice around them vociferously and actively"; their collaboration a consequence of "silence and inaction" in the midst of manifest wrongdoing (TRC Report, vol.5, ch.6, par.151).

The TRC Report's discussion of collaboration focuses largely on institutions, and mostly those institutions that were featured in the sectoral hearings convened as an attempt to widen the ambit of the TRC's deliberations beyond individual victims and perpetrators, and to include at least some aspects of the collective context of GHRVs. In the main, the Report ventures little beyond this domain of specific 'sectors' and their collaboration, either with particular practices of violation, or with the apartheid system more generally (see also Mamdani 2002). But the logic of the argument would extend to individual collaborators, along with institutional ones. In the TRC's schema, the category of collaborators could encompass all those who didn't speak up or take a stand against apartheid. This did not require supporting the liberation movements; the TRC acknowledged ideologically disparate ways of speaking out.

The Report seemed more tentative in going even further into a diagnosis of complicity one that would have found communities of individuals, or the society at large, collectively accountable for apartheid, simply by virtue of having inhabited it and reproduced its habits of thought, its racial common sense. Recognising, no doubt, that this was politically delicate territory – given the *realpolitik* of reaching a political compromise in the midst of lingering violence – the Report nevertheless did venture to suggest:

> A pertinent question is the extent to which individual South Africans can be regarded as responsible for the premises and presuppositions that gave rise to apartheid. (Vol.6, ch.5, par.105)

In the main, however, this question marks the limit of the TRC's own exploration of complicity – even if in the very act of acknowledging the importance of continuing beyond that limit. The Report is open and upfront about its failures to breach this limit:

> ... the varying degrees of moral responsibility that should be adopted by all South Africans have (both by design and by default) not been given sufficient emphasis by the Commission. (Vol.6, ch.5, par.106)

> [The] focus on the outrageous has drawn the nation's attention away from the commonplace violations. The result is that ordinary South Africans do not see themselves as represented by those the Commission defines as perpetrators, failing to recognise the "little perpetrator" in all of us. (Vol.6, ch.5, par.108)

Constrained by the terms of its mandate and the wider politics of its operation, the TRC Report acknowledged that the Commission could not delve sufficiently into the everyday practices that rendered ordinary South Africans "complicit in the banality that leads, step by step, to the kin of outrageous deeds that have left many 'good' South Africans feeling that they can never be expected, even indirectly, to accept responsibility for them" (vol.6, ch.5, par.109) – at the same time as acknowledging how crucial a confrontation with this dimension of complicity was, for exactly the TRC's own project of reconciliation (*ibid* par.103).

So the TRC Report doesn't go where it recognises it ought, finally, to have gone: to confront 'the little perpetrator in all of us', and the consequences thereof for individuals far removed from the political and military battlefields, but implicated in the ways the apartheid system worked. But even so, it went a long way down the road of locating complicity as the nub of the apartheid mode of being, and in recognising the need to grapple with the legacy of this in the effort to produce a more humane future with 'reconciliation' across the brutalising breaches of the apartheid past.

Reconciliation as mutual civility

Predictably perhaps, annulling the category of pure, unsullied victimhood was the TRC's most controversial move. Furious at the prospect of being implicated in gross human rights violations, the ANC sought a high court interdict to block the publication of the five-volume, so-called Interim Report, in 1998. They failed, but it was clear nevertheless that a complicitous version of the liberation struggle would not gain much political traction. Nor was there much openness to acknowledgements of complicity within the National Party, or within the white population generally. One of the major ironies of the "reconciliation" process enabled by the TRC was the space conceded to white South Africans to *disclaim* responsibility for apartheid, as if the system was an historical aberration for which only a few "bad apples" could be help responsible (Posel 2002). The "little perpetrator within every one of us" was little in evidence. So opportunities for greater degrees of collective and personal acknowledgement of complicities with a blighted past were squandered.

The political life of South Africa's new democracy has largely moved beyond the discourse of "reconciliation" – predictably, for some, as a sign that the honeymoon of the transition is over; sadly, for others, who see unfinished business in the process initiated by the TRC. The political prospects of revitalising or refashioning the project of reconciliation are beyond the scope of this essay; suffice to conclude by pulling together the threads of the argument I have mounted in a reflection on the version of reconciliation (understood here as an ethical project) that a frank encounter with our collective complicities might produce.

This essay has shown that complicities come into view when the lens to our human condition shows up the irrevocable mutuality of our lives as social beings. And this is a mutuality marked by a dialectic of proximity and distance. Our sociality does not homogenise us; being social is about being involved, inevitably, in relationships that simultaneously differentiate and connect. The conditions of positive ethical community are at the same time the ground of mutual complicities that produce harms inflicted on others, with varying degrees of deliberate malice and foresight. Reconciliation is, in the first instance, becoming reconciled to these conditions of collective and ethical life, with the humility and respectfulness that comes with acknowledging a shared moral fallibility and imperfect judgement (even if to varying degrees).

The logic of the argument developed in this essay also suggests that "reconciliation" need not – and may be more persuasive if it does not – entail an effusive embrace of others from whom we feel different, and whose ways of living and senses of self seem remote and unfamiliar. The existential premise of a project of reconciliation is that we are in it together, whether we like it or not. Ethically, there need be no prescription that we have to grow more alike or become more involved in each other's lives; "reconciliation" need not be an injunction to friendship or affection, an emotional embrace. It is, more plausibly, a commitment to mutual *civility*. Less indifferent and detached than mutual tolerance, civility is a mindful concern for, and acknowledgement of, the needs and interests of others, in the intersection between respectful distance and responsible closeness. Civility is the counterpoint to complicity; they are opposite sides of the same existential coin. As Christopher Kutz puts it,

> the collective project of living ethically may find as great support in what it deplores as in what it prizes. The hidden promise of complicity is the conception of community upon which it draws: a world where individuals shape their lives with others, in love mixed with resentment, and in co-operation mixed with discord. (Kutz 2000:59)

Reference List

Biko S. 1987. *I write what I like: Selected Writings.* Aelred Stubbs (ed). London: Heinemann.

Borer T. 2003. A Taxonomy of Victims and Perpetrators: Human Rights and Reconciliation in South Africa. *Human Rights Quarterly* 25(4):1088-1116.

Clingman S. 2005. On ethical grounds. *Law and Literature* 17(2):279-290.

Constitutional Court, South Africa. 1995. *State vs Makwanyane.* www.saflii.org/za/cases/ZACC/1995.3.html

— 1997. *T. Soobramoney vs Minister of Health, KwaZulu-Natal.* www.escr-net.org/usr_doc/Soobramoney_Decision.pdf

Klaits F. 2005. Review article: postcolonial civility. *Journal of Southern African Studies* 31(3):649-662.

Kutz C. 2000. *Complicity: Ethics and Law for a Collective Age.* Cambridge Studies in Law and Philosophy. New York: Cambridge University Press.

Makgoro Y. 1997. *Ubuntu* and the law in South Africa. Paper delivered at the first Colloquium Constitution and Law held at Potchefstroom on 31 October.

Mamdani M. 2002. Amnesty or Impunity? A Preliminary Critique of the Report of the Truth and Reconciliation Commission of South Africa. *Diacritics* 32.2-4:33-59.

Manganyi C. 1973. *Being-Black-in-the-World.* Johannesburg: Ravan Press.

Nagy R. 2002. Reconciliation in Post-Commission South Africa: Thick and Thin Accounts of Solidarity. *Canadian Journal of Political Science* 35(2):323-346.

Posel D. 2001. Race as Common Sense. *African Studies Review* 44(2):87-114.

— 2002. The TRC Report: What kind of truth? What kind of history? In: D Posel & G Simpson (eds). *Commissioning the Past: Understanding South Africa's Truth and Reconciliation Commission.* Johannesburg: Wits University Press. 147-172.

Republic of South Africa. 1993. *Epilogue to the Interim Constitution of the Republic of South Africa.* Pretoria: Government Printer.

— 1995. Promotion of National Unity and Reconciliation Act, no. 34. http://www.doj.gov.za//trc/legal/act9534.htm

— 1996. Constitution of the Republic of South Africa. http://www.info.gov.za/documents/constitution/1996/index.htm

Sanders M. 2002. *Complicities: The Intellectual and Apartheid.* Durham: Duke University Press.

Thomas CG. 2008. *Ubuntu*: The missing link in the rights discourse in post-apartheid transformation in South Africa. *International Journal of African Renaissance Studies – Multi-, Inter- and Transdisciplinarity* 3(2):39-62.

Truth and Reconciliation Commission. 1998. *Truth and Reconciliation Report of South Africa*, 6 vols. www.justice.gov.za/trc/report

AN AFRICAN THEORY OF DIGNITY AND A RELATIONAL CONCEPTION OF POVERTY

Thaddeus Metz

Poverty is degrading, but of what precisely? What is it about human nature that is treated disrespectfully when a state and other agents in society fail to prevent poverty? And what is it that they should be doing to prevent it? What kinds of policies and practices would treat the poor as having dignity? I suggest answers to these philosophical questions by drawing on a large strand of southern African moral thought that instructs us to develop *ubuntu* (in Nguni languages, or *botho* in Sotho-Tswana), that is, to realise our humanness or to live a genuinely human way of life.

In other work, I have articulated and defended a moral philosophy grounded on ideas associated with *ubuntu* that avoids problems of being too vague to understand, too abstract to apply to real life dilemmas, too metaphysical to serve as a public morality, or too implausible to take seriously in the light of recent philosophical insights into ethics (Metz 2010; Metz & Gaie 2010). Here, I briefly spell out my interpretation of *ubuntu* as a contemporary moral philosophy, in order to present under-explored and promising ways to understand the relationship between dignity and poverty in the context of South African society.

I begin by summarising the way that I approach *ubuntu* philosophically (section 1), which will set the stage for presenting a new conception of human dignity that has a sub-Saharan pedigree and constitutes a promising rival to the Kantian conception of dignity that dominates discussion in contemporary Western ethics and jurisprudence (section 2). According to my African-based theory of dignity, a being has it roughly in virtue of a substantial capacity for communal relationship, a view that contrasts with the characteristically Western view that 'internal' or 'non-relational' properties of rationality or autonomy constitute our dignity. Next, I invoke the Afro-communitarian conception of dignity to answer the questions of why poverty is morally problematic, which goods the state ought to distribute to the needy, and how much they ought to receive, along the way noting respects in which the implications of the sub-Saharan theory of dignity differ from those of the more Western approach (section 3). I briefly conclude by suggesting some additional avenues of research into the indignity of poverty (section 4).

A philosophical interpretation of *ubuntu*

My approach to *ubuntu* and southern African morality generally is philosophical and constructive, meaning that I draw on values salient in the region in order to create a fundamental theory indicating which actions, laws and policies are morally right. I do not seek to recount what a particular indigenous people believes about morality, as an anthropologist would. Instead, I appeal to many of the values shared widely among peoples in the region with the aim of proposing a basic principle that plausibly provides sound guidance about how we morally ought to treat one another.

It should not be expected that any traditional peoples have actually believed the ethical theory I present, for two reasons. For one, it is an abstract interpretation of morality that could likely come only from a professional philosopher critically engaging with indigenous southern African ideas, a relatively new creature to be found on the sub-Saharan landscape. For another, in seeking to create a philosophically attractive theory, I have used independent judgement, meaning that rather than seeking to unify any and all ideas recurrently associated with *ubuntu*, I spell out a principle that captures only those that I and other contemporary experts in ethics across the globe would tend to find appealing. If someone were to suggest, say, that I cannot obtain *ubuntu* because I am white, then I would deem that to be a poor *philosophical* interpretation of *ubuntu* (regardless of its *anthropological* accuracy), relative to one according to which in principle anyone, regardless of race or culture, is capable of living a genuinely human way of life.

Despite the fact that a professional philosopher, and a foreign one at that, has conceived the moral theory below, it is apt to call it 'southern African', or simply 'African', because it is principally informed by many piecemeal ideas about ethics that have been recurrent among traditional Nguni, Sotho-Tswana and Shona speaking peoples, among others, in the region.

Any promising interpretation of *ubuntu* as a moral philosophy is wise to start with the ubiquitous judgement, '*Umuntu ngumuntu ngabantu*', in Nguni languages, and '*Motho ke motho ka batho babang*', in Sotho-Tswana, which is usually translated as, 'A person is a person through other persons'. That overly literal translation means virtually nothing to a non-African English speaker, at best connoting empirical banalities to the effect that children cannot survive without parenting or that human beings are always part of a community. However, when those in southern Africa claim that a person is a person through other persons, they are typically (also) making a moral assertion, that is, a recommendation about how to live one's life. It is characteristic for them to think that personhood is an ideal, a virtuous state that is something to be striven for in life.

More specifically, one's proper goal should be to try to become a *full* person or to live a *genuinely* human way of life (Menkiti 2004). To say that a person is a person through other persons is to endorse the aim of becoming a complete person or of having exhibited *ubuntu* to a superlative degree, something that ancestors and elders are thought to have achieved but that the rest of us need to keep seeking out. Just as a jalopy is not a *real* car (Gaie 2007:33), so those who fail to behave properly are not *real* persons, and are occasionally labelled 'animals' (Bhengu 1996:27), beings who stereotypically do not exhibit what is valuable about human nature.

In virtue of what does one realise one's humanness? The answer 'through persons' tells us something, but not very much on the face of it. I interpret this phrase to say that the *only* way to become a real person is in the context of a positive relationship with others, specifically, prizing community with them. As Augustine Shutte, one of the first professional South African philosophers to publish a book on *ubuntu*, sums up the basics of the ethic: 'Our deepest moral obligation is to become more fully human and this means entering more and more deeply into community with others. So although the goal is personal fulfilment, selfishness is excluded' (2001:30).

In a traditional context, the 'others' with whom to commune include ancestors, God and animals that have a spiritual significance such as totems (Ramose 1999; Murove 2007). However, since I seek a philosophical understanding of *ubuntu* that could serve as a basis for public morality in a pluralistic society, I tend not to highlight the more contested, immaterial facets of indigenous sub-Saharan ethics. Most useful is the core, secular notion of communal relationship that is constitutive of one's humanness. In other work, I have sought to clarify with some analytic rigor what community involves, suggesting that it is well understood in terms of the combination of what I call 'identity' and 'solidarity'. Let me spell out these ideas.

To identify with each other is largely for people to think of themselves as members of the same group – that is, to conceive of themselves as a 'we', as well as for them to engage in joint projects, coordinating their behaviour to realise shared ends. For people to fail to identify with each other could involve outright division between them, i.e. people not only thinking of themselves as an 'I' in opposition to a 'you' or a 'they', but also aiming to undermine one another's ends.

To exhibit solidarity with one another is for people to engage in mutual aid, to act in ways that are expected to benefit each other. Solidarity is also a matter of people's attitudes such as emotions and motives being positively oriented toward others, say, by sympathising with them and helping them for their sake. For people to fail to exhibit solidarity would be for them either to be indifferent to each other's flourishing or to exhibit ill-will in the form of hostility and cruelty.

Community in characteristic African moral thinking is the condition in which one finds people *both* identifying with and exhibiting solidarity toward one another, or, as former Constitutional Court Justice Yvonne Mokgoro puts it, where one encounters 'close and sympathetic social relations within the group' (1998:3). Now, the combination of people identifying with each other or being close, on the one hand, and of them exhibiting solidarity with one another or being sympathetic, on the other, is more or less what people mean by 'friendship' or a broad sense of 'love'. A loving relationship is plausibly nothing other than thinking of oneself as a 'we' with another person, participating in joint activities with her, going out of one's way to help her, and doing so on the basis of compassion and for her sake. So, one attractive philosophical way to understand southern African morality is to read it as telling us, at bottom, to become human by prizing friendly or loving relationships with other human beings (*cf* Tutu 1999:34-35).

From *ubuntu* to dignity

So far in spelling out a moral philosophy grounded on salient ideas associated with talk of *ubuntu* (and cognate terms), I have not mentioned anything about human dignity. The sense of 'dignity' that I am interested in is the one that is thought to be equal among (nearly) all human beings and is plausibly taken as the foundation of human rights, as is done in the Universal Declaration of Human Rights (United Nations 1948). I set aside more variable and hierarchical senses of 'dignity', according to which those who have accomplished much in life, such as elders (real persons), may be said to have a 'more dignified existence' than others. So, the question I seek to answer now is this: given a philosophical interpretation of *ubuntu* that prescribes prizing communal or loving relationships with others, which conception of dignity, as the basis of an equal moral worth among human beings warranting respect, does it underwrite?

A plausible answer is to be found in the way one is to develop one's personhood, namely, 'through persons', i.e. by entering into community with others. One does not become a real person by tending rose bushes or saving beached whales, supposing these actions have no bearing on the lives of other human beings. Instead, in typical southern African thinking, one lives a genuinely human way of life only by communing with other human beings. What is it, then, about human beings that makes them the proper objects of community or love? My suggestion is this: they are the most important beings on the planet and demand our love in virtue of their superlative capacity to be part of a loving relationship. Human beings are sensibly deemed to have a dignity insofar as they have a great capacity for communal relationship, and an African ethic, as I have interpreted it, instructs us to respond to beings with a great capacity for community in a way that prizes community with them, i.e. that draws out, or actualises, this capacity.

Compare this conception of human dignity with the conception that is so influential in Western philosophy, based on the work of the German Enlightenment philosopher Immanuel Kant. Imagine that you are driving a bus that is careening down a hill, and that you must choose between running over a normal, adult human being or a cat. Supposing you must strike one of these beings, it would be right for you to hit the cat, the intuitive explanation of which is that the human is worth more than the cat. The Kantian would say that what makes the human worth more than the cat, or that gives it a dignity, is that it has the capacity to live autonomously, or to exhibit intelligence, or to act out of conscience. That is the conception of dignity that one finds most often in United Nations documents, in judgements by courts with dignity-based constitutions, in recent work by former Constitutional Court Justice Laurie Ackermann (n.d.), and in the influential moral and political philosophies of John Rawls (1971) and Ronald Dworkin (2000). In contrast, the African theory of dignity that I have proposed would say that the reason to run over the cat rather than the human is that the latter is capable of love in a way that the former is not. Even if the human has not utilised this capacity well, and has been rather nasty, he retains a dignity that demands respect simply in virtue of being able to act otherwise.

Dignity and poverty

I now apply this Afro-communitarian notion of what makes a human being special to several issues regarding poverty. To illustrate the novelty and attractiveness of my construal of poverty as an indignity, I often contrast it with the Kantian approach and do so in the context of South African issues. As I point out, there is a clear sense in which the Kantian conception of poverty is 'individualist', while the African one is 'relational' – and is revealing for being so.

Why poverty is morally problematic

When we speak of 'poverty', we are usually referring to a situation in which some people are lacking external, material goods and others could alleviate their plight, at least without enormous sacrifice on their part. What is at bottom morally wrong with that kind of situation?

Influential is the answer that avoidable poverty is fundamentally unjust insofar as it is inhuman or is an indignity, a condition in which some people are not treated as the most special beings in the world. However, a more precise answer will turn on the property in virtue of which humans are deemed to have a dignity. A Kantian, for example, believes that people have a dignity in virtue of their ability to make free decisions for themselves, and she will therefore understand the wrongness of poverty as a degradation of that capacity. Roughly, poverty is wrong, on this view, because it is a(n unnecessary) lack of individual freedom. When one is poor, one is less able to make a variety of choices that the rich can make.

That explanation of the wrongness of poverty is 'individualistic' in the sense that a feature utterly internal to a human being is what poverty degrades. In contrast, my Afro-communitarian theory of dignity is 'relational', in that it entails that poverty is an injustice to the extent that it degrades people's capacity to commune with others. Basically, poverty is something that stunts people socially, that impairs their ability to engage in loving relationships. I once attended a National *Ubuntu* Imbizo where an elderly African woman said that the reason she found poverty so troublesome is that it renders her *unable to give to others*.

What should be distributed to the poor?

Politicians usually think that the way to fight poverty is by increasing the gross domestic product or the amount of income that people receive. More sophisticated economists realise that income is not an ethically basic category, i.e. that poverty can be fought only roughly by giving people more money or some other exchange value such as shares of stock. Most often, they suggest that what ultimately matters with regard to fighting poverty is distributing external, material goods in a way that enables people to satisfy more of their preferences.

A focus on preference satisfaction ('utility') accords reasonably well with a Kantian conception of dignity, as friends of capitalism have often maintained. If what confers a dignity on people is their capacity for freedom, then it appears that poverty is to be fought by doing more to give people what they want or to satisfy their demand in a marketplace. Other Kantians have a related, but different, understanding of what it is the poor should receive. Rawls (1971) and Dworkin (2000) have maintained that since what is special about people is, basically, their capacity for autonomy, what the poor primarily ought to receive are *general-purpose means*, goods that can be used to achieve a wide variety of ends. Money is obviously one such good. However, there are additional forms, such as certain types of technology (nuclear), property (oil, land), and education (literacy, maths). Both the ability to obtain preference satisfaction and the possession of general-purpose means are again 'individualistic' in the sense that they are states of a human being that make no essential reference to others.

The Afro-communitarian conception of poverty is different, conceiving of the relevant external materials to distribute in essentially relational terms. What the state and other wealthy agents ought to provide to the poor are goods that are likely to foster, or otherwise respect, communal relationships (*cf* Nkondo 2007). Money will obviously be included among those goods, but there will be many others that differ from the satisfaction of demand on a market and from the provision of general-purpose means. What follow are five suggestions about what these could include, with a focus on South Africa (but with broader implications).

1. *Women's Shelters*. Poor women are often forced to stay with abusive men because they and their children have nowhere else to go. Providing temporary shelter for them, and eventually subsidised housing, would help end unloving relationships, and enable many women and children to seek out more positive ones.

2. *Counselling and Rehabilitation.* Broken families, households headed by orphans, by teenagers or by grandmothers, alcoholism, and an inability to resolve conflicts with emotional insight and communicative clarity are widespread problems. Familial relationships, which have the potential to be the most tight-knit, would be greatly facilitated by the provision of therapeutic social services.
3. *Neighbourhood Parks.* The combination of a car-culture and widespread criminal activity makes it difficult for people in urban environments to feel a sense of community. Funding safe, well-kept parks in neighbourhoods, not to mention inclusive activities in them such as fairs and musical events, would help overcome local residents' isolation.
4. *Reconciliatory Projects.* Society is splintered among many dimensions beyond the obvious fault-line of black/white, including: young/old, urban/rural, female/male, rich/poor, locals/foreigners and criminals/law-abiding residents. Some of these fractures would begin to mend if programmes such as the following were supported: restorative justice in which offenders work off debt to their victims, including the wider community, and youth service in which unemployed matriculants would, say, build houses for the elderly.
5. *Integrating Students.* Students should be instructed in a way that would be likely to foster identification with one another, discourage cliques based on wealth and status, fight stigma and alienation, and unite while leading to respect for difference. The above are five examples of the kinds of projects that a state that prizes communal relationships would be sensible to fund or otherwise support.

Note how different the above projects are from the kinds of programmes most often promoted by the ANC, the DA and COSATU. What all these political agendas have in common is a primary focus on money or other general-purpose means as the relevant goods to distribute to the poor. However, the friend of the Afro-communitarian conception of dignity would also propose, plausibly, that people are more wealthy, the more that their state funds things likely to foster communal relationship, such as shelters to house battered women and their children, therapy for those suffering from depression, addiction and neurosis, parks for local residents, programmes in which members of alienated groups labour for one another, and schools in which children engage in activities that are likely to foster cohesion.

How much the poor should receive

The conception of the right pattern by which economic goods should be distributed is informed by a motivating conception of human dignity and its companion conception of what the relevant goods are. If what is to be honoured about human beings is their capacity for autonomy, so that what the state should allocate to the poor is either preference satisfaction or general-purpose means, then it makes sense to want to *maximise* these things in some sense. For example, economists typically favour the principle of Pareto optimality, according to which, if relative to a given distribution, a different distribution would offer more income to someone and no less to anyone else, then the latter distribution is more just. Kantian philosophers of economic justice tend to favour a distribution of wealth known as the 'difference principle', according to which inequality is permissible if and only if it would make the worst-off group in particular the best off it can be, relative to any other possible distribution. It is typical of these perspectives to entail that any reduction in inequality would be irrational and unjust if it gave the poor less income (or other relevant economic goods) than they would have under a scheme with greater inequality.

The ANC and DA share this inegalitarian but nonetheless 'poor friendly' standpoint. These two parties favour private ownership of the means of production coupled with a substantial redistributive taxation of the income of those who have prospered on the market. Taxation of property (for non-compensatory reasons) is deemed just in order to provide money, shelter or electricity to the poor and to enable them to obtain the education or other qualifications needed to compete for work. However, neither political party objects, on grounds of economic principle, to market 'winners' garnering extreme amounts of wealth, so long as it results in the 'losers' being somewhat better off than they otherwise would have been.

In contrast, the Afro-communitarian conception of human dignity, with its relational conception of economic goods, entails that a large Gini coefficient reliably causes outcomes that are economically unjust. From this perspective, property must be distributed in a way that expresses esteem for communal relationships, and there is some economic injustice when property is held in a way that disrupts them. Such a view entails less of a tolerance for inequality than what is typical under welfare state capitalism, for a sense of togetherness is extraordinarily difficult to foster when some have much greater wealth than others (as Magesa 1997:277-278 points out). Large inequality not merely prevents the positive relationships of people thinking of themselves as a 'we', engaging in cooperative behaviour and helping one another for their sake, but also fosters their opposites, namely 'division' and 'ill-will'. When some are poor and have expectations that are frustrated in the face of others holding enormous amounts of wealth, then people turn to crime.

My claim is not that a market system, or even capitalism, is necessarily unjust, and I naturally recognise that fewer goods such as money going to the poor is a relevant economic harm to take into account when ascertaining which property distribution is most just. What I suggest, though, is that there is a *prima facie* relevant facet of distributive justice that the Kantian approach neglects and that the Afro-communitarian perspective highlights: one moral cost of substantial inequality (even when the poor marginally benefit in terms of income thereby) is the loss of communal relationship and the likely promotion of discord such as theft and violence. If a competitive economy is justified, then, given a need to respect the dignity people have in virtue of their capacity for community, there is *some* strong reason to regulate it to a much greater degree than the dominant political players have suggested.

If the present conception of the indignity of poverty is indeed more attractive in various ways than the dominant, Kantian view, then in future work it should be compared with additional rivals, such as the influential capabilities approach (e.g. Nussbaum 2000). If the Afro-communitarian perspective is to be taken seriously for public policy, then we need to explore what it might mean to measure the extent to which communal relationship is respected by a certain allocation of economic goods. Such abstract, theoretical analysis should be undertaken if South Africa's people are ever going to live genuinely human lives.

Reference List

Ackermann L. n.d. Human dignity. Unpublished manuscript.

Bhengu MJ. 1996. *Ubuntu.* Cape Town: Novalis Press.

Dworkin R. 2000. *Sovereign Virtue.* Cambridge, MA: Harvard University Press.

Friedman M. 1962. *Capitalism and Freedom.* Chicago: Chicago University Press.

Gaie J. 2007. The Setswana Concept of Botho. In: J Gaie & S Mmolai (eds). *The Concept of Botho and HIV/AIDS in Botswana.* Eldoret: Zapf Chancery. 29-43.

Magesa L. 1997. *African Religion.* Maryknoll, NY: Orbis Books.

Menkiti I. 2004. On the Normative Conception of a Person. In: K Wiredu (ed). *A Companion to African Philosophy.* Malden, MA: Blackwell. 324-331.

Metz T. 2010. Human Dignity, Capital Punishment, and an African Moral Theory. *Journal of Human Rights* 9(1):81-99.

Metz T & Gaie J. 2010. The African Ethic of *Ubuntu/Botho. Journal of Moral Education* 39(3):273-290.

Mokgoro Y. 1998. *Ubuntu* and the Law in South Africa. *Potchefstroom Electronic Law Journal* 1(1):1-11.

Murove MF. 2007. The Shona Ethic of Ukama with Reference to the Immortality of Values. *The Mankind Quarterly* 48(2):179-189.

Nkondo GM. 2007. *Ubuntu* as a Public Policy in South Africa. *International Journal of African Renaissance Studies* 2(1):88-100.

Nussbaum M. 2000. *Women and Human Development.* Cambridge: Cambridge University Press.

Ramose M. 1999. *African Philosophy Through Ubuntu.* Harare: Mond Books.

Rawls J. 1971. *A Theory of Justice.* Cambridge, MA: Harvard University Press.

Shutte A. 2001. *Ubuntu.* Pietermaritzburg: Cluster Publications.

Tutu D. 1999. *No Future Without Forgiveness.* New York: Random House.

United Nations. 1948. *The Universal Declaration of Human Rights.* Geneva: The Office of the High Commissioner for Human Rights.

A DIGNITY-ENRICHED HUMANISM

Russel Botman

The greatest ideas and the best innovations occur when humanity experiences a fresh genesis of humanism through the rediscovery of what it means to be human in a new context. Currently an emerging humanism stands in the balance between the needs of the being human and the wants of a technological society. This raises the question whether this new humanism will derive from a rebirth of human morality or from technological achievement. This new humanism must be contextually related to the new millennium if it is to be meaningful. It must be driven by the morality that substantiates the Millennium Development Goals of the United Nations, a dignity-enriched humanism that is essential for the transformation project in South Africa at a time when it is in danger of losing its humanist core. This must frame the way the new generation will become agents of responsible action locally and globally.

The 20th century was a time when powerful governments were committed to the selfish interests of the nation-states. As citizens of nations we have been overwhelmed by the demands, protections, secrecies and fears of the "state" of our nations. Somehow at the advent of the 21st century the question of the nation state and its rights to protection and secrecy are again demanding central stage. The genesis of a new humanism can bring to governments, the world and the many international institutions a new sense of urgency and responsibility focused this time on the dignity of the human being rather than the sovereignty of the state.

Humanity stepped into the 21st century with knowledge of the outcomes of the best international research. This was packaged in the Millennium Development Goals announced by Kofi Annan, the first African General Secretary of the UN whose term of office coincided with the turn of the century. After centuries of accepting that humanity will always have the poor with them, a new humanism arose from the idea of a humanity committed to making poverty history. Through knowledge regarding the achievability of the outcomes of these millennium goals we are looking at the possibilities of a world that will promote democracy, human dignity, health, peace, security of food and water, and a green environment.

The first manifestation of this new humanism is therefore in the moral realm, in a new planetary ethics. The first generation of the 21st century must be clearer about the objects and subjects that they value. They must have a good understanding of the roots of that which guide them to value some things above the ideologies and indoctrinations of their parents. The roots could be religious or secular. Every person rooting their actions in the values of a new humanism must re-examine their roots. The good and substantial morality of a new humanism can only come from a re-evaluation of our being human and of human agency in the 21st century. The humanness of the new generation will focus on values that embrace the wellness of humanity as a whole and of the environment as its home. The moral grounding of a new humanism depends on hard choices human beings must make. Such choices can also push society and the planet towards a future of misplaced despair and false hopes. The question of the next revolution that our children will lead is defined by the nature of such a new humanism. In Christian terms it will be a confession of hope in anticipation of the future that God projects.

The following values are the mainstays of this new emerging humanism:

Transparency

It is not the internet that is driving current sociality, but the worldwide value of human openness that's behind it. We are moving away from a cloistered, closed and whispering culture, breaking out of the mould of secrecy, to embrace a more open sociality. The virtual realism of technology provides a great tool for this new humanness. We find it in the social networks on the worldwide web. We see it as people step out of the "closet" (a word best describing the thought-world of my generation) at a much younger age, even when confronted by social repression, unfair criminalisation and familiar exclusions.

Valuing the future

The indescribable greed of my generation brought the world more than often to the brink of the abyss. This abyss has often threatened the future of the planet and of next generations. The threat occurred because my generation valued survival, dominance and fear more than anything else. Yes, more than the wholeness of the ozone layer, the balance of temperature in the climate, the greening of the physical world we have inherited, and much more. We can already feel the emergence of this new valuation process as the rights of future generations top the local and global charts of being and acting as truly human beings.

Embracing inclusivity and diversity concretely

Herein lies the challenge of humanism for Africa, America, the East and Europe in the 21st century. As resources dwindle, job opportunities evade the poorest of the poor of every country, and the results of the greed and corruption of my generation reach the end state of play, learning to live together, care about one another and investing in people that are different from one will become the hallmark of the genesis of a new humanism.

Material but not materialistic

The materialism of the next generation will be rooted in a new humanism. It will not simply mimic the materialism of the past, but present itself at first as a soundless pantomime of what can be described as humanist. The call of our time is to turn around the very meaning of humanism on the basis of what is important on the balance of things. The new humanism will seek a balance between the poor and the rich. We will, therefore, see a more giving humanism emerging from the rich and a more entrepreneurial humanism growing among the poor. This is the challenge for a more integrated world community. Immigration will show itself up as the most important solution presented by a new humanism, balanced by a proper and wisely targeted philanthropy of the rich.

Entrepreneurial initiatives and philanthropy must take on a new form, linked to the emergent humanism. For centuries entrepreneurial initiatives and philanthropy were caught up in the social welfare paradigm, where the private individual does good to another individual or family, or in the custodian paradigm where the community lets the government assume responsibility for all poor people on behalf of the rich. In exchange for this responsibility the government raises taxes. Tax strategies can be used for both welfare and guardianship purposes. The new innovative driver of entrepreneurial initiatives and philanthropy in the 21st century will be anchored much more in the development agenda of the world. The question is no longer how we can ensure social stability in a world of haves and have nots. The question now is how we can eradicate poverty with a new development strategy. In the 21st century the overarching concern is sustainable development. In this way sustainable development becomes the driver of a new humanism.

The new humanism will thus be a dignity-enriched humanism. This will change the world and the fate of many. No longer shall we pay homage to the will of the people in the abstract. Much more we shall learn to serve the dignity of people, the dignity of future generations and the integrity of their environment. This is the challenge of a generation in transition at the turn of the 21st century. But can humanity hold governments to the values they are beginning to share, to the vision of a future that they see together and to the mission of standing for the rights of future generations and the environment they know they can hope for in the 21st century? And, can they hold on to such hope against all hope? Will the people of our world, even at a cost to themselves summon the courage to be stronger than their most revered leaders in governments and religious communities everywhere in the world? If we can't achieve this, there will be no planet left. My generation succeeded in creating the biggest hole in the ozone layer. Plugging that hole requires a new humanism, a new way of being among all the people and the ecosystems of the world. My generation succeeded in dividing the world, the humanism of the next generation must deal of justice and unity. We have nowhere else to go, nowhere else to leave a footprint.

HUMAN RIGHTS IN A MORE HUMANE WORLD

Mary Burton

What does it require to live a humane life, in this country, at this time? We are bombarded by critiques, demands, complaints and accusations which are flung by one sector of our society against another, and we are ourselves conditioned to respond in ways which may contribute to these tensions, motivated by our own fear, rage or greed.

Our country (as indeed the world) is characterised by inequality, with a small slice of humanity having access to power and resources, and a much larger population living in relative or abject poverty, cut off from many of the benefits of modern knowledge and technology.

Enormous advances in the sciences have changed the world in many ways, and given human beings the capacity to achieve objectives which could scarcely be imagined even a few decades ago. The future promises even more astonishing developments and discoveries which will have unanticipated effects on our lives: communication, transport, health care and the environment. We exist in a world on which we can now have a tremendous impact, for good or ill, and yet we are still dependent on and responsible for the natural sphere and all that exists in it.

Our ability as human beings to relate to one another and to the world around us does not seem to have evolved as rapidly as other forms of knowledge. Over the centuries most of us have chosen to live in communities built on mutual relationships, and one could say that humankind has survived because of its ability to co-exist in societies governed by rules and values. Those societies, however, have often been disrupted by prejudice, conflict, exploitation and oppression. Peace and justice, and relationships built on mutual understanding and respect, sometimes seem unattainable.

When I look back at what I have written above, I am conscious that it could have been written at any time, and in any place, over the past several hundred years, by my grandmothers and great-grandmothers. Now in the 21st century, change is faster and more dramatic than ever before, because it builds on all the scientific and technological advances that have preceded it. The process of globalisation has brought people of different cultures and languages into closer contact with one another, with results that are both positive and negative. Yet, the issues that face humankind continue to be the same:

- How do we live together in justice and harmony?
- How do we protect our natural environment?
- How do we celebrate and protect diversity – of belief, of language, of origins, of abilities?
- How do we resolve conflicts and distribute resources?
- How can we harness economic and intellectual wealth to serve all societies instead of individuals or privileged groups?

The symposia at STIAS (the Stellenbosch Institute for Advanced Study) have considered these and other questions in exploring whether conditions exist for the rise of a new humanism, a new way of building human relationships, which could thereby contribute to a better world. Are there lessons to be learned from past humanist movements, and could there be particular lessons to be learned from the African experience?

Participants in these discussions came from within South Africa and beyond, from the fields of science, law, jurisprudence, education, literature, music, theology, anthropology, sociology, economics, business and civil society. They recognised that there is evidence of the emergence of a new global debate about what might be meant by humanism, about a view of the world which is based on concern for human dignity and human life, but also for the cosmos within which that life is contained and shared with other creatures.

That global debate has been stimulated by a quest for new ways to deal with the strife and cruelty which characterise many of the relationships of the present-day world. Countries have sought to codify and protect human rights by means of laws and constitutions; most of the world's religions have taught values of peace and justice and mutual respect. Still it is clear that this has not been enough.

What have we in South Africa to contribute to new understandings of human rights and human dignity, of how to live in a way which bestows nobility on every person, not only on those with economic and political status? When one travels outside our borders, one finds that the world is hungry for answers from a country which is seen as having found a way out of an abusive and conflict-ridden past into a new form of reconciliation.

We may know all too well how many disappointments and disillusionments have followed the initial prospect of a transformation of our society. Yet, there are aspects of our experience which do offer some possibilities for shifts in our own attitudes and in the relationships of the world. Traditional African societies had evolved mechanisms for resolving disputes which were inclusive, transparent, and had as their goal not the defeat and humiliation of one party, but an outcome which provided the best option for all. It is easy to deride romantic notions of *ubuntu* and rainbow nations, but it would be more useful to examine what lessons they may have for us.

We have eleven officially recognised national languages, and South Africans come from a variety of cultures and belief systems, each one of which has something to offer towards creating a rich store of knowledge. We should use this to build a common understanding of our history, a process which was given a special impetus by the Truth and Reconciliation Commission, but which could take up many more strands from our past.

This would enable us to see more clearly the way in which past abuses of human rights and human dignity impact on our present relationships. It could help us to find ways of living which break down barriers, create better understanding between people and groups, and relieve suffering and deprivation.

In working towards building a more humane country and a more humane world, and towards sharing its resources, we can draw on the experience and skills which are found in all sectors of society, the stories and the poetry, the knowledge and creative arts which can be used for the enrichment of all.

TO LEAD FOR HUMANITY

Peter Willis

As in any country, there are many positional leaders in South Africa. Every organisation and institution provides the opportunity for and requires such formal, positional leadership. We also have our fair share of informal leaders, people who express leadership through the way they influence others, even though they lack positional authority. Perhaps the most fundamental question that can be asked of any leader is "Leadership *for what*?" Taking the question to its highest potential, "What kind of world are you seeking to create through the way you lead?" I take as my starting point the assumption that any good leader will have the intention of promoting a humane world, that is, one in which each individual may flourish, not at the expense of others but in ways that will increase their well-being. With this in mind, there are two fundamental questions that should be asked and answered by any leader who intends to offer the kind of leadership that can create such a world.

The context for leadership

The first question concerns the context within which leadership takes place and seeks to achieve its specific ends. "Looking at the world around you, to what trends or patterns do you pay attention? Which of them do you think actually matter?"

The importance of this question has grown enormously over the last two decades and continues to grow. Whereas in previous generations it may have been both possible and excusable to focus one's leadership attention on a relatively local field of concern around one's organisation and its specific sector, as the reality has come home of our all sharing a small planet, now connected to one another in myriad ways through communications, trade and globalised culture, it is essential that leaders recognise the interdependence of their organisation with pretty much everything else that is. This need not be a recipe for paralysis, but the arts of discernment and discrimination have never been more important for leaders as the information at their fingertips multiplies. Wise leaders are recognising that in order to survive and thrive in an increasingly joined-together and speeded-up world they must understand their organisation as one system nested within and intersecting with multiple other systems, all of them dynamically adaptive to one another in varying degrees.

The challenge comes in ranking these multiple contextual systems as to their relevance to and potential impact on one's own system or organisation. Here it may help to think of the management of a company or institution of government or civil society as a game. One plays within a certain roughly defined field, one has one's team, one has a goal or set of goals to which one directs the team's efforts, and one plays to a set of rules. Some fields are larger than others. At the smaller end one might find a company that competes to be the best in its sector within a geographical region. Winning or losing at this game may matter to those immediately concerned but the implications do not normally spread much wider. At the other end of the spectrum we are all, whatever our organisation and its affiliations, playing on the field of Humanity-on-Earth. Here the rules are determined by the laws of physics and the principles of biology, ecology and so on. They tend to trump the man-made laws of commerce and government. Because this field is apparently so large an individual leader may believe his or her role in making decisions that affect play on that field is relatively insignificant, so rather concentrate on a smaller field where one can see one's impact more clearly. In fact many business people see the welfare of Humanity-on-Earth as being the concern of government, the NGOs, the religions or academia. But this is to mistake the way in which one field of play can be nested within another and to underestimate the degree of their interdependence. There is in reality a strict hierarchy of relevance and rank between these fields of play. In the words of US Senator the late Gaylord Nelson, "The economy is the wholly-owned subsidiary of the environment, not the other way around."

Why is this recognition of relative importance so critical for leadership today and in the coming times? The reason is simply that things are not going well on that larger field of play. It is one of the most challenging ironies of our age that the pursuit of economic growth and business advantage continues unabated at a time when natural scientists, sociologists and system thinkers are providing ever more compelling evidence that our tenure as the dominant species on planet Earth is no longer assured, this being precisely the unintended consequence of the pursuit of economic growth and business advantage.

If we as a species are to have any chance of reversing this trend and creating a platform upon which the next generations can build a genuinely sustainable global society, those who have influence within the most influential organisations in society have to awaken to the crucial relevance of the pictures being painted with increasing detail by the climate scientists, the biodiversity specialists, the social scientists and their ilk. Alongside the pragmatic case for being aware of that upon which one is dependent, there is the ethical case. Whether or not I chose you as my leader, you have some part of me in your care and I must place my trust in your superior access to information about the terrain we must traverse and your superior vision regarding our direction of travel. It is therefore beholden upon you to do whatever you can to inform yourself on both counts and reflect with all your skill and intelligence, drawing on whatever help is available, before making your decisions.

Our dominant narrative

The leader asks the second question, "What story do you think you (and we) are in?" It is quintessentially human to construct narratives and tell stories. They are indeed a primary way whereby we make sense of the world and our place in it. We do this as individuals; each of us has our own evolving 'life story' and we constantly seek to fit events and relationships into that narrative in order to reinforce our sense of being to some extent in charge of our life. We also do it as groups, as families, communities, companies and nations. The power of the story we created in South Africa around the first democratic elections in 1994, with metaphors like 'the rainbow nation', plays a vital role in our national discourse even today and was recently reaffirmed and re-told by the nation during its hosting of the FIFA World Cup.

All our narratives, at whatever level, affect the way we conceive of our future possibilities. They do this in a general way through the universe of assumptions they suggest. More specifically, most good stories contain consequences (e.g. "he did this and that's what happened to him"), which in turn imply a moral ("do this and this will happen to you"). In the case of South Africa's democratic transition, "If we treat each other with respect and are ready to listen and forgive, we can overcome what look like insuperable barriers between us and reach common ground beyond". For all our failings, this and other related story lines have been powerful national – even international – reference points during the last 16 years. There must have been uncountable times when individuals have been able to reference the story as a justification for behaving in a more humane way to a fellow being. This is but one way in which we South Africans can be said to be living within that familiar South African narrative of mutual respect in the service of a wider sense of being one nation, even if we may notice it for its absence as much as we notice it for its active presence.

Beyond personal, group and national narratives there is, in our time, something more – a dominant *global* narrative. This is the narrative that tells us that the ultimate earthly goal is to acquire material wealth and comfort for oneself and one's kin. I call it The Narrative of Consumption (at the level of the individual) and Growth (at the level of the company or national economy). I would suggest that, although less than a hundred years old, this is in fact the first and only truly globally dominant narrative. Others, such as for example the narratives of Islam, Christianity, Communism, all of which have commanded the adherence of vast numbers across different nations, have never been comprehensively global in their reach, whereas increased Consumption is the aspiration of most people everywhere today and Growth is the aspiration of virtually every company and nation. While earlier grand narratives have been constructed and maintained by various elite groups or priesthoods, the high priests of Consumption and Growth can be recognised everywhere today in the ranks of economists, bankers, technologists and advertising executives. It barely needs mentioning that this narrative has the attention of most leaders in government and business here in South Africa and worldwide. One must acknowledge that it has released the most extraordinary amount of human creativity, ingenuity and sheer energy during the past sixty years, a heady and probably highly addictive cocktail from which it will be correspondingly hard to withdraw. Like any great story, it continues to shape what is held up in the public discourse as possible and desirable for our future.

Yet, if we refer to the pictures being painted by the climate scientists, biodiversity specialists, etc., we can see that a counter-narrative is emerging, one I call the Narrative of Constraints. It tells us that our planet is finite, that Nature operates according to strict principles and that all the Earth's resources and sinks are being heavily used by humans to the point where many are close to their limits. With every passing year the evidence in support of this Narrative of Constraints mounts up.

What is important here is that, provided one gives credence to the scientific method and provided one pays at least fleeting attention to the accumulating data, one finds that the Narrative of Constraints whisks the rug of credibility from underneath the Narrative of Consumption and Growth. It is impossible to hold the two as true in one's mind simultaneously. For all that Consumption and Growth still continue to hold the high ground as of now, their days as a dominant narrative are numbered. Though we will deny the ill effects of our favourite story for as long as we are able, those ill effects will be increasingly self-evident and so we can expect more and more people to surrender their solid attachment to the story.

But here lies a dilemma. The Narrative of Constraints can clearly be shown to have superior logic and explanatory power to the Story of Consumption and Growth, yet, whereas the latter story held out the promise of a material heaven on earth as the reward for following its rules ('work hard, be smart, compete well and you will accumulate'), the Narrative of Constraints offers no such happy ending. If you reduce your carbon footprint there is no suggestion that you will reach carbon heaven; the moral of this story is simply that continuing with Consumption and Growth is suicidal. The natural scientists and systems thinkers have not seen fit to develop a happy ending to accompany their warnings of collapse, and nor should they have. So humanity is entering a double-sided crisis. For the first time and even without ever willing it so, we have created the real possibility of our collective demise. This in itself is serious enough. Simultaneously, however, we face a crisis of narrative. We have effectively started to run out of story.

On the face of it, and if one considers that we humans seem to have been dependent for the whole of our history upon stories – preferably with happy endings we can look forward to – having our dominant narrative taken away from us with no immediate prospect of a suitable replacement is worrying. Indeed, there is every reason to suspect that, as the pillars of our Consumption and Growth world start to crumble many people will be tempted to panic and act out of selfish desperation.

There are of course other possibilities. One is that qualities, values and attributes that have been systematically undervalued or suppressed in the Consumption and Growth world will resurface with a vigour commensurate with the force of the other's collapse. The feminine, for instance, has had a hard time expressing itself over the last three millennia and was certainly selected against under Consumption and Growth. Other casualties of this narrative have included the spirit of generosity and the emphasis on fellow-feeling or *ubuntu*. Another is sufficiency, or the concept of 'enough' – heresy under the dominant global paradigm where one defines oneself through one's wants. These and many other half-hidden treasures of the human spirit can be expected to make a resurgence in the near future, indeed are already doing so. This in itself may be cause for optimism.

But perhaps we should stretch our imagination a little further. Surely one of our era's defining features has been the way in which the human family, begun in South Africa and then for most of its history dispersed and separated by geography, language and belief, has sought so powerfully to come together in the past handful of decades. This may turn out to be the most important unintended consequence of the era of Consumption and Growth, when capitalists and technologists teamed up to link everyone together in what looked like markets but were also webs of human connectedness.

Although the formal discourse of national and international politics and business still uses the language of national boundaries and corporate identities, many currents now run across these, threatening to break them up and render them irrelevant in the foreseeable future. One need only look at the web- and cell phone-enabled youth, for whom national pride or loyalty to a company are weak signals compared to their membership of the wider world community, to realise that when it is their turn to run things they will do it very differently to us.

It can be argued that human history is marked by a progressive (if uneven) expansion of the circle of what is perceived to matter to us, from just ourselves and our immediate kin to our clan, to our church or state, to an ideal, to a global brand, to the galaxies, to ... perhaps we are getting ready to acknowledge *en masse* that, much as we still care about ourselves, our kin and our clan, the well-being of the whole Earth family, all of us and all of our neighbours, matters vitally, too. It not only matters, it excites us, it draws out the best in us. Is this wishful thinking? Put another way, what ultimately matters to us is what we love, what speaks to our heart. Perhaps the evolution of human consciousness can be understood as the widening of the circle of what we can love. In this case we can look at the self-serving, highly competitive ethos of the era of Consumption and Growth and speculate that the human heart has been treading water somewhat, mistaking narrow objects of desire for the full scope of the heart's capacity. There have been and are enough saintly and inspiring individuals to suggest that there is almost unlimited scope for the heart's expansion, so what might we not anticipate as the shackles of our attachment to our dominant narrative fall away?

The task for business leaders in particular

I see a period of immense challenge for those who work currently in the corporate world. Quite apart from the practical problems of continuing to run profitable enterprises as we run up against the limits of the ecological systems and social structures we have long depended on, I see a period in which the failing logic of the unrestrained, growth-oriented capitalist model will cause increasing stresses within individuals and whole organisations. Up until now the role of the corporate executive has been largely cast as heroic, certainly within the story of Consumption and Growth. What has happened in many countries to the public perception of bankers since the 2008 financial crisis is perhaps an indicator that this can no longer be assured.

Given the turbulence and uncertainty that's approaching, leadership will now be at a high premium. Fortunately there are in my experience many individuals within business, notably here in South Africa, with personal qualities of great potential value to the wider whole. I suggest here just three ways in which such leadership might be offered beyond the current requirements of the individual company:

1. Once they realise that the narrative of Consumption and Growth is flawed, executives can and should collaborate with their peers to work out what will be the next effective models for ensuring that society's needs (not its manufactured wants) are met within the constraints of nature. Designing the shape of businesses that will serve the widest possible whole is indeed a heroic and urgent undertaking.
2. Governments at all levels face enormous challenges in navigating the future. For too long business people have seen government in oppositional terms, and *vice versa*. Yet, in the face of certain kinds of challenge, business can often marshal resources with greater effect than government. There will be much opportunity here for creative collaborations, proposed in good faith and based in transparency. It will become increasingly obvious that nobody and no company can win while its surrounding community or country loses.
3. Within their companies there is enormous scope for leaders to nurture the humanity of their staff and through them all who come into contact with the company. We have come from an era where the organisation, the system, money,

even property and objects mattered more than the person. Having encountered some inspiring exceptions to the norm it is clear to me that a South Africa is possible where to be employed by a company means one is embarked 'in good company' on one's journey towards selfhood. If we are to evolve through this crisis rather than bow out altogether, such a shift is a necessity.

The last word must go to that great advocate of transformational corporate leadership, Ché Guevara. Try reading it substituting the word 'leader' – or even 'business leader' – for 'revolutionary'.

> At the risk of seeming ridiculous, let me say that the true revolutionary is guided by a great feeling of love. It is impossible to think of a great revolutionary lacking this quality ... We must strive every day so that this love of living humanity will be transformed into actual deeds, into acts that serve as examples, as a moving force.[1]

1 "Socialism and Man in Cuba", a letter to Carlos Quijano, editor of *Marcha*, a weekly published in Montevideo, Uruguay; published as "From Algiers, for Marcha: The Cuban Revolution Today"
by Che Guevara on 12 March 1965.

The Conversation

A narrative of the second symposium | *Stephen Martin*

Participants & Contributors

Indices

Names
Subjects

THE CONVERSATION

A narrative of the second symposium

Stephen Martin

Each of the five sessions of the symposium comprised the presentation of papers followed by discussion. We have highlighted some of the salient features of each paper and the interventions that followed. Based on a verbatim report, the narrative has been significantly shortened. But it may help the reader gain some sense of how the discussion developed.

DAY ONE

Introductory Remarks

John de Gruchy: "Widening the Conversation"[1]

The purpose of the gathering is to engage in ongoing conversation about issues arising out of the conversation at the first symposium of the New Humanism project

[1] De Gruchy's paper was read by Bernard Lategan. Part of this paper is included in the Introduction.

and to widen the conversation by incorporating new voices and more directly engaging societal matters. This is both a South African and a global conversation. The aim is to move from analysis to possibility and to give full expression to our hope for human flourishing.

Bernard Lategan: "Recurrent Themes at the first symposium"

General Contours

A New Humanism should be characterised by the following general features:

1. historical
2. contextual
3. dynamic and principled
4. critical and self-critical
5. de-centred
6. relational and inclusive
7. integral
8. imaginative

Specific Features

More specifically, a New Humanism should

1. explore *alternatives to violent overthrow* on the one hand and mere *reformism* on the other
2. develop a *more complex anthropology* and reconsider the idea of a human nature
3. address the *dehumanisation of poverty* and rethink values for a humane society
4. be aimed at *living well and being at peace together*
5. acknowledge *human agency and responsibility*, looking to change through interactions of ordinary persons rather than heroic leaders (or the imposition of grand theories)

Ethical Aspects

A New Humanism should

1. be *normative*, not merely descriptive, proceeding from a vision, and articulating a moral compass
2. replace "an ethics of *accumulation*" with "a principle of *sufficiency*"
3. rethink *dignity*, *equality*, and *freedom* in the present context
4. address balance of *rights* and *responsibilities*
5. be a "*reparative* humanism" in which values consolidate a culture of care in a violent context
6. explore *ubuntu* as source of African humanism

Trends and Debates in the African Context

With specific reference to the African context, a New Humanism should take into account

1. the new, democratically elected governments
2. the decline of transnational conflicts
3. the growth of market economies
4. new ways of appropriating modernity
5. the assertion of local identities in response to globalisation
6. the dominant discourse of transformation and Black empowerment and oppositional discourse of "corruption"
7. the concern with crime, entitlement and "culture of denialism"
8. the problem of xenophobia
9. the gap between human rights discourses and practices
10. populism and its view of institutions such as the courts
11. fundamentalisms and their view of science

Operational Issues

In thinking about how a New Humanism might be applied, there's need to

1. survey various *traditions* of humanism in South Africa
2. address the *systems* underlying society
3. embrace *complexity* thinking
4. include the total human and non-human *environment*
5. consider *race* and *gender* issues
6. provide a *research agenda* for different disciplines

Negative Factors

Finally, in recognition that no conversation is innocent, this particular conversation needs to be aware of

1. the historic failure of humanism, including its "dark side"
2. the present way humanism is talked about behind secure walls
3. the recurrent danger of humanism as a discussion of historical ideals
4. the dilemmas of transitional justice and the continuing presence of the past

Lategan argued that the present is an opportunity to re-examine the tradition of humanism. In doing so we need to make efforts to explore new traditions. This New Humanism would have at least seven features. It would

1. be self-critical and humble
2. shift away from anthropocentricism to biocentricism

3. be inclusive of all humans
4. mine religious and secular sources
5. be aware of complexity, multidimensionality, and contextuality
6. be dialogical and participatory
7. be prescriptive and normative.

Crucial to a New Humanism here would be attending to the *contextual contours* of South Africa. There are also negative aspects of the older humanism that would be obstacles to overcome, including the legacy of naive optimism. **Comaroff** raised the existence of other humanisms (classical and Islamic) which also need to be attended to.

First Session

Russel Botman: "A Pedagogy of Hope"

The transformation project in South Africa has lost its humanist core. It needs "a dignity-enriched humanism" which names things correctly. Is the task of government "service delivery", or furthering the human project in South Africa? Crucial to naming correctly is education – as a *humanising* project. Since the benchmark of a healthy, human society is its youth, something more than socioeconomic analysis is required. *An imaginative pedagogy of hope* captures the challenge to think about the kinds of people who will make up this imagined future world. Such a pedagogy takes us beyond a fragmented humanity to a global community, where analogous struggles are taking place.

Jean Comaroff: "Engaging Populism"

We live in the tension between a *humanitarian* world on the one hand, and a *post-humanist* world on the other. While human rights jurisprudence has spread across the world, we live in a world where life is abject. This is the paradox of humanism in late-modernity. Humanism names "an orientation shared by any vision that assumes the world is 'made', in significant respects, by human agency". While the term is often seen as part of the discourse of elites, a humanism "from below", articulates the elemental politics as a struggle for water. It does this in a world where projects of liberation have given way to a market model, where the citizen is consumer. At the same time, the Enlightenment idea of the sovereignty of the *people* has given way to the exclusionary membership of the *group*. This is evident in both populist and religious movements, and intellectual and theological movements. For both, humanism is heresy. Other kinds of populism point back to a "humanism from below", for instance new social movements in South Africa such as the Treatment Action Campaign.

Njabulo Ndebele: "Africa in the Modern World"

Recent elections in Africa are significant indications of ordinary people engaging with political processes and market economies. The relative decrease in conflict creates an "enabling environment", with fewer resources spent on managing conflict.

In South Africa, the election of Jacob Zuma after the decline of participation in the Thabo Mbeki years also carries great promise. The new social movements pressing a "service delivery" agenda understand this promise. But there seems to be a lack of awareness of their significance for the current historical moment. Needed is a "guiding mind" emerging from interactions between citizens and the state. The use of the genre of *biography* to examine how a family engages, at local levels, with the complexities of the system, and how structures respond is one approach to exploring this. This approach will take into account regional diversity and statistical matters, though its thrust will be qualitative rather than quantitative.

In response **George Ellis** said that the dehumanising abstraction of bureaucracies needs to be addressed in any humanist account. There is an illusion of participation that needs to be unmasked in the hope that real participation may come to pass. But as **Comaroff** noted, people live in a world of *multiple abstractions* and *multiple mediations*, creating closeness and distance simultaneously. **Lategan** found the case-study idea interesting as a strategy to explore humanism. He suggested that fiction allows the possibility of imaginatively reconfiguring the world. This is the strength of a literary – not just a social scientific – investigation of issues of delivery. **Huber** agreed and suggested that humanistic education in the classical sense (with its emphasis on literacy and literary education) has the virtue of confronting people with narratives other than their own.

Bobby Godsell: "Rethinking the Meaning of Wealth"

Despite talk of "a third wave of humanism" after the Second World War, what actually developed was a stronger, *mechanistic* worldview where education was subordinated to technical purposes. South African political discourse displays two problems. The first is *a wrong concept of wealth*. While the roots of the term are about health ("weal"), now wealth is about "metrics". The second problem is *a failure of solidarity*. The banking crisis has issued in a failure of trust, pointing to a lack of social coherence. The mechanistic world view is passing, and the rule of Anglo-Saxon capitalism is over. The situation within which we now think of a "good society" is politically polarised, xenophobic, and socially divided. Within this situation we have to think of what a "good society" is. An African way must be found.

Jannie Hofmeyr: "Integrating Humanity into the Web of Life"

We need a model of what a human being is in an unpredictable, uncontrollable world. The idea that "God will bail us out" allows people to opt out of taking responsibility. There are no deities to throw us lifelines. But neither can we escape our evolutionary past. We have a brain with a 50-year lifespan and are hard-wired to think locally, and for our immediate generations. The challenge is not easy in a world where humanity is being commodified. How can we bootstrap ourselves beyond this to a view that sees us as part of the web of life?

Wolfgang Huber: "Reflexive Humanism"

A *Reflexive Humanism* situates itself in dialogue with the multiplicity of humanisms, critically evaluating them and attending to their overlaps. It also monitors the particular anthropocentrism in each, questioning how each relates the human to creation. There are two specific challenges for our conversation. The first is the challenge of acknowledging the different as equal, addressing motivation and behaviour. Why does the ethical motive of attending to the other seem to pale next to the economic impulse? This is a question that renews interest in religion, however inconsistent its witness has been. A second challenge concerns dignity. Renaissance humanists distinguished *honour* from *dignity*. But what's a substantial definition of dignity? This is an occasion for the coming together in conversations of different understandings (humanisms). A Christian understanding sees dignity as "radically eccentric", rather than being grounded in an aspect of human being. Dignity is not self-grounded. While this can be explained in secular terms, the motivational power of Christian traditions, rituals, and convictions should not be underestimated.

Mark Solms: "Humanism and Human Biology"

The search for the good life is rooted in biology, and can be excavated by "affective neuroscience". Values are rooted in evolutionary predispositions, while not being reducible to evolution. Values, in turn, point to consciousness, which has its roots in the periaqueductal. Good sensations have an evolutionary advantage, pointing to actions that enhance chances of survival. While the human *drive* is to homeostasis, the basic sensory *affects* concern anything that stimulates receptors to be avoided. What lies between drives and affects are *instincts*. There are seven instincts that are built into the brain – from basic emotions to complex behaviours: seeking, pleasure, rage, fear, attachment, care, and play. Through such instincts we form relations and map our world in order to enhance pleasure. But instincts can be over-ridden, albeit with difficulty. We *can* act against our instincts, and the possibility for this is also biologically rooted in the frontal part of the brain.

Njongonkulu Ndungane: "African humanism"

African humanism is linked to an African world view that sees humans (and God) as inter-related, including *the living* and *the living dead*. This relationship includes the land, which has sacred value, and the animals. It's relationship all the way down.

In response **Ebrahim Moosa** said that the classical notion of a humanist education is now challenged by a view aimed at preparing people with values for the "real" world of business. While it's encouraging to see dialogue between the natural sciences and the humanities, as **Botman** noted, macroeconomic questions continue to drive the agenda in education. The perception is that academic discourse doesn't represent "the real world". Or perhaps it is, as **Moosa** suggested, simply that the critical humanities speaks a language not understood outside. While it may be true that humans share a common evolutionary background, they follow a diversity of values that can be understood through "sympathetically" putting ourselves into the narratives of others. Agreeing with **Huber** on this point, **Denise Ackermann** worried about the language of "hard-wiring" compromising human agency. What is the relation between the biological limitation of the human brain and the opening up of new imaginative possibilities? **Alexander** noted that the meeting of basic needs, such as those instinctually rooted, understood as basic *economic* needs, is a prerequisite for imagining a different future.

The paradox and ambiguity that seem inherent in humanism are related. In fact, as **Comaroff** said, ambiguity makes the key categories of older humanism, such as "secular" and "sovereign", problematic. The destabilisation of such concepts opens up a humanism from below. Think of **Ndebele**'s idea that the taxi industry was a way of contesting apartheid's control of movement. New public spaces that can't be mapped onto an older account of "public", are now being created, as in a taxi itself, which is also a site of political conversation and contestation.[2] Is the call for a "New Humanism" a call for a "new modernism?" Is this New Humanism intended to be *universal*? The terms used to describe it such as "solidarity", "inclusion", and "no line drawing" make it seem so, at least for **Hendrik Geyer**. But it's not a conceptual concern that brings the group together, responded **Alexander**, rather, it's a shared concern about the barbarism of the twenty-first century as it's shaping up. The challenge is to find ways of thinking and speaking that change conditions on the ground, right *now*. For that reason, it may be better to speak of a humanism *for the twenty-first century*, rather than a "New Humanism". It's the quest for a *humane*, society in South Africa.

Georg Fodor expressed concern that the group not overlook what has been achieved in South Africa since 1994. **Peter Willis** returned to the notion of imagination. An "ecology of images" could liberate creativity and steer dialogue about the kind of world we'd *like* to live in. At the same time, **Mary Burton** stated the sober fact that 4 percent of the people in the world control the wealth of the world, while 73 percent live in poverty. All the planning is in the hands of the 4 percent. Like it or not, this is *us*. The challenge is for us to listen to the 73 percent, so that ideas flow both ways.

Second Session

Achille Mbembe: "On African Humanism"

The new engagement with the theological, especially around recovering a tradition of "Christian Humanism", suggests that fundamental questions are on the agenda. These questions are appropriate to our disjointed world of radical uncertainty, where "making it from day-to-day" is the principle cultural act. This uncertainty includes questions such as "who is my neighbour?" and "what's the relation between truth, justice and freedom?" But in South Africa, race accents questions of what it means to be human. Race has been the principal method for the production of surplus/superfluous people. Since in South Africa's history of capitalism, the human becomes a form of waste, a New Humanism needs to be thought of in terms of liberation from production of the human as waste. There are multiple genealogies of African

2 There are two dimensions to this: as Ndebele had pointed out, taxis represent the incursion of black entrepreneurialism onto apartheid's attempt to control movement. In this regard, a taxi is an interruption of urban planning. But the space *inside* a taxi is also a space of discourse and of debate.

humanism. *African humanism as ubuntu* presents the latter as a metaphysical/aesthetic concept overcoming the dyads of slavery/self-affirmation, subject-object/singular. It's a reinvention of the African self, but also allows us to think of African humanism in relation to universal humanism. A second genealogy is *African humanism as the dead hand of legitimation*. This is based on Fanon's criticism of a future-oriented African humanism. We can't know what it is to be human without mapping it onto a history of servitude. Is there a future community of hope and possibility while living in the present? A final genealogy is *African humanism as negotiation*. Whatever Africans might mean by humanism has to be related to the twin concepts of "wealth" and "multiplicity". "Wealth" has three forms: wealth as *people*, wealth as *things*, and wealth as *knowledge*. Humanism means negotiating people, things, and knowledge in such a way as to promote future possibility and potentiality.

In his response **Moosa** commented on the danger and hope of "the return to the theological". The particularism of some theological movements is a matter of concern, while the collapse of traditional metaphysics opens the possibility of new ways of thinking. Further, since the coloniality of power gives rise to that of knowledge, an African humanism will have to deal with power *and* knowledge.

Drucilla Cornell and Kenneth Panfilio:[3] "Ubuntu"

Neoliberalism as an ideology is destructive in that it bleeds a humanism of teleology. It is crucial to get a teleological humanism back. This does not imply a single, total view of what it means to be human, but rather identifying a symbol that can invoke the whole in a "radical epistemological openness", pointing us toward a New Humanism that moves ahead of us. *Ubuntu*, understood as "a universalisable activist ethic". In dialogue with **Achille Mbembe**'s criticism of "frozen narratives of [African] subjectivity", they propose a view of *ubuntu* that sees relationality "all the way down". One is born into a language, a kinship group, a nation. While these make it possible to develop as a moral agent, he or she cannot be reduced to them as a shared world is ongoingly realised, not only for the agent, but for other agents. This shared world is a harmonisation of individual interests. A disruption of the agency of one person is thus a violation of the agency of others. Justice looks to a situation of restoration rather than punitive intervention. Justice is the "moral repair" of society. Obviously this also contests neoliberalism as private property and dispossession give way to the idea of a "commons".

Comaroff expressed concern that identifying genealogies of African humanism with *ubuntu* forecloses discussion of more complex movements. **Ndebele** expressed suspicion towards the whole *ubuntu* concept, as it seems to elevate "codes of courtesy" into a philosophy declared "essentially African" over-against colonialism. The idea that every civilisation *has* to have a governing philosophy is colonialist romanticism. But this, suggested **Alexander**, necessitates reinventing concepts,

3 As Cornell and Panfilio were unable to attend the second symposium, their paper was read by Ebrahim Moosa.

giving them new content. A syncretic position is viable, especially in South Africa where African, European, and Asian traditions flow together.

Coming back to his presentation, **Mbembe** noted how African values are related to structural factors such as *mobilisability* and *multiplicity*. Innovations present themselves in relation to changing structural conditions. The question is how do people interpret their lives? The goal of investigation into this question is a "singularity", something original and irreducible, but which is also transportable. Agreeing with **Comaroff**, **Moosa** said that the romanticisation of particularities in response to liberalism could also become anti-humanistic. Particularity must be affirmed while steering clear of the danger of universalisation.

Third Session

André du Toit: "Humanisms in South Africa: Who Were/Are the Humanists?"

Du Toit suggested that General Jan Smuts could be called a humanist despite his white supremacy and racism. If Smuts' humanism can be demonstrated, does this not place *any* humanism in moral question? In his education, he learned that "humanising" was "civilising" done through the "humanities". It was this heritage (borne by white Europeans in Africa) that Smuts was determined "not to see lost in the 'black pool' of Africa". Smuts is also known for his role in drafting the United Nations Charter, and its championing of human rights. Yet, Smuts rejected the use of the term by Africanists within South Africa. Did the term apply only to those who stood in the traditions linked to classical humanism? There are other readings of the Charter's option for "human rights", such as an effort to move away from the failed League of Nations' idea of "minority rights". Either way, in talking about a New Humanism, we have to address the question of why the old humanism failed, and whether something "new" can avoid its pitfalls.

In the nineteenth century, **Huber** remarked, humanism could speak both *universally and generally*, but also with a deep distinction among *kinds* of humans. Further, while Smuts was involved in drafting the 1945 UN Charter, the Universal Declaration of Human Rights was rejected by South Africa three years later. Even documents framing equality as self-evident are subject to interpretation, as was the American Declaration of Independence, formulated as it was in a society where slavery was practiced. But history is messy, said **Godsell**. Great leaders are not all great. At the same time we must avoid using contemporary norms to evaluate historical situations. There was no humanism in sixteenth century Italy if we apply today's standards. But humanism does have a dark side, replied **du Toit**. Be aware of a politics of "the moral high ground", especially one that claims to be unaligned.

Religion and Humanism

Denise Ackermann: "Becoming More Fully Human: The Relational and the New Humanism"

For religious communities to be vehicles for developing a new humanism requires a theology of relation. The contours of this relationality in biblical religion begin with Israel as a covenant people. This relationship is voluntary and governed by love. Justice means right relationship – something carried in the message of Jesus. But classical theism lost the centrality of relationship, the intimacy and immediacy of the covenant. A more relational view of God is being recovered by contemporary feminist theologies, and points to five features of "a humanising relational praxis":

1. Being in relation is a fact.
2. Being in relation is embodied.
3. Part of embodied relations is justice – people live in dignity as agents of their own destiny.
4. Hallmarks of justice include respect for the rights of the other and taking moral responsibility for our intentions.
5. Interrelatedness means sensitivity to the difference that arises from our common humanity.

Several participants commented that the idea of covenant creates problems, notably the idea of a "chosen people". Even in biblical tradition, said **Mbembe**, the relation between the elector and the elected is fragile, with an immense amount of energy spent on maintaining/repairing the relationship. A more inclusive understanding of covenant, suggested **Huber**, comes by starting not with Abraham but with Noah. Here the covenant is with *all creation*, something that **Ackermann** suggested that the Christian Eucharist links us to. In the history of Israel the covenant is always in broken form. However, dealing with this brokenness gave the community a language for speaking about God, and to God. The language of lament is a product of this dynamic. In biblical covenant discourse, observed **Willis**, there is an inbuilt reward system to virtuous behaviour. This is something that religious discourses have that a New Humanist discourse would have to develop.

DAY TWO

Fourth Session

Humanisms in South Africa Continued

Neville Alexander: "Let us Return to the Source: In Quest of a Humanism of the Twenty-First Century"

Modernity signals a rupture which must be addressed through Africa "owning" modernity for itself. The Black Consciousness Movement (BCM) understood liberation *psychologically* as well as socio-economically. From this *liberation of consciousness* came a host of community development *programmes*, including community organisations spawning a creativity and a vision which looked to a different South Africa. But after 1994, the new elite adopted the same socio-economic values as the apartheid regime. This sent the wrong signal to black youth. Fifteen years later an ideal of success undermines the morality of the liberation movement. We must imagine a different moral economy, based on two dictums: "enough is as good as a feast", and gifts are given for the benefit of others. This swims against the cultural tide. But there are already signs of this hope where farmers have decided to withhold their taxes and fix the potholes in the roads themselves. Reading clubs, literature groups, and co-ops are arising. Government should be called upon to assist such initiatives.

In discussion it was suggested that a constructive way to preach this "secular sermon" to businesspeople might be to rethink key terms such as wealth. As **Godsell** suggested, the etymology of "wealth" is the old English word "weal" as in "commonweal", which has to do with the health of a society. "Doing well" need not be bank-balance defined. **Alexander** affirmed this, though the challenge is getting those historically advantaged to recognise that Apartheid was a massive affirmative action programme from which they benefitted, and thus to make their wealth available to the majority. There was an opportunity to do this in the early nineties, which whites regrettably missed. **Manganyi** also identified a pedagogical imperative in recovering the traditions of empowerment developed by the BCM.

The Constitution and Human Dignity

Laurie Ackermann: "The Constitutional Law Concept of Human Dignity and the New Humanism"

While human dignity is the lodestar for equality in South Africa, what is a judge to make of the fact that dignity, equality and freedom are not defined in the Constitution? Lawyers need to attend to the philosophical and theological sources for understanding the meaning of human dignity. The core provisions in post-war German law (influential in South African Constitution-making) stipulate that human dignity is inviolable and extra-constitutional (that is, human dignity exists prior to the making of a constitution). But the norm of human dignity in understanding the meaning of equality is something that continually challenges law-making. The South African Constitutional Court has understood dignity and worth (the development of one's potential) as synonymous. It is difficult to see how the concept of dignity can be applied more widely (animal rights), or the idea that "barbarous acts" committed by humans (stripping the rain forests, for example) were a violation of *natural* dignity. It is better to regard this consequentially as violating the dignity of later *human generations.*

Huber suggested that human dignity be thought of in the context of human *duty*. Hence **Denise Ackermann**'s underscoring of the necessity of a New Humanism and her asking what a human being is – a question that also must be asked within law. **Fodor** observed that, from the perspective of group psychology our position is defined strongly by the group, and the affirmation of our individual dignity remains through the group. **Laurie Ackermann** responded saying the Constitution protects *associational* rights, while the group itself has no reasonable personality. The recognition of human dignity can only come through other humans; but the distortions of this idea which say one can only find one's true identity in the *volk* are to be avoided. **Metz** observed a tension between the two accounts of dignity: as grounded in *individual self-recognition* and on *the ability to form relationships*.[4] **Laurie Ackermann** responded that if the person achieves self-recognition in interrelation with other people, there's no tension. Nonetheless, individuality needs careful explanation, and **Huber** noted that possessive and relational individualities are very different. **Leon Wessels** was less sanguine about the Constitution's refusal to define "dignity, equality, and freedom". The drafters could have said that "the right to life", for instance, means "the right to a better life". It's fine to speak of procedural rights, but this assumes that all subjects of the Constitution have *equal access* to the instruments that guarantee this. **Mbembe** pointed out the ambiguity of a figure like Kant, whose idea of human dignity doesn't include races that aren't white. We have to work with him *and* against him. **Laurie Ackermann** insisted that the one side of Kant does not necessarily follow from the other.

Thaddeus Metz: "African Conceptions of Human Dignity"

There are two understandings of human dignity in African moral thought: humans are special *because they contain or embody life force* (vitality), or humans are special *because they are relational* (community). The African *communal* conception is better than the Western Enlightenment conception that says humans are special because of their *freedom/autonomy*. The vitality understanding can be argued *supernaturalistically* (with respect to the divine) or *naturalistically*; and with regard to *substance* (we have a soul) or *force* (which may or may not be bound to a metaphysics). For some, the community understanding of dignity comes from *actual* being in community. But what if someone is in solitary confinement and has no *actual* relations? The *potentiality* for forming relations marks humans as special. There are two logically distinct kinds of relationship: *identity* and *solidarity*. One can have identity without solidarity, and vice-versa, but much African philosophy is a combination of identity and solidarity. Hence, an African answer to the question of why poverty is wrong would have to do with its depriving the person of the ability to share.

Huber asked whether it was better to leave the question open, allowing the poor person to answer *for him or herself*? **Metz** replied that it is indeed important to be able to say *why* poverty is bad, as this will determine one's response. **Moosa** affirmed the use of *ubuntu*, though he granted the danger of essentialising and romanticising the term. **Metz** concurred. South Africans spend too much time trying to define *ubuntu* when they *could* be talking about how to live. But isn't the community model still highly idealised? How to account for inconsistencies in its outworking? Does it not

4 See also Metz's paper for more on the difference between a communal and a Kantian account.

neglect power and violence, leading one to look away from existential reality? What he's trying to do, **Metz** replied, is not to describe, but to articulate a concept that is recognisably African and philosophically attractive. The limits of the Kantian model also concern non-Western and non-African views which nonetheless play a role in South Africa's context. **Hofmeyr** suggested a need to engage Asian views such as Taoism. And **Fodor** returned to the contrast between Kantian and communitarian approaches, especially to poverty. In different cultures, people have different ideas of what constitutes poverty. How much people need is a culturally relative question.

Dignity, Community and Technology

George Ellis: "Science, Technology and Humanity"

Technology embraces all of life's aspects. Its overwhelming effects are more significant than politics. It can be used for good or for ill. Technology creates opportunities, but also changes the ways we think, determining the ways cultures develop. For better or for worse, the founders of civilisations are the engineers, not the artists, and the technology created by a civilisation will outlive the demise of that civilisation. Science and technology are related. And yet, the development of the latter usually follows "blue skies" research of the former. One cannot therefore promote technological development while neglecting basic research. Even abstract technology (the development of languages, theories, models) develops social indicators and models of human happiness. Technology marks an important difference between human making and natural invention through evolution. Since it always embodies human values, technology can enhance or constrain life. How are we to *choose* and *shape* the technology of the future? Value choices need to be imposed on technological applications. These choices come down to two questions: *who benefits* from a particular application of technology? and, how will this application *improve human life*? [To these two questions, **Lategan** added a third: *who decides*, especially when the "beneficiaries" are often anonymous.] But these "purpose" choices also presuppose a set of values that guides them, including justice, participatory freedom, and economic development for humans, and sustainability.

The question was raised in discussion: if a new way of being human prioritises living in relationship, how does living with an overload of information from different sources/people affect this? For **Denise Ackermann**, the convenience of e-mail, and the way it can facilitate relationships is one side of the coin, but the fragmentation of families is the other. Another question concerned the theoretical limit of technological development. We're rapidly moving from hip replacements to the possibility of replacing *everything*. At what point do we stop being human? The ethical question, suggested **Ellis**, is how to *shape* what's done to good, rather than destructive, purpose. This means some kind of intervention to limit possible applications. Indeed the law faces challenges from technology, said **Laurie Ackermann**. If *society* doesn't decide what's appropriate and what's not, the *courts* will decide. Reiterating a point in his own presentation, in the instance of cloning the question of whether human dignity extends beyond death has to be dealt with. **Geyer** wondered whether, when we talk about human beings in this discussion, we are talking about human beings *as they have historically been*, or human beings *as they are becoming in the 21st century*. The latter especially takes into account the relationship humans have with the contexts they design (including technologies) – and, as **Moosa** said – the way humans are subjects of technology. Human beings would have been very different without the developments of fire, agriculture, and so forth.

Fifth Session

Memory, Interpretive Excess and Solidarity

Bernard Lategan: "Exploring the Contours of a New Humanism"

There is a convergence of values around the table in which terms like "reflective", "pluralistic", "relational", "complex", "decentred", and "dialogical" portray a critical humanism. Yet, while the conceptual building blocks are in place, we can't translate them into social reality. South Africa has a Constitution, a Bill of Rights, and democratic structures which are, while necessary, *in themselves* insufficient to bring about social transformation. "More" is needed. Based on the antitheses in the Sermon on the Mount, Lategan suggested that this "going beyond" imagines creative alternatives in dealing with specific situations. While the *lex talionis* could point to basic instincts, a *default* position, we can conceive alternatives. South Africa's transition embodied this by putting on hold the natural consequences of the struggle, but the persistence of violence is a consequence of our inability to conceive alternatives. There are analogies to "going the second mile" in the South African context. With regard to property rights, we can stay true to the *intent* of the law, yet take the liberating *possibilities* within the situation much further. Here dialogue and negotiation come to the fore. This is also a "going beyond", a refusal to be satisfied with equilibrium.

In discussion, **Comaroff** spoke of a dialectic between reparation and affirmative action. An excess takes us beyond apology and leveling the playing field, allowing us to deal with things more assertively through debates around basic income grants and so forth. There's already been a cue here which could kickstart a process, suggested **Lategan**, in the surplus generosity of members of the liberation movements at the beginning of South Africa's democratic project. But how to make the state do what it's *supposed* to do? **Burton** said there has to be a mental shift so that people with power think differently, acting in light of information in front of them, as well as [democratic] values. **Ndungane** referred to the significance of the poverty hearings and African Monitor. As long as the *lex talionis* remains the default position, there's no place to end the cycle of retribution, and thus to get to the "beyond". Ireland and Israel are examples. Government should be brought into the process of moving into an "excessive" future, but only if values are presented in such a way as to make "the way things are" resistible. **Willis** asked what a humane state might be in practical terms. Can we think about a government that sees a person as a person? "A humane state" appeals to the common sense of humanity and seems to have more purchase than "a developmental state". But perhaps since 1994 there has been too much of an expectation for government to act on behalf of people. **Alexander** spoke of the challenge of persuading communities and neighbourhoods to act. While Section 9 of the Constitution does speak along the lines of the *lex talionis* of "restitutionary equality", it assumes that there can be *unwilling* beneficiaries. One doesn't have to be guilty in order to bear an obligation of restitution. At the same time, it's important to be aware that people can *overestimate* what the Constitution and the courts can do. The Constitution will only succeed if social transformation is a reality. It borders on the obscene to preach "human dignity" to homeless and starving people. How to communicate the values of civil society to "an iPod generation"? Perhaps one way might be to consider community service as an essential component of education. Indeed, concluded **Lategan**, this disconnection between values and social involvement was the reason for the demise of civil society. There must be a constant interaction between the values and actions of liberation.

Harry Kunnemann: "Autonomy and Solidarity"

The challenge within humanism concerns combining the search for a meaningful life with deep experiences of being human together with others. These two core concepts, *autonomy* and *solidarity*, are in tension with each other. This is something humanists have to attend to, especially since there's growing support for xenophobic politics, all in the name of autonomy and freedom. As Kunnemann's paper is not included in the book, we provide a brief summary of its three parts.

- *The development of the modern concept of autonomy* as something possessed prior to relationship with others. Hence the modern problem has been to account for the conditions under which autonomous individuals engage morally for the sake of other people.
- *A post-modern idea of autonomy* articulates a distinction between "surface" and "deep autonomy". The depth is a vulnerability in which we are tied to the other. This remains tacit until through loss of the other "we are undone" by a lost relationality neither wholly possessed by the self or the other. But this relationality may be held at the depths without losing autonomy in a deeper sense: that of accepting our vulnerability, our limitation, our needs. Deeper autonomy means letting go of possessiveness in relation to an other, but without letting go of agency. However, this leaves unattended the question of violence in human relations. The self exists in an illusion of omnipotence, by which we continually (and violently) construct the other as an object. So constructed, the other is always in our shadow. The constructed other (alter) and the ego make up an intra-psychic dynamic. But we have to move from intra-psychic to inter-subjective relations by "stepping out of the shadow", rejecting the projections without destroying the relationship. In this way we block the omnipotent self while offering a new relationship on another basis. We learn we can be safe without controlling the other. In this other space we can experience intimacy, but only as we accept our vulnerability.
- *Applying deep autonomy to "normative professionalism".* In professional relationships (such as that of a health care worker to a patient) the dynamics of mourning and longing remain in play, as do the dynamics of "containment" in which they deal with the omnipotence of those they seek to serve. Professionalism

becomes a site for relating the search for a meaningful life to the challenges of others (and more contextual factors professionals have to cope with, such as efficiency, transparency, and economic frugality) in deepening autonomy.

Comaroff asked how this model translates into a politics. Can you confront the state in such a way as to move it to fulfil its promises? **Kunneman** suggested that the key here is *rehabilitating professionalism*. The idea is to encounter persons as *subjects*, rather than as objects to control. Perhaps the idea of civil or "professional" society captures this as well. The term *professio* (which has an originally religious meaning) means there's something *beyond yourself* to appeal to. Does this not place too much faith in professional society, **Moosa** wondered. There's need for vigilance. After all, a whole professional class in South Africa justified apartheid. Indeed, claimed **Godsell**, South Africa has seen a continued conflation of party, state, and society.

DAY THREE

Final Discussion

The final session consisted of final thoughts on the project.

1. It's important not to lose the distinctiveness of South African experience around the more abstract questions of what it means to be human. At the same time, suggested **Raenette Taljaard**, talking about a distinctive, concrete South African experience we can't lose sight of the current "global moment", with the crisis in financial institutions especially.
2. The "global moment" is also about the question of power. **Fodor** noted that *Geweigt* is power/violence, but also something necessary to preserving the dignity of the individual. Ironically, there can be no humanism without *Geweigt*.
3. In addressing the discouragement that many South Africans experience about the post-apartheid project, the note of hope must continue to sound. **Lategan** suggested that Paul Ricoeur's idea of "second naivety" could help articulate what needs to be grasped. **Eugene Klaaren** suggested that the idea of dignity could carry the element of hope. **Moosa** suggested concretising this "dignity in hope" in the areas of economics, life-sciences, and technology – all places where dignity is vulnerable.
4. Is there a danger in focusing too much on academic (or journalistic) writing in considering the outworkings of the Project? For instance, a musical performance can also provide seeds for conversation, as well as bring into relief the contested relation between commodification and the arts.[5] But even here, there's need to maintain connection to the biological, **Solms** remarked. Humans share with mammals the use of music to facilitate bonding, but also to express the pain of separation. In recognising the "uniquely human" character of music, we mustn't differentiate it from our prehistory.

---

5 To illustrate this, Hans Huyssen played a movement from one of the Bach cello suites.

5. "A vision is like the polar star when you are navigating the Atlantic" (**Fodor**). Perhaps "vision" says best what the group was trying to articulate over these three days. While representing a diversity of professions (academic and non-academic), disciplines, and ideological/religious (and non-religious) perspectives, what emerged was a vision which saw the past fifteen years in South Africa, while nowhere near the darkness of apartheid, as nevertheless a time when important values have been either lost or forgotten. The vision that expressed the values which led South Africa to move toward transformation needs to be recaptured. But South Africans are now more "worldly wise", and more aware of how the wider world impinges on its transformation project, for good or for ill. That there is a conversation is surely a sign of hope. And the agreement on concepts like *wealth as weal*, *valuing personhood*, and *respecting difference* is significant. Perhaps this is what a New Humanism is: something that emerges as a gift from a painful past and reaches toward a positive future of flourishing.

An Analysis of the Discussion

Steve Martin[6]

The conversations took into account both the *historical* and changing development of humanism as unfolding in particular *contexts*. The contemporary European and African contexts raised the question of its continued viability, particularly in South Africa. Thus the humanism spoken of was *dynamic* in being a tradition both handed down and taken up afresh. The ethical concerns enumerated throughout the conversation demonstrate that contextuality does not mean relativism. The concerns point to a *principled* reading of the humanist tradition. Despite differences in understanding how to ground human dignity most participants seemed to agree that there is an ethical imperative that obtains for humans *as such*. And it's this imperative that leads the participants to *criticise* much of what's been happening in South African society since 1994. At the same time, the conversation was only too aware of its own limitations. Even those who still used the language of autonomy understood autonomy against a background of shared sociality and *relationality*. Finally, the conversation exemplified *creativity* as well as identifying the capability to think differently, to think otherwise, to create alternatives as fundamental to human activity.

Specific features

The idea of developing *a more complex anthropology and reconsidering the idea of a human nature* was developed linked to the criticism of anthropocentrism, but also related to questions of building just social structures. In the case of individual or physical anthropology, the question concerns whether we are biologically determined by the instinctual apparatus we share with other mammals, or free as a distinctive

---

6 This analysis returns to the recurrent features identified by Lategan from the first consultation in 2009 (see above), tracing their development in the second consultation in 2010. These are also developed in Lategan's essay in the book.

species. While no one suggested that humans are determined, several participants saw a danger in tracing human values to brain activity. Not only was there a danger of reductionism, there was also a failure to account for human imagination, to think a different possibility for the world, and thus to think transformation. This was a creative conversation, because even a physicalist account supplied purchase for metaphors: how do we create these possibilities for action beyond instinct? There's a basic minimum requirement for humans to exist as humans. But a "good society" must go beyond this if such a society is to flourish as one in which people are *living-well and at peace together*. A New Humanism *should acknowledge human agency and responsibility, looking to change through the interaction of ordinary persons rather than heroic leaders*. A New Humanism must seek to trace the ways humans *collectively* make their world (and under what conditions).

Ethical aspects

The discussions saw New Humanism as an ethical project whose tenets *should be normative, not merely descriptive, proceeding from a vision, and articulating a moral compass*. One of these value shifts concerned replacing *an ethics of accumulation with a principle of sufficiency*. How we should think about *dignity, equality, and freedom in the present context* was debated with reference to different interpretations of Immanuel Kant, namely treating others as ends and not just means to an end, human autonomy, and an ambivalent Eurocentric upholding of human dignity. Any viable concept of autonomy has to overcome the violence of a self that constructs the other to fulfil its own needs. Gifts exist to be shared for the greater good; autonomy, has to co-exist within communality. Much discourse finds the answer to both in the vision of *ubuntu*. A distinctively African contribution to the wider human debate, *ubuntu* is deeply rooted in African sociality and religion. But the danger of the essentialisation of the concept, along with a romantic view of the notion and its co-optation by self or group interests, has to be avoided.

The contemporary African context

The *new democratically elected governments* and the *decline of transnational conflicts* have actually created the conditions for the *growth of market economies* in Africa. But capitalism is deeply ambiguous. While new religious movements represent *new ways of appropriating modernity* they are also located within the paradox of a system that manufactures disposable human beings. This is the legacy of apartheid that South Africa is struggling to overcome. But it's also part of globalisation. Likewise, the local is being "manufactured", packaged, and sold abroad in "authentic" foods and music. Capitalism ingests every particular, including music, rendering it "consumable". At the same time, capitalism creates opportunities for redistributing the necessities of life. Unquestionably, capitalism raises ethical issues for New Humanism. While the metaphor of the market challenges traditional ideas of citizenship there's something distinctively African about a market. The idea of exchange helps account for how Africans appropriate ideas.

Within South Africa, a democratic government, the decrease of civil strife, and the growth of the market economy do not automatically mean social *transformation*.

In fact, that term "transformation" is another contested concept, having become synonymous with "Black empowerment". There are deep concerns expressed about *crime, entitlement and "the culture of denialism"*. In response to this, the notion of wealth was considered, firstly, in terms of the meaning of the word (which is closer to the modern idea of "welfare") and secondly, in terms of what wealth is *for*. Even taking the common-place idea of wealth as *geld*, the purpose of material prosperity is to benefit the whole, rather than to separate rich from poor. If the icons of success are those conspicuously so, it's not surprising that people otherwise disadvantaged turn to crime as a means of attaining and maintaining that status.

The different humanist traditions in South African history were discussed ranging from liberal humanism to anti-apartheid humanisms, including the Black Consciousness Movement. The ambiguity of certain strands of the humanist tradition in South Africa was its blindness to matters of race, class, and gender. Complexity thinking was mentioned several times, but with only a tantalising hint of what it might mean for the project. Are we talking about "multidimensionality" and "multidisciplinarity"? Or is there something within the physical sciences that could be translated into a larger paradigm for rethinking the human? One social category that showed great potential is "system", especially the systemic structures that limit human imagination and possibility. This gets at the question of the necessary conditions for human flourishing. What then are the systemic conditions under which 21st century South Africans can exercise their creative imagination? And how do dysfunctional systems take such possibilities away?

Negative factors

All four negative factors (the failure of humanism, the problem of discussing humanism behind secure, academic walls, the danger of a-historical and a-contextual accounts, and the ever-present South African past) were assumed in most of the discussion, either tacitly or focally. This was not a conversation that could have taken place "anywhere, at anytime". Nor was it a conversation in a space marked off from engagement. Indeed, the concern with dissemination was precisely the concern to enlarge the conversation. Finally, the urgency with which the ideas for incorporating more voices was precisely because the opportunity is here, now. South Africa's democracy is now a teenager, at times looking full of potential, at other times unruly and chaotic. The conversation about a New Humanism is a quest for a wisdom that can allow all its citizens to grow toward adulthood.

PARTICIPANTS & CONTRIBUTORS

BOTH SYMPOSIA

ACKERMANN, DENISE
Extraordinary Professor of Practical Theology, Stellenbosch University

ACKERMANN, LAURIE
Retired Judge of the South African Constitutional Court

ALEXANDER, NEVILLE
Director of the Project for the Study of Alternative Education in South Africa (PRAESA), University of Cape Town

BURTON, MARY
Former Commissioner of the TRC, and founder of the Home for All Campaign

CILLIERS, PAUL
Professor of Philosophy and Complexity, Stellenbosch University

DU TOIT, ANDRÉ
Emeritus Professor of Political Studies, University of Cape Town

ELLIS, GEORGE
Emeritus Professor of Applied Mathematics, University of Cape Town

GEYER, HENDRIK
Professor of Theoretical Physics and Director of the Stellenbosch Institute for Advanced Study

KUNNEMANN, HARRY
Professor of Philosophy, University for Humanistics, Utrecht; Stellenbosch Institute for Advanced Study

LATEGAN, BERNARD
Emeritus Professor of Religious Studies, Stellenbosch University; Stellenbosch Institute for Advanced Study

METZ, THADDEUS
Professor of Philosophy, University of Johannesburg; Stellenbosch Institute for Advanced Study

MOOSA, EBRAHIM
Professor of Islamic Studies, Duke University; Stellenbosch Institute for Advanced Study

NDEBELE, NJABULO
Former Vice-Chancellor of the University of Cape Town; Association of African Universities; Stellenbosch Institute for Advanced Study

SMIT, DIRKIE
Professor of Theology, Stellenbosch University; Stellenbosch Institute for Advanced Study

WILLIS, PETER
Cambridge Programme for Sustainability, Cape Town

SUPPORT STAFF

HOLNESS, LYN
Director, Emerging Researchers' Programme, University of Cape Town

FIRST SYMPOSIUM ONLY

CORNELL, DRUCILLA
Professor of Political Science, Comparative Literature, and Women's Studies, Rutgers University; University of Pretoria

DE GRUCHY, JOHN
Emeritus Professor of Christian Studies, University of Cape Town; Extraordinary Professor, Stellenbosch University; Stellenbosch Institute for Advanced Study

DU PLESSIS, LOURENS
Professor of Law, Stellenbosch University

ESACK, FARIED
Professor of Islamic Studies, University of Johannesburg

GOBODO-MADIKIZELA, PUMLA
Professor of Psychology, University of Cape Town

KROG, ANTJIE
Author, poet and Extraordinary Professor in the Arts Faculty, University of the Western Cape

PANFILIO, KENNETH
Professor of Politics, Illinois State University, USA

SCHWEIKER, WILLIAM
Professor of Theological Ethics, University of Chicago

SUPPORT STAFF

SCHWEIKER, PAUL
Student at Johns Hopkins University

SECOND SYMPOSIUM ONLY

BOTMAN, RUSSEL
Rector and Vice-Chancellor, Stellenbosch University

COMAROFF, JEAN
Distinguished Service Professor
of Anthropology and of Social Sciences, University of Chicago; University of Cape Town

FODOR, GEORG
University of Cape Town

GODSELL, BOBBY
Chairman, Business Leadership South Africa; National Planning Commission

HUYSSEN, HANS
Department of Music, University of the Free State; Stellenbosch Institute for Advanced Study

HOFMEYR, JAN-HENDRIK
Professor of Biocomplexity and Biochemistry, Stellenbosch University

HUBER, WOLFGANG
Honorary Professor of Systematic Theology, Humboldt University, Berlin, and
former Bishop of Berlin and Chairperson of the Council of the Evangelical Church in Germany (EKD);
Stellenbosch Institute for Advanced Study

KLAAREN, EUGENE
Professor of Theology, Wesleyan University, Connecticut

MANGANYI, CHABANI
Senior Research Fellow, Unit for Advanced Studies, University of Pretoria;
Stellenbosch Institute for Advanced Study

MBEMBE, ACHILLE
Research Professor in History and Politics, University of the Witwatersrand

NDUNGANE, NJONGONKULU
African Monitor; former Anglican Archbishop of Cape Town

SOLMS, MARK
Professor of Neuropsychology, University of Cape Town; Stellenbosch Institute for Advanced Study

TALJAARD, RAENETTE
Department of Political Studies, University of Cape Town

WESSELS, LEON
Former Commissioner of the South African Human Rights Commission;
Stellenbosch Institute for Advanced Study

INVITED BUT UNABLE TO ATTEND

POSEL, DEBORAH
Professor of Sociology and founding director of the Institute for Humanities in Africa (HUMA) at the University of Cape Town; Stellenbosch Institute for Advanced Study

SUPPORT STAFF

MARTIN, STEPHEN
Associate Professor, King's University College, Edmonton; Beyers Naudé Centre, Stellenbosch

INDEX: NAMES

A

Ackermann, Denise 28, 266, 270, 271, 273
Ackermann, Laurie 26, 237, 271-273
Alexander, Neville 28, 269
Annan, Kofi 244
Appiah, Kwame 102
Arieli, Y 214
Azad, Abul Kalam 111, 112, 115

B

Baudelaire, Charles 145
Baxter, W 139
Bereng, David Cranmer Theko 175
Berridge, K 45, 47
Biko, Steve 12, 198, 224
Bin Laden, Osama 108
Bonhoeffer, Dietrich 65
Botman, Russel 264, 266
Brockman, John 101, 102
Bronowski, Jacob 134
Burton, Mary 267, 274
Bush, George W 108

C

Calvin, John 67
Cassirer, Ernst 146, 147
Cicero 68
Cilliers, Paul 33, 34, 37, 160, 161, 182
Clark, Kenneth 135
Coetzee, JM 176
Comaroff, Jean 21, 189, 264, 265, 267-269, 274, 276
Cornell, Drucilla 28, 146, 149, 151, 266
Critchley, Simon 103
Cueva, Mateo 196, 202

D

Da Gama, Vasco 168
Darwin, Charles 60, 69, 78, 158, 162, 183
De Gruchy, John W 11, 67, 68, 102, 204, 261
De Sousa Santos, B 113, 114
Díä!kwãin 168, 169, 170
Dickson, Kwesi 171
Diop, Birago 171
Dürig, Günter 213, 218
Du Toit, André 29, 269
Dworkin, Ronald 237, 238

E

Eagleton, Terry 62, 160
Einstein, Albert 78, 80, 141, 197
Ellis, George 28, 265, 273

F

Farley, Margaret 71
Fernado, Keith 174
Fodor, Georg 267, 271, 273, 276, 277
Foster, John Bellamy 196
Freud, Sigmund 42, 44, 50, 197

G

Gandhi, Mahatma 111, 118
Geyer, Hendrik 12, 18, 267, 273
Ghazali, Abu Hamid al- 113-115
Gobodo-Madikizela, Pumla 173
Godsell, Bobby 29, 78, 265, 269, 271, 276
Gorz, André 200
Grootboom (Mrs) 26
Guyer, Jane 191
Gyekye, Kwame 171, 174, 175

H

Haarhoff, TJ 123, 124
Habermas, Jürgen 103
/Han≠kassó 168, 169
Hewitt, Roger 169
Hoffmeyer, Jan F 183
Hofmeyr, Jan-Hendrik S 27, 129, 265, 273
Hollmann, Jeremy 169, 170
Horler, Vivien 196
Huber, Wolfgang 28, 103, 214, 265, 266, 269-272
Huyssen, Hans 278

K

//Kabbo 170
Kant, Immanuel 49, 73, 104, 213-215, 218, 234, 237, 238, 240, 272, 273, 278
Kelsen, Hans 129
Klaaren, Eugene 276
Koestler, A 158
Krog, Antjie 23, 173, 176
Kunnemann, Harry 275
Kutz, Christopher 222, 230

L

Langa, Pius 216, 224, 226
Laszlo, Ervin 182, 183
Lategan, Bernard 12, 18, 27, 261-263, 265, 273-277
LeDoux, J 50
Lentsoeane, HML 173
Lovelock, James 157, 158, 181
Luxemburg, Rosa 147, 148, 153

M

Ma`arri, Abu al-Ala al- 110, 111
Macmurray, John 69, 74
Mamdani, Mahmood 151, 228
Mandela, Nelson 23, 172, 176, 226
Manganyi, Chabani 224, 225, 271
Marais, Eugène 169
Margulis, Lynn 157, 158
Marks, Shula 125, 126
Martin, Stephen 18, 277
Marx, Karl 190, 197, 198
Maturana, Humberto 157
Mazower, Mark 128-130
Mazrui, Ali 171
Mbeki, Thabo 22, 78, 226, 267
Mbembe, Achille 22-24, 148, 149, 267-270, 272
McFague, Sallie 72, 74
Meadows, D 182
Menkiti, Ifeanyi 149, 174, 235
Metz, Thaddeus 26, 64, 272, 273
Ming, Tu Wei 196
Mokgoro, Yvonne 224, 236
Moosa, Ebrahim 18, 113, 266, 268, 269, 272, 274, 276
Morales, Evo 101, 198
Moshoeshoe (King) 23, 175
Mqhayi, SEK 172
Murray, Gilbert 123, 124

N

Nadvi, Abul Hasan Ali 111
Ndebele, Njabulo 12, 64, 264, 267, 268
Ndlovu, RL 172
Ndungane, Njongonkulu 266, 274
Nehru, Jawaharlal 111
Nelson, Gaylord 252
Ngewu, Cynthia 173
Nkurmah, Kwame 78

P

Panfilio, Kenneth 145, 146, 149, 268
Panksepp, J 45-47, 50
Philip, John 118-122, 126, 130, 131
Prozesky, Martin H 168, 176

R

Ramphele, Mamphela 12, 13
Rees, Martin 57
Rhodes, Cecil John 125, 126
Robinson, Marilynne 61
Rolls, E 45
Roosevelt, Eleanore 128

S

Sachs, Albie 152, 223
Sagan, Carl 182
Sahtouris, Elizabeth 156-159, 161
Said, Edward 100
Sanders, Mark 175, 176, 221, 224
Schreiner, Olive 118
Setiloane, Gabriel 174
Shaka (King) 23, 175
Shutte, Augustine 171, 174, 216, 235
Sijistani, Abu Dawud al- 112
Smuts, Jan 29, 78, 118, 123-131, 271
Socrates 68
Solms, Mark 27, 28, 47, 50, 53, 266, 276
Soyinka, Wole 173
Spencer-Brown, G 182

T

Taljaard, Raenette 276
Taylor, Charles 100
Tempels, Placide (Father) 171
Terreblanche, Sampie 151
Tutu, Desmond 118, 174, 175, 226, 236

V

Van der Walt, André 26

W

Welker, Michael 73
Wessels, Leon 272
Wilberforce, William 118
Williams, Bernard 214
Willis, Peter 267, 270, 274

X

Xuma, AB 129

Y

Yali-Manisi, DLP 172

Z

Zikode, S'Bu 153

INDEX: SUBJECTS

A

Aborigines Protection Society 118
Abrahamic
  concept of human dignity 214
  — faiths 58
  — religions 217
Adam, myth of 62
aesthetic
  — design 62
  — existence 65
aesthetics
  art 23, 62, 65, 66, 69, 104, 110, 115, 124, 130, 135, 159, 162, 165, 182
  beauty 62, 65, 204
  music 62, 135, 155, 156, 159-165, 170, 182, 191, 248, 276, 278
  poetry 17, 111, 114, 115, 249
affirmative action 271, 274
Afghanistan 107, 108
Africa
  — in the modern world 264
  new scramble for — 189
  sub-Saharan 234, 235
African
  Christianity 58-61, 64, 70, 72, 118, 119, 122, 130, 254
  communitarianism 149, 224
  contemporary context 163
  — customs 23, 126
  — ethics 176
  — humanism 23, 146-148, 153, 262, 266-268
  moral wisdom 168
  — spirituality 146
  See also ***ubuntu***
African National Congress *See* ANC
Afrikaner organisations 227
Afro-radicalism 148
Aging Lantern (Purane Chiragh) 111
agnosticism 69
Allah 207
al-Qaida 108
ANC 129, 226, 227, 229, 239, 240
ancestors 45, 149, 171, 235
animals 28, 42, 43, 54, 63, 134, 137, 169-171, 182, 235, 266
anthropocentrism 28, 71, 102, 206, 266, 277
Anti-Slavery Society 118
apartheid
  collaboration 227
  collusion 227
  complicity 221, 222, 227-230
  denialism 200, 263, 279
Arabs 110
atheism 69, 70
Athens 99
Atlantic Charter 127, 129
authority 25, 27, 112, 115, 120, 121, 201, 202, 208, 212, 251
autonomy 29, 100, 122, 148, 214, 215, 223, 224, 234, 238, 239, 272, 275-278

B

Bahrain 109
barbarism 124-126, 130, 196, 197, 199, 267
being human
  commonality of 196
  differences in 43, 119, 277
  image of God 59, 63, 171, 206, 214
  in relationship 60-62, 64, 69, 70, 273
  See also **human relationships**, ***ubuntu***
Bethelsdorp 121
Bible 61
biocentric 263
biography 124, 265
biology 183, 266
  biosemiotics 183
  molecular — 183
  relational — 183
birds 45, 89
black
  — consciousness 198, 221, 224, 270, 279
  — empowerment 263, 279
  — intellectuals 188
  — labour 225
  — middle class 190
  See also **African**, **identity**, ***ubuntu***
Black Community Programmes 198

Black Consciousness Movement 198, 270, 279
Blombos Caves 14
body
resurrection of 61
See also **embodiment, identity, material/ism, sexuality**
bondage of the will 62
brain 15, 34, 42-46, 48, 50, 52, 53, 61, 142, 190, 197, 265, 266, 278
amygdala 48, 49, 53
periaqueductal grey (PAG) 44
prefrontal lobes 53, 54
Buddhists 207
bureaucracies 265
Bushmen 169, 170
and animals 169
language 169
tales 169
business 32, 80, 107, 108, 136, 227, 229, 248, 252-257, 266
— leaders 257

C

Canadian Charter of Rights and Freedoms 213
Cape Colony 122
Cape High Court 26
Cape liberal tradition 118
Cape Library 169
capitalism 32, 80, 101, 109, 145, 148, 151, 189, 190, 196, 197, 199, 200, 238, 240, 265, 267, 278
and waste 267
See also **economics, poverty, wealth**
child/ren 13, 25, 51, 111, 126, 141, 170, 171, 173, 191, 195, 202, 214, 235, 238, 239, 244
Christian 12, 17, 24, 28, 58, 59, 60, 61, 62, 64, 65, 66, 68, 69, 70, 72, 73, 74, 99, 102, 104, 110, 119, 126, 183, 203, 206, 208, 209, 214, 244, 266, 267, 270
— Church 24
fundamentalism 58
Christianity 58-61, 64, 70, 72, 118, 119, 122, 130, 254
— and civilisation 119
and colonialism 64
— and commerce 122
and democracy 64
and injustice 63
and women 25, 68-70, 72, 108, 110, 123, 128, 195, 238, 239
civilisation 54, 62, 78, 119-121, 123-131, 134, 161, 205, 268, 273
agricultural 54, 119
industrial 77, 78, 119, 200
Civilisation 135
civility 229, 230
civil society 128, 202, 218, 248, 252, 275
claims 33, 34, 36, 37, 39, 59, 63, 120, 156, 191, 193, 194, 201, 206, 209, 223, 224, 269
class 15, 42, 58, 61, 73, 78, 79, 80, 148, 149, 190, 196, 198, 201, 202, 224, 276, 279
exploitation 198, 202
— struggle 201, 202
Codex Hammurabi 24
colonial/ism 64, 78, 79, 108, 111, 115, 118-120, 122-124, 130, 150, 176, 188, 191, 204, 205, 208, 221, 268
— settlers 119, 122
common good 15, 17, 29, 59, 60, 63-65, 68, 71, 201
Communism 60, 254
Soviet — 60
communitarian 224, 234, 237-240, 273
See also **community, social, *ubuntu***
community 23, 60, 61, 63, 65, 66, 71, 73, 100, 107, 121, 124, 138, 149-152, 165, 171, 174-176, 188-191, 194, 198, 201, 202, 204-207, 212, 216, 221, 223, 229, 230, 235-237, 239, 240, 245, 255, 256, 264, 268, 270-272, 275
See also **social relations**
compassion 65, 66, 173, 207, 236
complexity 21, 31-33, 35-39, 45, 57, 62, 104, 137, 141, 142, 146, 147, 156, 160, 161, 183, 263, 264
and critical thought 115
ethics of — 31, 37
frameworks 36
systems 29, 33-36, 141, 156
computer science 183
Constitutional Court 26, 212, 213, 215, 216, 222, 223, 226, 236, 237, 271
Second Certification case 215
Constitution of South Africa 12, 117, 151, 212, 217, 271
Bill of Human Rights 23
Preamble 24, 129, 212
religion and 217
consumerism 32
corruption 11, 16, 245, 263
COSATU (Congress of South African Trade Unions) 239

cosmology 59
covenant 70, 270
Cradle of Humankind Heritage Site 15
creation 71, 73
integrity of — 74
See also **ecology, environment, evolution**
creativity 31, 32, 59, 66, 114, 197, 254, 267, 271, 277
See also **aesthetics**
crime 11, 16, 73, 140, 226, 240, 263, 279
critical theory 146
culture 14, 22, 33, 58, 61, 101, 102, 114, 119, 121-124, 134, 148, 160, 162, 168, 170, 171, 189, 190, 192, 200, 201, 212, 216, 217, 234, 239, 244, 252, 262, 263, 279

D

DA (Democratic Alliance) 239, 240
death 16, 17, 57, 61-64, 71, 113, 175, 206, 216, 273
— penalty 216
democracy 11, 12, 14, 21, 24, 25, 58, 60, 77, 122, 139, 152, 153, 188-190, 192-194, 197, 222-224, 226, 229, 244, 279
as a community of life 188, 189, 194
liberal 15, 60, 62, 109, 110, 118, 125, 146, 197, 200, 223, 279
social — 60
See also **Constitution of South Africa**
development 15-17, 22, 24, 26, 27, 62, 65, 79, 80, 100, 101, 119, 129, 134, 135, 139-143, 146, 149, 153, 183, 187, 198, 201, 211, 214, 215, 217, 245, 271, 273, 275, 277
dialogue 27, 28, 58, 59, 68, 109, 150, 151, 218, 265-268, 274
difference/diversity 12, 13, 26, 47, 53, 61, 63, 72-74, 102, 103, 114, 115, 120, 129, 131, 148, 156, 159-161, 164, 188, 190, 192-194, 200, 202, 205, 208, 209, 222-224, 239, 240, 245, 248, 265, 266, 270, 272, 273, 277
Dumbarton Oaks Conference 127, 128

E

earth 67, 68, 89, 114, 145, 147, 157, 171, 182, 206, 254
ecological 34, 176, 187, 195, 196, 200, 256
— collapse 195
— sustainability 187
See also **environment**
ecology 183, 252, 267
planetary ethics 27, 32, 59, 60, 63, 68, 157, 182, 195, 196, 207, 208, 236, 244-246, 252-254
economics 33, 80, 151, 200, 205, 248, 276
See also **capitalism, consumerism, labour, poverty, socialism, wealth**
ecumenism 68
education 11, 13, 16, 58, 65, 99, 100, 111, 118, 121, 123, 124, 130, 140, 152, 183, 196, 198, 201, 217, 238, 240, 248, 264-266, 269, 275
classical — 123, 124
Egypt 109
elites 78, 80, 109, 196, 264
moral crisis of 196
embodiment 61, 72, 148
See also **body**
empire 77, 79, 103, 120, 122
ambiguities of — 120
employment 81, 139, 142
See also **affirmative action, labour, work**
England 78, 123
Victorian — 123
enlightenment 99, 100, 119, 126, 214, 223, 237, 264, 272
Scottish — 119, 126
enough 192, 197, 200, 202, 255, 271
See also **poverty, wealth**
environment 21, 24, 28, 32, 33, 35, 36, 43, 46, 62, 67, 71, 72, 74, 136, 139-142, 157, 158, 165, 180, 192, 203, 217, 244, 246-248, 252, 263, 264
See also **ecology**
epistemological openness 147, 268
ethics 25, 31, 32, 36, 37, 67, 78, 102, 103, 110, 115, 148, 176, 208, 217, 222, 224, 227, 233-235, 244, 262, 278
Ethiopians 168
ethnicity 14, 15, 32, 79, 108, 119
See also **race**
Europe 12, 23, 77, 78, 100, 108, 124, 130, 200, 216, 245
Evangelical Revival 119
evolution 12, 49, 60, 119, 124, 134, 256, 266, 273
experience 13, 14, 46, 49, 50, 54, 58, 59, 61, 63, 64, 72, 80, 103, 119, 129, 165, 169, 188, 189, 193, 194, 204, 223, 225, 248, 249, 256, 275, 276
foundations of — 188

F

faith 13, 15, 17, 58, 59, 64, 65, 68-72, 74, 108, 109, 111, 115, 128, 227, 256, 276
claims 58
— communities 13, 65, 68, 71
Fascism 124
Football World Cup 79
Four Power plan 127
fundamentalism 58, 68, 100, 139

G

Gaia 27, 156-158, 181
See also **earth, ecology**
gender 13, 15, 25, 32, 58, 61, 64, 73, 224, 263, 279
generations 36, 37, 43, 101, 119, 187, 198, 200, 223, 224, 243-246, 275
future — 13, 24, 63, 65, 101, 217, 245, 246
genes 43, 45, 50
genetics 26, 53, 78, 134, 142, 196, 214
German 78, 101, 146, 148, 169, 196, 197, 211-214, 237, 271
— Basic Law 211, 212
— jurisprudence 213, 214
Germany 79, 99, 124, 211, 213
global 13, 15, 21, 22, 62, 65, 78, 81, 101, 103, 108-110, 121, 136, 139, 156, 158, 160-162, 193, 196, 199, 200, 202, 204, 208, 212, 223, 245, 248, 253-255, 262, 264, 276
— markets 204, 208
— narrative 254
globalisation 22, 32, 102, 110, 156, 160, 248, 263, 278
God 27, 28, 58, 59, 62-64, 68-70, 72, 74, 78, 100, 104, 112, 119, 171, 206, 207, 214, 235, 244, 266, 270
as creator 70
as trinity 70
the "God-debate" 59
See also **transcendence**
government 11, 32, 80, 108, 122, 136, 142, 149, 153, 189, 192, 198, 202, 218, 245, 252, 254, 256, 264, 274, 278
Grameen bank 138
Greek 123, 124, 165
Griqua 120
Gugulethu mothers 173

H

Hindus 111, 207
historical, the 15, 70, 100, 114, 117, 118, 123, 124, 127, 129, 163, 205, 226, 277
history 15, 21, 23, 25, 52, 59, 63, 69, 70, 72, 73, 78, 118, 127, 130, 145, 147, 148, 150, 151, 153, 188, 190, 192, 193, 196, 204-206, 214, 222, 224, 225, 244, 249, 255, 267-270, 279
of difference 73, 74, 103, 148, 188, 193, 194, 222
reified 148, 151, 153
HIV/AIDS 16, 196
homophobia 68
hope 13, 16, 17, 50, 61-65, 74, 78, 79, 103, 115, 151, 189, 190, 193, 198, 206-208, 244, 246, 262, 264, 265, 268, 271, 276, 277
hospitality 175
housing 13, 16, 26, 139, 151, 152, 197, 238
human
— agency 244, 262, 264, 266, 278
— and animal 42
— autonomy 278
— behaviour 159
— choices 62
— consciousness 209, 256
— dignity 211
emotions 52
— equality 111, 112
feelings 46-50, 52, 194, 196, 200, 206, 228, 255, 257
— flourishing 203, 207, 208, 262, 279
— freedom 188
free will 53, 206
— fulfilment 65, 66
future 12-15, 23, 24, 27, 38, 39, 57-59, 63, 65, 66, 68, 71, 101, 113, 125, 126, 135, 139, 140, 146, 150, 151, 179, 180, 188-190, 193, 194, 196, 202, 206, 209, 217, 229, 240, 244-247, 253-256, 264, 267, 268, 273, 274, 277
greed 62, 63, 81, 245, 247
— mutuality 190, 192, 194, 223, 225
— perception 209
— potential 202
vulnerability 50, 187, 190, 208, 209, 275
waste/surplus 24, 27, 267, 274
— wholeness 69, 103, 176, 245

— worth 63, 207, 209, 211, 212, 214, 215, 217, 218, 237
See also **being human, instincts, mammals, social relations**
humanisation 13
dehumanisation 107, 188, 226, 262
over- 63
under- 63
humanism
— African 23, 146-148, 153, 262, 266-268
as moral imperative 12, 14
Christian — 267
classical — 123, 124, 126, 127, 130, 131, 269
cosmopolitan — 99, 102
critical — 189
dark side of 29, 130, 134, 263, 269
dignity-enriched — 243, 246, 264
entrepreneurial — 245
European 12, 15, 23, 99, 100, 124, 130, 245, 269, 277
indigenous — 15
liberal — 15, 60, 62, 279
Muslim — 110, 111
reflexive — 28, 117
relational — 181
Renaissance — 61, 69, 99, 124
secular 27, 58-60, 103, 104, 181, 187, 244, 264, 267
socialist 15
third culture — 102
tragic — 62
Humanistic International 100
humanists 12, 14, 15, 17, 29, 58, 59, 61, 64-69, 71, 74, 110, 111, 117, 118, 121-126, 129-131, 159, 163, 167, 203, 243, 245, 248, 264-266, 269, 277, 279
humanitarianism 118-121, 130, 131
evangelical — 118, 119, 130, 131
humanities, the 59, 102, 167, 266
human rights 120
— as civil rights 119
— violations 129, 130, 226, 227, 229
humility 28, 78, 206-209, 229
hunger 32, 188, 190, 192

I

identity 12, 13, 15, 22, 27, 29, 58, 61, 78-81, 148, 157, 160, 180, 188, 215, 235, 272
multiple 22
ideology 15, 160, 268
IFP (Inkatha Freedom Party) 227
imagination 27, 32, 39, 52, 115, 146, 147, 192, 194, 197, 200, 255, 267, 278, 279
imperialism 120-122, 126, 130, 146, 148
British — 120
utopian — 122
inclusivity 245
India 79, 111, 115, 123, 129
Indian Civil Service 123
indigenous peoples 120-122, 146
and "latecomers" 167
individualism 80
individual rights 215, 217
associational — 215, 217, 272
instincts 27, 28, 43-45, 47-49, 52-54, 160, 266, 274
anger 48, 107, 108, 110
care 51, 110, 114, 141, 209, 245, 247, 253, 255, 262, 266, 275
desire 46, 50, 62, 70, 113, 206, 213, 256
fear 50, 53, 73, 81, 134, 172, 187, 245, 247, 266
grief 16, 50
panic 50
play 51
pleasure 41, 44, 45, 47, 48, 266
sadness 50
seeking 17, 50, 64, 113, 214, 234, 235, 251, 266
survival 28, 44, 50, 124, 158, 187, 190, 195, 245, 266
instrumental thinking 33
intellectuals 12, 187, 188, 196, 223
organic 196, 223
interconnectedness 23, 28, 29, 74, 167, 168, 176, 224, 225
See also **relationships,** ***ubuntu***
interfaith dialogue 109
International Humanist and Ethical Union 100
Iraq 107, 108

Islam 58, 107, 108, 110-113, 254
and terrorism 107, 109
in Middle Ages 110
in South Africa 108
See also **Muslim/s**
Israel 70, 270, 274
Istanbul 107

J

Jains 111
Jerusalem 99
Johannesburg 14
Judaism 58
justice 11, 12, 16, 24, 45, 64-66, 70, 72-74, 109, 120, 125, 126, 140, 146, 150-152, 163, 189, 190, 193, 203-209, 212, 226, 239, 240, 246, 248, 263, 267, 270, 273
creative alternatives 25, 274
distributive — 240
even-handedness 24
jus talionis 24
punishment 24
restorative — 140, 150, 206, 239
retribution 206
See also **law**

K

Kabul 107
Kantian ethics 213-215, 234, 237, 238, 240, 272, 273
categorical imperatives 213
Karachi 107
Kat River settlement 121
Khoi 119-122, 168
Kimberley 125
King Williamstown 172
knowledge 13, 15, 22, 23, 26, 31, 33, 35-37, 39, 48, 51, 61, 65, 71, 74, 77, 102, 110, 112-115, 128, 138, 141, 148, 156, 191, 212, 214, 222, 227, 244, 247-249, 268
emancipatory 114, 188

L

labour 115, 139, 148, 190, 198, 204, 208, 217, 225, 239
cheap — 148
domestic 225
workers 13, 148, 176, 189, 190, 225
See also **class, COSATU, unemployment**
land 15, 16, 28, 64, 72, 120, 125, 139, 152, 168, 170, 181, 204, 238, 266
occupation of 26, 170
redistribution of 192, 194
language 33, 54, 62, 69, 79, 104, 123, 133, 134, 136, 140, 145, 147, 149, 153, 163, 169, 173, 193, 202, 206, 216, 217, 226, 248, 255, 266, 268, 270, 277
Language and Myth 147
languages 111, 167, 204, 233, 235, 248, 249, 273
African 79
Afrikaans 79, 124, 125, 173
Greek 123, 124, 165
Latin 100, 123, 124, 200
Nguni 233-235
Sotho-Tswana 233-235
Latin America 100, 200
law 11, 24, 26, 59, 63, 70, 120, 121, 129, 140, 187-190, 192, 194, 198, 211-213, 216, 217, 225, 239, 248, 271, 273, 274
Anglo-Saxon 213
German 211-214, 271
Roman-Dutch 216
See also **justice**
Laws of Form 182
leadership 108, 251, 252, 256, 257
League of Nations 127, 128, 130, 269
legal systems 24, 135, 213
See also **justice**
liberation 22, 24, 72, 100, 101, 103, 111, 115, 149, 153, 192, 197, 198, 226-229, 264, 267, 270, 271, 274, 275
psychological — 198
— struggle 22, 115, 226, 229
Libya 109
life
as story 253
integrity of — 203, 207-209
meaning of — 55, 57
quality of — 11, 12, 24, 65, 142
literature 69, 111, 115, 118, 123, 169, 182, 216, 248, 271
See also **aesthetics, language**
locality 204-208
historical — 205
natural — 206
social — 204, 205, 207
London 107, 118, 120, 122, 125, 126

love 51, 52, 58, 62, 64, 65, 68-72, 85, 87, 95, 111, 161, 197, 209, 230, 236, 237, 256, 257, 270
of God 68
of neighbour 68, 197, 209
redemptive — 58
suffering 58

M

Madrid 107
mammals 42-45, 50-52, 54, 170, 276, 277
mother/infant 50, 51
reproduction 61, 146, 193
See also **human, instincts**
mapping/morphism 183, 268
Maropeng 15
material/ism 29, 40, 61, 114, 188, 191, 218, 237, 238, 245, 254, 279
deprivation 189, 249
See also **body**
mathematics 136, 138, 140, 183
See also **science, technology**
Mecca 111
mechanistic 159, 265
mediation 22, 151, 152, 265
media tribunal 22
Melamet Commission 198, 199
memory/ies 16, 17, 27, 35, 54, 64, 136, 138, 205, 207
dangerous 64
historical 27
Message to Humanity 111
Middle East 108
migrants 148, 188, 193
Millennium Development Goals 243, 244
modernity 59, 147, 214, 263, 264, 270, 278
Moscow Declaration 127
motivation/al/s 44, 54, 55, 63, 69, 103, 104, 180, 266
deficit 103, 104
Mozambique 168
multi-cultural 15
multi-disciplinary 14, 157, 218
multinationals 139
multiple identities 22
music 62, 135, 155, 156, 159-165, 170, 182, 191, 248, 276, 278
See also **aesthetics**
Muslim/s 107-113, 115, 208
aesthetics 115
elites 109
Indian 111
intelligentsia 110
religious scholars 110
Sunni 112
terrorists 107, 109
theology 110
tradition/s 110, 113
See also **Islam**

N

narrative 14, 23, 58, 59, 62, 64, 114, 120, 148, 156, 188, 253-256, 261
crisis of — 255
— of constraints 254
— of consumption 256
Native Question 125
nativism 148
natural sciences 26, 77, 183, 214, 266
natural selection 43, 182
See also **evolution**
Nature and Destiny of Man 62
Nazism 60
neighbourhood parks 239
neurology 134
See also **brain**
New Humanism project 261
absent voices 13
first symposium 13, 17, 18, 261, 262
interdisciplinary 14
narrative account 14
participants 13, 14, 16, 28, 270, 277, 278
recurrent themes 262
second symposium 13, 16, 18, 261, 268
new humanism, the 245, 246
new humanity, the 60
New Testament 58, 124
New York 107
nihilism 63, 109
North America 77, 108
nuclear disarmament 67

O

Ordinance 50 120, 122
Origin of Species 60
other, the 52, 59, 63, 65, 72, 100, 104, 136, 142, 149, 173, 188, 190, 223, 266, 270, 275, 278
as people 152, 268
Oxford 123, 126

P

PAGAD 108
Paideia 123
Pakistan 108, 111
Parsis 111
paternalism 121, 126, 131
patriarchialism 22
peace work 147
peasantisation 147
perpetrators 109, 173, 227-229
Persian 111
person/hood 11, 12, 23, 24, 32, 34, 39, 65, 70, 71, 73, 99-104, 120, 146, 149-151, 155, 159, 168, 174-176, 188, 191-193, 196, 202, 213-216, 222, 223, 225, 235, 236, 244, 249, 257, 262, 268, 272, 274, 276-278
  See also being human, identity, soul
philosophy 23, 39, 63, 68-70, 102, 110, 114, 123, 124, 148, 149, 175, 214, 221, 233, 235-237, 268, 272
physics 80, 140, 141, 157, 183, 252
  See also science, technology
planet, the 27, 32, 59, 60, 63, 68, 157, 158, 182, 195, 196, 207, 208, 236, 244-246, 252-255
  as a living organism 27
pleasure principle 44, 45
pluralism 73, 103
  See also multi-cultural
poetry/poetics 17, 111, 114, 115, 249
political 15, 32, 38, 59, 60, 64, 68, 72, 77, 78, 109, 115, 120, 123-130, 134, 135, 138, 139, 148-150, 153, 156, 158, 159, 164, 182, 187-190, 192, 193, 197-202, 205, 206, 217, 222, 227-229, 237, 239, 240, 249, 264, 265, 267
  accountability 179, 191, 192, 221, 222
  conflict 60, 69, 101, 120, 124, 150-152, 179, 204, 239, 248, 249, 263, 264, 278
  See also aesthetics
politico-theological 188
politics 25, 101, 110, 114, 118, 123, 124, 129, 148, 179-190, 192-194, 201, 228, 255, 264, 269, 273, 275, 276
  affirmative — 189
  — of expediency 194
  of negotiation 128
  — of principle 194
  paralysis of 197
  transnational — 179
poor 13, 16, 22, 23, 32, 60, 73, 101, 102, 110, 118, 138, 139, 142, 190, 192, 194, 196, 199, 202, 209, 218, 233, 234, 237-240, 244, 245, 272, 279
  aspirations of 63, 204
  empowerment of 81, 263, 271, 279
populism 263, 264
post-human 206, 264
postmodernism 113, 156
poverty 13, 15, 67, 72, 73, 151, 188, 192, 199, 204, 233, 234, 237, 238, 240, 244, 245, 247, 262, 267, 272-274
  and crime 16, 199, 240, 263, 279
  indignity of 234, 240
  See also poor, unemployment
power
  — and knowledge 268
  — relations 160
prejudice 146, 248
privatisation 149, 152, 189
  See also economics, land, property
professionalism 275, 276
property 26, 120, 121, 134, 141, 151, 160, 171, 183, 191-193, 200, 225, 237, 238, 240, 257, 268, 274
  private — 151, 268
  — rights 26, 134, 141, 200, 274
public accountability 179

Q

Qur'an 110, 111

R

race 13, 15, 32, 61, 73, 78, 79, 108, 119, 125, 148, 171, 173, 176, 188-190, 192, 222, 224-226, 234, 263, 267, 279
racial classification 224, 225
  See also apartheid
racism 41, 72, 125, 198, 200, 269
  See also apartheid
rationality 74, 100, 104, 206, 234
reconciliation 16, 151, 173, 229, 249
  projects 228, 229
  with universe 168
  See also TRC
reductionism 41, 197, 278
relational praxis 71-74, 270
relationships 12, 17, 28, 29, 31, 33, 34, 36, 37, 39, 51, 60-62, 64-74, 80, 104, 113, 149, 150, 158, 159, 163, 170, 183, 188,

190-194, 197, 204, 213, 215, 229, 234-236, 238-241, 248, 249, 253, 266, 270, 272-275
life-affirming — 70
religion 15, 32, 33, 58-61, 63, 77, 79, 104, 108, 111, 188, 201, 207, 217, 266, 270, 278
religious institutions 68
reparation 149, 151, 193, 274
Researches in South Africa 120
research strategy, an open 34
resources 32, 79, 110, 113, 138, 148, 152, 153, 190, 192, 196, 203, 205, 209, 225, 245, 247-249, 254, 256, 264
control of 28, 32, 62, 138, 267
scarce 192
responsible/ity 13, 26, 29, 32, 37, 59, 63, 69, 71, 73, 74, 81, 125, 149, 153, 182, 203, 207-209, 216, 224, 227-229, 244, 245, 262, 265, 270, 278
action 62, 243
retaliation 24, 25, 27
See also **justice**
revelation 113
Roman-Dutch law 216
Rome 99, 120
classical — 120

S

San 119, 167
San Francisco 123, 127-129
scientific knowledge 33
scientism 59
secularism/sts 13, 17, 59, 207, 214
segregation 15, 123, 126, 164, 189, 224
self, the 27, 41, 63, 71, 80, 85, 100, 104, 110, 113, 115, 173, 176, 192, 256, 275
fulfilment 213, 215
worth 213
See also **human, identity, person/hood, soul**
September 11, 2001 108
Sermon on the Mount 25, 70, 274
service delivery 13, 190, 199, 264, 265
settlers 78, 79, 119, 122
as "latecomers" 167
sexism 24, 68
sexuality 61
Shackdwellers Movement 152
Sikhs 111
sin 62, 174
slavery 15, 29, 64, 176, 188, 204, 268, 269
social
— contract 203
— hierarchies 52
— interconnectedness 23
— relations 23, 25, 150, 236
solidarity 22, 24, 28, 29, 61, 72, 81, 103, 174, 176, 197, 200, 235, 236, 265, 267, 272, 275
— welfare 81, 245
social Darwinism 60, 69
social sciences, the 59
society 11, 13, 15, 16, 21-26, 28, 29, 33, 58, 64, 65, 68, 69, 71-73, 78, 80, 81, 102, 111, 113, 119, 120, 121, 124, 125, 128, 134, 140, 142, 146, 148, 150, 151, 159, 161, 174, 175, 189-194, 198, 200-204, 207, 218, 226, 228, 233-235, 243, 244, 247-249, 252, 253, 256, 262-265, 267-269, 271, 273, 275-278
humane — 16, 21-25, 29, 200, 262
soul 61, 62, 66, 67, 111, 112, 114, 115, 164, 165, 199, 272
and body 61
as being-in-relation 61
immortality of 61
See also **being human, social relations, (the) self**
South Africa 11-17, 22, 25, 26, 29, 58, 64, 65, 68, 78-81, 101, 108, 112, 115, 117, 120, 123-125, 130, 139, 141, 142, 150-152, 168, 176, 180, 189, 190, 192-195, 197-202, 204, 205, 207-209, 211, 212, 214-218, 221-225, 229, 238, 241, 243, 248, 249, 251, 253-257, 263-265, 267, 269-271, 273, 274, 276-279
Christianity in 58
future generations 13, 24, 63, 65, 101, 217, 245, 246
humanism in — 117
Islam in 58, 108
National Assembly 212, 215
national crises 67, 195
national identity 12, 78-81
post-apartheid — 117, 198, 201, 202
transformation 37, 38, 64, 100, 109, 121, 142, 150, 189, 193, 201, 209, 243, 249, 263, 264, 274, 275, 277-279
See also **apartheid, Constitution of South Africa, politics, TRC**
South African Institute of Race Relations 126
South Asia 108

Soweto uprising 173
Spirit
pluralism of 73
spirituality 33, 61, 66, 146
Stellenbosch Institute for Advanced Study (STIAS) 12, 13, 18, 204, 248
Sterkfontein Caves 14
stranger 175, 176, 188, 193
students 13, 125, 141, 202
subjectivity 61, 113, 115, 268
suffering 29, 57, 58, 61-63, 67, 101, 174, 188, 221, 226, 239, 249
sufficiency 200, 201, 255, 262, 278
principle of — 200, 201, 262, 278
symbolic
— forms 146, 147
— world 147
systems 23-25, 27, 29, 31-37, 39, 42-54, 65, 67, 81, 113, 114, 123, 126, 130, 134-142, 151, 153, 156-158, 160-163, 167, 183, 195, 199-202, 204, 213, 224-226, 228, 229, 240, 249, 252-254, 256, 263, 265, 270, 278, 279

T

Taliban 108
taxi industry 267
tax strategies 245
technology 28, 59, 133-142, 238, 244, 247, 273, 274, 276
abstract — 273
— and civilisation 134
— and crime 140
— and daily life 135
— and democracy 139
— and education 140
— and environment 139
— and values 139
appropriate — 137, 142
benefits of 247
control of 136, 137
design 136-139, 142
development of — 134
fear of — 134
information — 136
learning 138, 140
nano 196
priorities 142
usability of 136, 142
See also **science**
The Ascent of Man 134
The Death of Adam 61
theism 70, 175, 270
theology 59
— of relation 69-71, 74, 270
See also **Christianity, Islam**
Theopolis 121
The Systems View of the World 183
The White Man's Task 125, 126
third culture 99, 102
tolerance 102, 204, 205, 207-209, 230, 240
Torah 25
torture 63, 187, 227
totalitarianism 29, 64
tradition 13, 15, 17, 23, 27, 28, 57-59, 61, 62, 64, 68, 70, 74, 99, 102, 104, 110-115, 117, 118, 124, 130, 149, 162, 164, 165, 167, 188, 193, 207, 208, 214, 263, 266, 267, 269-271, 277, 279
African — 15, 23, 121, 174
Judaic-Christian — 28
reconstructing 208
Reformed — 68
transcendence 70, 190
See also **God**
transparency 256, 276
Treason Trial 172
truth 58, 62, 65, 71, 72, 74, 110, 114, 148, 172, 176, 188, 190, 197, 206, 208, 267
Truth and Reconciliation Commission (TRC) 16, 27, 151, 222, 223, 225-229, 249
counselling and rehabilitation 239
reparations 149, 151, 193, 274
See also **reconciliation**
two cultures 101

U

ubuntu 146, 149, 205, 216, 223, 224, 238, 268
UDF (United Democratic Front) 227
uhuru 201
unemployment 16, 139, 190
UNESCO 196
United Nations Charter 123, 127, 269
United States of America (USA) 77, 100, 101, 204, 213
Universal Declaration of Human Rights 127, 129, 211, 214, 236, 269

V

values 11, 12, 15, 22, 24, 26, 29, 34, 37, 43-45, 47, 48, 51, 52, 58, 63, 70, 73, 74, 78, 80, 81, 111, 126, 129, 130, 138, 139, 142, 143, 162, 174, 195, 197-201, 204, 205, 208, 212, 216-218, 223, 224, 234, 244, 246, 248, 255, 262, 266, 269, 271, 273-275, 277, 278
victims 63, 121, 173, 199, 226-228, 239
violence 13, 23, 25, 27, 59, 63, 67, 107-109, 111, 120, 148, 151, 187, 194, 205, 226, 228, 240, 273-276, 278
voluntarism 197

W

war 63, 66, 67, 78, 79, 109, 124, 128, 130, 138, 147, 158, 187, 189, 195, 198, 205, 271
Washington 107
water 133, 135, 138, 141, 142, 147, 152, 153, 172, 244, 256, 264
wealth 13, 29, 32, 78, 80, 81, 142, 188-192, 194, 195, 202, 239, 240, 248, 254, 265, 267, 268, 271, 277, 279
— accumulation 80
distribution of — 240
See also economics, poverty
white 12, 13, 22, 79-81, 123, 125, 126, 130, 131, 146, 172, 183, 190, 223-225, 229, 234, 239, 269, 272
— males 12, 13, 146
— supremacy 123, 126, 131, 269
See also race
will-to-power 62, 63
wisdom 13, 65, 66, 158, 168, 279
witnessing 22, 188, 189, 199
women's shelters 238
World Council of Churches 74
worldviews 60, 156, 159, 160, 167, 182, 183, 265
World War II 101, 131, 211

X

/Xam 170
Xhosa 119, 120, 153

Y

Yemen 108
youth 198, 199, 201, 202, 239, 255, 264, 271

Z

Zion Christian Church 24